THE TECHNIQUE

of

RADIO PRODUCTION

THE LIBRARY
OF COMMUNICATION TECHNIQUES

THE TECHNIQUE OF

RADIO PRODUCTION

A Manual for Local Broadcasters

by

ROBERT McLEISH

**Foreword by Ian Trethowan,
Director General of the B.B.C.**

Focal Press • London
Focal/Hastings House • New York

🅱🅛 British Library Cataloguing in Publication Data

McLeish, Robert
   Technique of radio production. —
   (The library of communication techniques).
   1. Radio broadcasting. II. Series
   791.44'0232   PN1991.75

ISBN (excl. USA) 0 240 51008 9
ISBN (USA only) 0 8038 7186 4

First edition 1978

Text set in 11/12 pt Press Roman by Donald Typesetting, Bristol.
Printed and bound in Great Britain by A. Wheaton & Co. Ltd, Exeter

CONTENTS

FOREWORD

During the great expansion of television in the 1950s, it was often assumed that the days of radio were numbered. When the picture of an event was going to be so widely available — be it a train crash or a play — who would be interested in a medium relying solely on sound? Over the ensuing twenty years or so, there have certainly been great changes in radio, but in Britain, about half the population still listens to it each day. Once television becomes the norm in a country, people no longer turn to the radio as the main source of family evening entertainment, as in the days of programmes such as our own 'In Town Tonight' and 'ITMA'. Instead, radio has developed a whole new role as informant and friend during the day-time. It has, in particular, come to fulfil certain special functions: it is a major source of cultural experience, particularly through such specialised services as the BBC's Radio 3, or the National Public Radio stations in the United States. It is also increasingly the main source of community broadcasting.

The first forty years of radio in this country were heavily tilted towards national services. The BBC wanted to move into local radio in the 1950s, but were not able to do so because of restrictions in available frequencies until the late 1960s. Once the first new community stations were opened, however, it was clear that this was going to be the main growth area, and we have seen in Britain the development first of BBC stations, then of commercial stations. A pattern of Local Radio in many parts of the world is that the station attempts to serve its community by being not simply the mouthpiece of the decision makers, but part of the process whereby decisions are made. It helps the community to reach a concensus, to do its thinking 'out loud'. Its appeal lies in the fact that its programmes can deal with those matters which are close to us and probably affect us most — local transport and industry, our jobs, medical facilities, the education of our children and how we spend our leisure.

11

It is in the field of community radio that the author, Robert McLeish, has made his own most important personal contribution. He writes on the basis of over twenty years' experience in radio, and particularly of experience in local radio dating from the very earliest days of the BBC's development. He was Programme Organiser at one of the original stations, Radio Nottingham, and then when in 1970 the BBC decided to more than double its stake in local radio in a very short time, he took charge of what was probably the single most crucial area: the training of about three hundred new local radio staff in a matter of a few months. The achievements of the new BBC stations in the mid 1970s owed a great deal to the grounding which the staffs and contributors received from Robert McLeish, and during the succeeding years he developed an increasingly wide range of training schemes for community broadcasters.

It is on the basis of this experience that this book will, I believe, provide fresh insights for all radio people. Much of its content deals with techniques which are of universal application, but there is a special emphasis on some of the aspects of radio particularly important in a community setting.

Radio has a wide range of roles, from the fastest possible carrier of international news to the relaxing familiarity of a personal friend. Radio serves as a cultural stimulus as much as it provides practical advice, neighbourly contact or simply background atmosphere. Its programmes can be designed to cover a continent or meet the needs of the small isolated community. Radio is still very much alive — the listeners to a thousand million radio sets around the world can't be wrong!* — and it is invaluable to have here such a thorough source book of radio technique.

IAN TRETHOWAN
Director General,
British Broadcasting Corporation
July 1978

INTRODUCTION AND ACKNOWLEDGEMENTS

If ever there was a book which needed a soundtrack, this is it. Chapter by chapter we shall want to imagine things in their 'radio state'; to 'hear' the smile in the voice of a programme presenter or the correct level of crowd noise behind a commentary, to judge the right length of pause after an introduction, or the meaningful inflection in a spoken sentence. The intention is to encourage the reader to listen more carefully to radio. By doing so, he will not only pick up points of technique but come to know the difference between the adequate and the superlative; and more importantly, the reasons for using a specific technique.

Some producers seem to have an instinctive approach to aural communication, effortlessly turning what they want to say into attractive easily understood radio. Others, probably most of us, have to work hard; gathering, assembling and refining material with considerable care so that what comes out of the loudspeaker will *sound* effective. This book, which is based on the experience of many, provides an analysis of programme making, and indicates short cuts, so that the practitioner can quickly reach acceptable standards, and make fewer mistakes on the way.

Much of the book is based on the BBC's practical approach to community broadcasting, and the public response to it. The small local radio station does more than provide programmes, it also acts as a communication catalyst encouraging members of the community to take part in the making of these programmes. One indicator of the success or failure of a station is the degree to which the non-professional broadcaster regards his own participation in it as worthwhile. I trust the professional broadcaster finds this book both stimulating and useful, but it is primarily to those who take seriously the two-way role of radio in its own community that this work is dedicated. I hope they will find here encouragement to further involvement.

I gratefully acknowledge the immense contribution made in this field by the BBC Local Radio Managers and their staff, and the countless contributors who had to find out 'the hard way'. In particular I want to thank the instructors of the Local Radio Training Unit and visiting lecturers, who have helped us all towards a better understanding and a surer technique.

A word of apology to women readers. I have referred throughout to producers, writers and others as 'he'. I hasten to discount any implication that I have deliberately excluded the feminine: it is only for the sake of simplicity that I have avoided the more laborious form 'he or she'. Both sexes are included in the application if not the construction. The word 'broadcaster' I have used to denote anyone involved in the broadcasting process, not just the person at the microphone.

Finally, a word of thanks to those directly involved in the production of this book: to Michael Barton, Controller of BBC Local Radio for permission to publish, to BBC Publications for the extract from 'Richard Dimbleby, Broadcaster', reprinted on page 208, and to the Royal Navy Public Relations Department for the use of their press release on page 118. My personal thanks go to Frank Gillard for his encouragement and advice with the draft, to Dave Wilkinson who produced the ideas for the illustrations, and to Ann Hamman who wrestled with the script.

ROBERT McLEISH

1

CHARACTERISTICS OF THE MEDIUM

FROM its first tentative experiments and the early days of wireless, radio has expanded into an almost universal medium of communication. It leaps around the world on short waves linking the continents in a fraction of a second. It brings that world to those who cannot read and helps maintain a contact for those who cannot see.

It is used by armies in war and by amateurs for fun. It controls the air lanes and directs the taxi. It is the commonplace of business and commerce, the normality for fire brigades and police. Broadcasters pour out thousands of words every minute in an effort to inform, educate and entertain, propagandise and persuade; music fills the air. Community radio makes broadcasters out of listeners and the Citizen Band gives transmitter power to the individual.

Whatever else can be said of the medium, it is plentiful. It is fast losing the sense of awe which attended its early years, becoming instead a very ordinary and 'unspecial' method of communication. To use it well we may have to adapt the formal 'written' language which we learnt at school and rediscover our oral traditions. How the world might have been different had Guglielmo Marconi lived before William Caxton.

To succeed in a highly competitive marketplace where television, newspapers, cinema, theatre and the gramophone record jostle for the attentions of a media-conscious public the radio producer must understand the strengths and weaknesses of his medium.

Radio makes pictures

It is a blind medium but one which can stimulate the imagination so that as soon as a voice comes out of the loudspeaker, the listener attempts to visualise what he hears and to create in the mind's eye the owner of the voice. What pictures are created when the voice carries an emotional content – an interview with wives gathering at the pit head after news of an accident in the mine – the halting joy of relatives on opposite sides of the world linked by a request programme.

Unlike television where the pictures are limited by the size of the screen, radio's pictures are any size you care to make them. For the writer of radio drama it is easy to involve us in a battle between goblins and giants, or to have our spaceship land on a strange and distant planet. Created by appropriate sound effects and supported by the right music virtually any situation can be brought to us. As the schoolboy said when asked about television drama, "I prefer radio, the scenery is so much better".

But is it more accurate? Naturally, a visual medium has an advantage when demonstrating a procedure or technique, and a simple graph is worth many words of explanation. In reporting an event there is much to be said for seeing film of say a public demonstration rather than leaving it to our imagination. Both sound and vision are liable to the distortions of selectivity, and in news reporting it is up to the integrity of the individual on the spot to produce as fair, honest and factual an account as possible. In the case of radio, its great strength of appealing directly to the imagination must not become the weakness of allowing individual interpretation of a factual event, let alone the deliberate exaggeration of that event by the broadcaster. The radio writer and commentator chooses his words so that they create appropriate pictures in the listener's mind, and by so doing he makes his subject understood and its occasion memorable.

The directness of radio

Unlike television where the viewer is observing something coming out of a box 'over there', the sights and sounds of radio are created within us, and can have greater impact and involvement. Television is in general watched by small groups of people and the reaction to the programme is often affected by the reaction between individuals. Radio is much more a personal thing, coming direct to the listener. There are obvious

16

exceptions, such as in the poorer countries where a whole village will gather round the set. However even here, the transistor revolution makes a radio increasingly an ordinary everyday personal item.

The broadcaster should not abuse this directness of the medium by regarding the microphone as an input to a public address system, but rather a means of talking directly to the individual listener. If the programme is transmitted 'live', then the broadcaster has the further advantage of an immediate link with the individual and with thousands like him. The recorded programme introduces a shift in time and, like a newspaper, is capable of some distortion.

The speed of radio

Technically uncumbersome, the medium is enormously flexible and is often at its best in the totally immediate 'live' situation. No processing of film, no waiting for the presses. A report from a correspondent overseas, a listener talking on the phone, the radio car in the suburbs, a sports result from the local stadium, a concert from the capital, are all examples of the immediacy of radio. This ability to move about geographically generates its own excitement. This facility of course is long since regarded as a commonplace, both for television and radio. Pictures and sounds are bounced around the world, bringing any event anywhere to our immediate notice.

The simplicity of radio

The basic unit comprises one man with a tape recorder rather than a crew with camera, lights and sound recorder. This makes it easier for the non-professional to take part, thereby creating a greater possibility for public access to the medium. In any case, sound equipment is better understood, with tape recorders and hi-fi equipment being found in most schools and homes. It is also probably true that whereas with television or print any loss of technical standards becomes immediately obvious and unacceptable, with radio there is a recognisable margin between the excellent and the adequate. This is not to say that one should not continually strive for the highest possible radio standards.

For the broadcaster, radio's comparative simplicity means a flexibility in its scheduling. Items within programmes, or even whole programmes can be dropped to be replaced at short notice by something more urgent.

Radio is cheap

Relative to the other media, both its capital cost and its running expenses are small. As broadcasters round the world have discovered, the main difficulty in setting up a station is often not financial but lies in obtaining a transmission frequency. Such frequencies are safeguarded by governments as signatories to international agreements and are not easily assigned.

Radio stations are financed in various ways including public licence, commercial advertising, government grant, private capital, public subscription, or any of these methods in combination.

The relatively low cost once again means that the medium is ideal for use by the non-professional. Because time is not so expensive or so rare, radio stations are encouraged to take a few gambles in programming. Radio is a commodity which cannot be hoarded, neither is it so special that it cannot be used by anyone with something interesting to say. Through all sorts of methods of listener participation, the medium is capable of offering a role as a two-way communicator, particularly in the area of community broadcasting.

Radio is also cheap for the listener. The development of the transistor, printed circuit boards, and 'solid state' manufacturing techniques allows sets to be mass produced at a cost which enables their virtual total distribution. The broadcaster should never forget that while he may regard his own installations (studios, transmitters, etc.) as expensive, the greater part of the total capital cost of any broadcasting system is borne directly by the public in buying receivers.

The transient nature of radio

It is a very ephemeral medium and if the listener is not in time for the news bulletin, then it is gone and he has to wait for the next. Unlike the newspaper which he can put down, then come back to or pass round, the broadcasting media impose a strict discipline of having to be there at the right time. The radio producer must recognise that while he may store his programme in tape archives, his work is only short-lived for the listener.

This is not to say that it may not be memorable, but the memory is fallible and without a written record it is easy to be misquoted or taken out of context. For this reason it is often advisable for the broadcaster to have some form of audio or written log as a check on what was said, and by whom. In some cases this may be a statutory requirement of a radio station as part of its public accountability. Where this is not so, lawyers have been known to argue that it is better to have no record of what was said – for example in a public phone-in. Practice would suggest however that the keeping of a tape of the transmission is a useful safeguard against allegations of malpractice, particularly from complainants who missed the broadcast and who heard about it at second hand.

The transitory nature of the medium also means that the listener must not only hear the programme at the time of its broadcast, but must also understand it then. The impact and intelligibility of the spoken word should occur on hearing it – there is seldom a second chance. The producer must therefore strive for the utmost logic and order in the presentation of his ideas, and the use of clearly understood language.

Radio is selective

There is a different kind of responsibility on the broadcaster from that of the newspaper editor in that the radio producer selects exactly what is to be received by his consumer. In print, a large number of news stories, articles and other features are set out across several pages. Each one is headlined or identified in some way to make for easy selection. The reader scans the pages choosing to read those items which interest him – he is using his own judgement. With radio this is not possible. The selection process takes place in the studio and the listener is presented with a single thread of material. Choice for the listener exists only in the mental switching off which occurs during an item which fails to maintain his interest, or when he tunes to another station. In this respect a channel of radio or television is rather more autocratic than a newspaper.

Radio lacks space

A newspaper may carry 30 or 40 columns of news copy – a 10 minute radio bulletin is equivalent to a mere column and a half. Again, the selection and shaping of the spoken material has to be tighter and more logical. Papers can devote large amounts of space to advertisements, particularly to the 'small ads', and personal announcements such as births, deaths and marriages. This is ideal scanning material but it is not possible to provide such detailed coverage in a radio programme.

A newspaper is able to give an important item additional impact simply by using more space. The big story is run using large headlines – the picture is blown up and splashed across the front page. The equivalent in a radio bulletin is to lead with the story and to illustrate it with a voice report or interview. There is a tendency for everything in the broadcast media to come out of the set the same size. An item may be run longer but this is not necessarily the same as 'bigger'. There is only limited scope for indicating the differing importance of an economic crisis, a religious item, a murder, the arrival of a pop group, the market prices and the weather forecast. It could be argued that the press is more likely to use this ability to emphasise certain stories to impose its own value judgements on the consumer. This naturally depends on the policy of the individual newspaper editor. The radio producer is denied the same freedom of manoeuvre and this can lead to the feeling that all subjects are treated in the same way, a criticism of bland superficiality not infrequently heard. On the other hand this characteristic of radio perhaps restores the balance of democracy, imposing less on the listener and allowing him to make up his own mind as to what is important.

The personality of radio

A great advantage of an aural medium over print lies in the sound of the human voice – the warmth, the compassion, the anger, the pain and the laughter. A voice is capable of conveying so much more than reported speech. It has inflection and accent, hesitation and pause, a variety of emphasis and speed. The information which a speaker imparts is to do with his style of presentation as much as the content of what he is saying. The vitality of radio depends on the diversity of voices which it uses and the extent to which it allows the colourful turn of phrase and the local idiom.

It is important, particularly for a local radio station, that all kinds of voices are heard and not just those of the professional broadcasters or the articulate spokesmen. Also, the technicalities of the medium must not deter members of a community from expressing themselves with a naturalness and sincerity which reflects their true personalities. Here radio, uncluttered by the pictures which accompany the talk of television, is capable of great sensitivity.

Radio has music

Here are the Beethoven symphonies, the top 40, tunes of our childhood, jazz, opera, rock and favourite shows. From the best on record to a quite passable local church organist, radio provides the pleasantness of an unobtrusive background or the focus of our total absorption. The range of music is wider than the coverage of the most comprehensive record library and radio therefore gives the listener a chance to discover unfamiliar forms of music. But unlike the domestic L.P., which we select to match our taste and feelings of the moment, the music on radio is chosen for us and may change our mood and take us out of ourselves. The listener's non-selection of music is really 'chance' listening — a surprise encounter with something unexpected. Broadcasters are tempted to think only in terms of 'format' radio where the music content lies precisely between narrowly defined limits. This gives consistency and enables the listener to hear what he expects to hear, which is probably why he switched on in the first place. But radio can also provide the opportunity for innovation and experiment — the risk involved must be taken if the medium is to be used by both broadcasters and listeners in a way which is creative and stimulating.

2

OPERATIONAL TECHNIQUES

BOOKS on the technical and operational aspects of broadcasting are listed under Further Reading and the subject is not dealt with in detail here. However to omit it altogether might appear to indicate a separation of programme production from its functional base. This can never be so. The listener is after all dependent on sound alone and he must be able to hear clearly and accurately. Any sounds which are distorted, confused or poorly assembled are tiring to the listener and will not retain his interest.

The quality of the end product depends directly on the engineering and operational standards. It scarcely matters how good the ideas are, how brilliant the production, how polished the presentation, because all will founder on poor operational technique. Whether the broadcaster is using other operational staff, or is in the 'self-operational' mode, the basic familiarity with the studio equipment has to be taken for granted − it must be 'second nature'.

Taking the analogy of driving a car, the good driver is not preoccupied with how to change gear, or with which foot pedal does what − he is more concerned with road sense, i.e. the position of his car on the road in relation to other vehicles. So it is with the broadcaster. His use of the tools of the trade − microphones, tape recorders, the studio mixer, the radio car, cartridge players, record turntables − these must all be at the full command of the producer. He can then concentrate on what broadcasting is really about, the communication of ideas in music and speech.

Good technique comes first, and having been mastered, it should not then be allowed to obtrude into the programme. The technicalities of broadcasting − editing, fading, control of levels, sound quality and so on, should be so good that they do not show. By not being obvious they allow the programme content to come through.

In common with other performing arts such as film, theatre and television, the hallmark of the good communicator is that his means are not always apparent. Basic craft skills are seldom discernible except to the professional who recognises in their unobtrusiveness a mastery of the medium.

There are programme producers who declare themselves uninterested in technical things, they will leave the jackfield or panel operation to others so that they can concentrate on 'higher' things. Unfortunately if you do not know what is technically possible, then you cannot fully realise the potential of the medium. Without knowing the limitations either, there can be no attempt to overcome them, you simply suffer the frustrations of always having to depend on someone else who does understand.

The studio desk (control panel, or control board)

This is essentially a device for mixing together the various programme sources to form the broadcast output. It contains three types of circuit function:

1. *Programme circuits:* A series of channels, their individual volume levels controlled by separate slider or rotary faders.
2. *Monitoring circuits:* A visual (meter) and aural (loudspeaker or headphone) means of measuring and hearing the individual sources as well as the final mixed output.
3. *Control circuits:* Provision of communication with studios or outside broadcasts by means of 'talkback' or telephone line.

In learning to operate the panel there is little substitute for first understanding the principles of the individual equipment, then practising until its operation becomes second nature. The following are some operational points for the beginner.

The operator must be comfortable. The correct chair height and easy access to all necessary equipment is important for fluent operation.

The first function to be considered is the *monitoring* of the programme. Nothing on a panel, which might possibly be on the air, should be touched until the question has been answered –

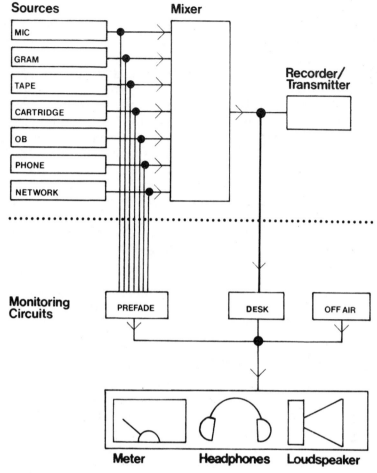

Studio control panel or board: typical programme and monitoring circuits.

What am I listening to? The loudspeaker is normally required to carry the direct output of the desk, as for example in the case of a rehearsal or recording. In transmission conditions it will normally take its programme 'off-air', although it may not be feasible to listen via a receiver when transmitting on a short wave service. As far as is possible, the programme should be monitored as it will be heard by the listener, not simply as it leaves the studio.

The volume of the monitoring loudspeaker should be adjusted to a comfortable level and then left alone. It is impossible to make subjective assessments of relative loudness within the programme if the volume of the loudspeaker is constantly being changed. If the loudspeaker is required to be turned down, for instance, so that a conversation can take place on the telephone, it should be done with a single key operation so that the original volume is easily restored afterwards.

In *mixing* sources together – mics, grams, tape, cartridge, etc. – the general rule is to bring the 'new' fader in before taking the 'old' one out. This avoids the loss of atmosphere between the various sources which will occur when all the faders are closed. A slow mix from one sound source to another is the 'crossfade'.

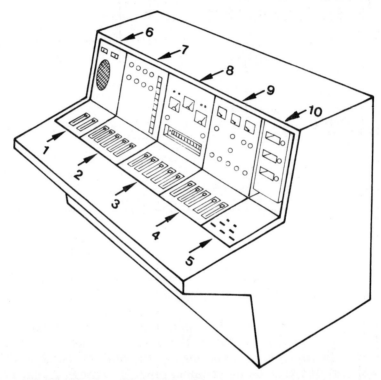

Studio control console based on BBC Local Radio MK3 desk. 1. Gram faders. 2. Outside source faders. 3. Microphone faders controlling two microphones in the adjacent studio plus two associated with the desk for 'self-op' work. Also 'echo return' fader. 4. Two tape and three cartridge channel faders. 5. Talkback and radio car calling keys. 6. Intercom loudspeaker. 7. Outside source selection. 8. Output and prefade monitoring meters. Transmission selector. 9. Loudspeaker and headphone monitoring controls. Voice-over and limiter keys. Tape recorder input selection and remote start facilities. 10. Three-stack cartridge machine. (Courtesy, BBC Engineering Information Department.)

In assessing the relative *sound* levels of one programme source against another, either in a mix, or in juxtaposition, the most important devices are the operator's own ears. The question of how loud speech should be against music depends on a variety of factors, including the nature of the programme and the probable listening conditions of the audience, as well as the type of music and the vocal characteristics of the speech. There will certainly be a maximum level which can be sent to the line feeding the transmitter, and this represents the upper limit against which everything else is judged. Obviously for the orchestral concert, music needs to be louder than speech. However, the reverse is the case where the speech is of predominant importance or where the music is already dynamically compressed, as it is with most popular records. This 'speech louder than music' characteristic is general for most record request or

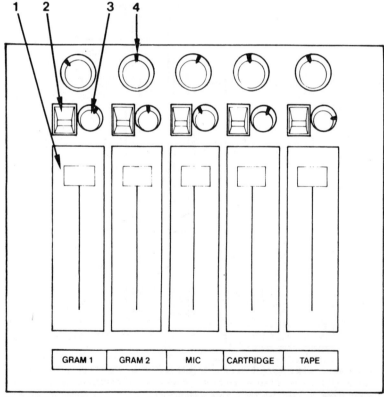

Simple 5-channel mixing unit for self-operation. 1. Channel fader. 2. Prefade key. 3. Prefade volume control. 4. Pan-pot for placing the source in a stereo 'picture'.

magazine programmes or when the music is designed for background listening. It is particularly important when the listening conditions are likely to be noisy, for example at busy domestic times or in the car.

However it is also true, and seems to be especially prevalent in a situation of fiercely competing transmitters, that maximum signal penetration is obtained by sacrificing dynamic subtlety.

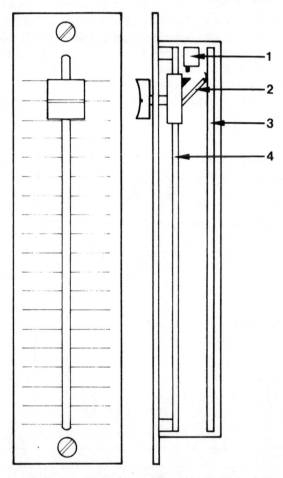

Typical linear or slider fader. BBC practice is to fade up by moving the slider towards the operator. This avoids inadvertent operation of backstop switch.
1. Backstop switch; operates 'remote start' equipment, mutes loudspeaker or switches on red 'on-air' lights. 2. Fine wire electrical 'brush' connectors. 3. Resistive block. 4. Guide rail.

The sound levels of all sources are kept as high as possible and the transmitter is given a large dose of compression. It is as well for the producer to know about this otherwise he may spend a good deal of time obtaining a certain kind of effect or perfecting his fades only to have them overruled by an uncomprehending transmitter!

Probably the most important aspect of panel operation is *self-organisation*. It is essential to have a system for the handling of the physical items; that is the running order, scripts, cue sheets, records, tapes, etc. The material which has been used should be put out of the way, and new material brought forward as it is needed. The good operator is always one step ahead. He knows what he is going to do next, and having done it he sets up the next step.

Records and turntables

Music, like speech, comes in sentences and paragraphs. It would be nonsensical to finish a voice piece other than at the

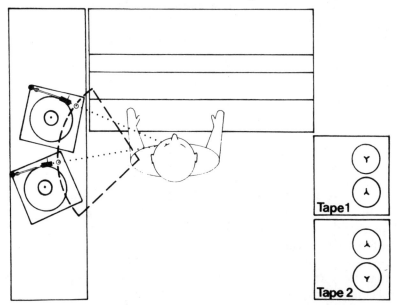

Operator position relative to gramophone turntables. The operational controls should be on the same radius from the operator's shoulder and lie on his sightline for easy 'setting up' at the start of the disc. This type of control desk offers full programme facilities and is relatively large. Smaller DJ desks often arrange turntables to be sited left and right of the operator.

end of a sentence, similarly it is wrong to fade a piece of music arbitrarily. A great deal of work has gone into the making of a record, it should not be treated like water out of a tap and be turned off and on at will — not unless the broadcaster is prepared to accept the degradation of music into simply a plastic filler material. The good operator therefore will develop an 'ear' for fade points. The 'talk-over' — an accurately timed announcement which exactly fits the non-vocal introduction to a song — provides a satisfying example of paying attention to such detail. Music handled *with respect to its phrasing* provides listening pleasure for everyone. The presenter must accept the responsibility when music and speech are mixed through an automatic 'voice-over' unit so that whenever he utters, the music is hurled into the background. It has its uses in particular types of 'immediately disposable' programme, but to use music as a semi-fluid sealant universally applied, seems to imply that the programme has cracks which have to be frantically filled!

The broadcaster's attitude to music is often typified by his care in the treatment of records. They are worth looking after. This includes an up-to-date library cataloguing system and proper arrangements for their withdrawal and return; thus avoiding records being left lying around in the studio or production offices. They should be held so that the fingers do not touch the playing surface, kept clean and free of dust and cigarette ash, played with the correct and fluff-free stylus, and replaced in the sleeve as soon as possible after playing. Very many broadcasters who use records professionally have domestic hi-fi equipment over which they take meticulous care. However, only too often is it possible to see in a radio studio naked records ground together under a pile of coffee cups, melting on a radiator or gently warping in the sun. The inevitable result is " . . . sorry Mrs. Jones, we don't seem to have that one . . ."

In playing a record, most control desks have a 'pre-fade', 'pre-hear' or 'audition' facility which enables the operator to listen to the record and check its volume before setting it up to play on the air. This provides the opportunity of checking that it is the right piece of music, but listening only to the beginning may give a false idea of its volume throughout. A glance at the grooves will often be sufficient to indicate whether there is a wide variation in dynamic range — grey grooves are loud, black ones are quieter.

Mistakes will occur and sooner or later a record goes on at

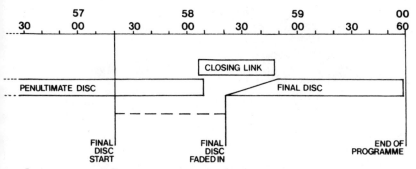

Prefading to time. This is the most usual method of ensuring that programmes run to time. In this example, the final disc (or tape) is 2'40" long. It is therefore started at 57'20" but not faded up until it is wanted as the closing link finishes. It runs for a further 1'10" and brings the programme to an end on the hour.

the wrong speed. (This should have been apparent at the setting up stage but just this once there was insufficient time to listen to it.) The best course generally is to do what is simplest and most natural — to fade out, apologise, change speed and re-start. It may throw the timing out but that is another problem. On the rare occasion it is just possible to get away with a disc at the wrong speed — certain types of string sound and harpsichord seem indifferent to treatment at 33⅓ or 45 r.p.m. If the composer is dead one may be safe (a movement of one of the Brandenburg concertos was a personal case in point!). If the incorrect speed has been applied to a record which is being prefaded to time, such as a closing signature tune, and the error is discovered before the record is faded up, the following formula is crude but effective and may save the situation:

1. When a 33⅓ r.p.m. disc is played inadvertently at 45 r.p.m.; then stop the record and while changing speed hold it at that place for a third of the time it has been running fast.
2. When a 45 r.p.m. disc is played inadvertently at 33⅓ r.p.m.; then play the record at 78 r.p.m. for half the length of time it has been running slow. Then change speed once again to 45 r.p.m. This is not a recommended method of treating records, simply a way of overcoming a problem when timing is crucial.

Tape reproduction

As with records, tapes should be checked before transmission

Open Reel

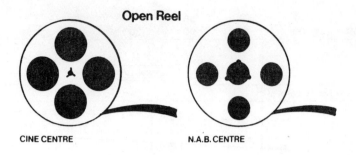

CINE CENTRE   N.A.B. CENTRE

Cassette

Cartridge

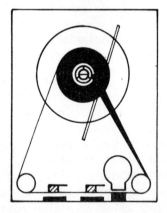

Tape formats. The most usual sizes for 'open' or 'reel to reel' spools are 12.5 cm (5 in) and 17.5 cm (7 in) for plastic spools with a cine centre, and 25 cm (10 in) for aluminium spools with a NAB centre. Tape is also used on one-sided spools or simply wound on a central 'former'. Cassettes are designated according to their total playing time — a C60 cassette has a 30 min duration for each side. In the cartridge, tape is drawn from the outside of the reel and returned to the inside so forming a continuous loop.

32

to ensure that the correct tape is played. This requires the words of the start of the tape to be matched against the information provided on the cue sheet. Recorded levels can vary considerably and the pre-transmission check is also used to adjust the replay volume to the existing programme level. Tape is used in the studio in at least three different formats — open reels, cassettes and cartridges.

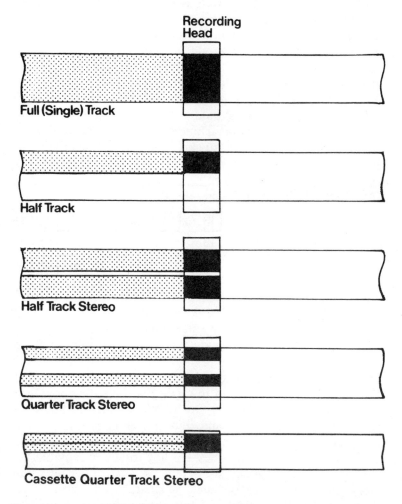

Tape track systems. Monophonically recorded cassette tape uses all the top half of the tape to ensure compatibility of playback with the stereo system. A recording system using only part of the tape enables a second signal to be recorded by 'turning the tape over', but results in a lower signal to noise ratio i.e. greater tape hiss.

Reel to reel tape recorders use spools of 6mm ('¼ inch) wide tape which vary in diameter from 12.5 cm (5 inches) to 25 cm (10 inches.) Playing speeds of professional tape machines are 9.5 cm/sec (3³/₄ inches/sec), 19 cm/sec (7½ inches/sec), or 38 cm/sec (15 inches/sec). It is important that, as far as possible, all producers within a single system adopt common technical standards for tape reproduction. This applies to the thickness and type of tape used as well as the actual tape speed. If for example 'standard play' tape is adopted for general use (acceptted BBC practice), it would be unwise to assume that the thinner 'long play' tape would perform equally well. In this instance applying the brakes while spooling at high speed is generally sufficient to reduce the tape to an unusable piece of 'stretched shoe lace'. The adjustment of the brakes can be critical and producers should call for engineering advice if they suspect any kind of machine problem. Faulty equipment, or faulty operation, can quickly destroy pre-recorded programme material.

TAPE LENGTH	SPEED – cm/sec (ins/sec)				
	38(15)	19(7$\frac{1}{2}$)	9.5(3$\frac{3}{4}$)	4.7(1$\frac{7}{8}$)	2.3($\frac{15}{16}$)
600ft	8m	16m	32m	1h4m	2h8m
1200ft	16m	32m	1h4m	2h8m	4h16m
2400ft	32m	1h4m	2h8m	4h16m	8h32m

Running times of recording tape in hours and minutes.

The cassette recorder uses a small 'closed' reel to reel device containing 3mm ('⅛ inch) wide tape of 30-120 minutes total duration at a tape speed of 4.7 cm/sec (1⁷/₈ inches/sec). Cassettes were originally developed for the domestic market but have steadily improved in quality so that they now have a number of applications in broadcasting. The cassette recorder is easily carried and unobtrusive in operation; it is this ease of handling which is the key to their increasing popularity. Nevertheless, they are not totally acceptable for widespread professional use. This is firstly because the mechanical tolerances on such small, relatively slow speed devices are fairly critical and there is no absolute guarantee that a cassette recorded on one machine will replay perfectly on another; and secondly because access to the tape itself is denied and a physical editing process requires that the cassette is first copied on to an 'open' reel tape. However, given a consistently satisfactory level of quality, the cassette opens the way to dubbing rather than cutting as a general method of editing, at least for speech material.

The cartridge is an enclosed single spool device, containing

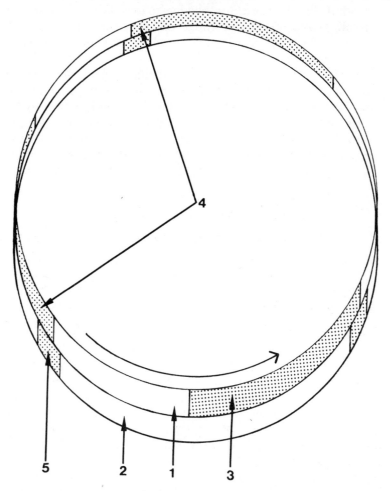

Cartridge tape loop. The top half 1 is the programme track, the bottom half 2 is the cue track. The programme item 3 is recorded on the tape with as many repeat record-ings 4 as will fit conveniently in the whole cartridge. This technique reduces the resetting time for a frequently used item. Each recording is associated with a stop pulse 5 on the cue track. This pulse ensures that the tape stops at the point where the recorded programme item is about to start. The total duration of a cartridge loop can be anything from 20 seconds to 10 minutes. Special lubricated tape is used.

a continuous loop of tape and is an ideal method of handling relatively short items, particularly those which need to be replayed a number of times, e.g. signature tunes, station identifications, jingles, commercials, programme trails. After replay, it is generally arranged that the tape automatically resets itself so that the material can be repeated as required. In addition to its use for playing material directly into the broadcast output, the cartridge also represents a convenient method of storing the one-off item for insertion into a magazine programme or news bulletin.

Relative to the open spool, cartridges take a little more time and trouble to record but are extremely simple to replay and being fast to change they offer the producer the advantages of very flexible programming. However they do not normally 'fast spool' and once started, e.g. to adjust the level, the tape must play through its entire duration in order to be reset once again at its start.

Tape editing

The purposes of editing recorded tape can be summarised as:

1. To rearrange recorded material into a more logical sequence.
2. To remove the uninteresting, repetitive, or technically unacceptable.
3. To compress the material in time.

Editing must not be used to alter the sense of what has been said or to place the material within an unintended context.

There are always two considerations when editing, namely the editorial and the mechanical. In the editorial sense it is important to leave intact for example the view of an interviewee, and the reasons given for its support. It would be wrong to include a key statement but to omit an essential qualification through lack of time. On the other hand facts can often be edited out and included more economically in the introductory cue material. It is also very often possible to remove some or all of the interviewer's questions, letting the interviewee continue. If the interviewee has a stammer, or pauses for long periods, tape editing can obviously remove these gaps. However it would be unwise to remove them completely, as this may alter the nature of the individual voice.

Mechanically, the process consists of identifying the beginning and the end of the unwanted section of the recording, marking both (generally using a light coloured 'chinagraph' pencil), cutting the tape with a single-sided razor blade at the marks using a diagonal slot in an editing block, removing the section of tape and joining together the tape ends with 3cms of appropriate adhesive tape. Initially, practice is required in listening carefully to a recording being played through the machine by hand at slow speed, so that the exact place where the tape is to be cut can be located. Since this generally coincides with the start of a word, this is not a difficult operation,

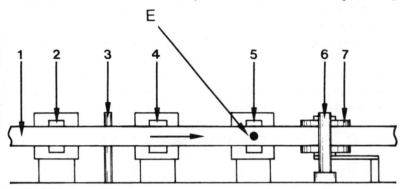

Tape machine head assembly. 1. Tape. 2. Erase head. 3. Guide pin. 4. Recording head. 5. Replay head. 6. Capstan. 7. Pinch wheel which holds the tape firmly against the capstan. During editing, the tape is marked on the replay head at point E.

especially if there is a small piece of silent tape immediately preceding it. These tiny silences are useful and the most frequent fault in editing is their removal so destroying the paragraph pauses which occur naturally in speech.

An alternative process of editing which avoids the physical cutting of tape is dubbing. Here, the sections of tape to be used are individually copied in the required order on to a second tape. It is not so precise as cutting, and two machines are required, but it does preserve intact the original reel of tape so that it can be used again. It may well be the more suitable method where long sections of the material are to be removed, or where the recorded levels vary and need adjusting, or where a number of studio links have to be inserted.

Care of tape

The proper reproduction of tape relies on the preservation of

37

the magnetic patterns as recorded, and their close and consistent contact with the replay head of the tape machine during the reproduction process. The enemies of tape are excessive heat, vibration or banging, and the influence of external magnetic fields, as for example from certain types of microphone. These things affect the magnetic elements on the tape and can cause loss of quality, particularly at the upper frequencies. In extreme cases the programme material may suffer partial or total erasure. It is possible for example for tapes to be 'wiped clean' by certain types of luggage search equipment used at airports. For the long term storage of tapes the recommended temperature is 10°C (50°F).

To ensure good quality at the replay stage it is important that the equipment, especially the replay head and the tape itself are all clean. A thin film of grease on the tape or remnants of marking pencil on the head will considerably impair the quality.

A characteristic of tape in storage is its remarkable anonymity. A disc is inseparable from its label but one piece of tape is precisely like another. A spool, cassette or cartridge, and its box should carry sufficient marking for the programme material to be identified. In the first instance it is the responsibility of the individual producer, interviewer or technical operator to ensure that the proper details are noted at the time of recording. These will include:

1. Subject matter.
2. Name and address of speaker, musicians or other participants.
3. Location of recording.
4. Date of recording.
5. Details of any copyright material – music, poetry etc.
6. Duration.
7. Details of any editing required prior to transmission.

Other than the last item, all this information should accompany a tape that is retained for archive purposes.

3

INTERVIEWING

THE aim of an interview is to provide, in the interviewee's own words; facts, reasons or opinions on a particular topic so that the listener can form a conclusion as to the validity of what he is saying.

The basic approach

It follows from the above definition that the opinions of the interviewer are irrelevant, he should never get drawn into answering a question which the interviewee may put to him — an interview is not a discussion. We are not concerned here with what has been referred to as 'the personality interview' where the interviewer, often the host of a television 'chat show', acts as the grand inquisitor and asks his guests to test their opinions against his own. Within this present definition it is solely the interviewee who must come through and in the interviewer's vocabulary the word 'I' should be absent. The interviewer is not there to argue, to agree or disagree. He is not there to comment on the answers he gets. He is there to ask questions. To do this he needs to have done his homework and must be prepared to listen.

The interview is essentially a spontaneous event. Any hint of its being rehearsed damages the interviewee's credibility to the extent of the listener believing the whole thing to be 'fixed'. For this reason, while the topic may be discussed generally beforehand, the actual questions should not be provided in advance. The interview must be what it appears to be — questions and answers for the benefit of the eavesdropping listener. The interviewer is after all acting on behalf of his listener and is asking the questions which the listener would want to ask. More than this, he is asking the questions which his listener would ask if he knew as much about the background to the subject as the interviewer knows. The interview is an opportunity to provide not only what the listener wants to know, but also what he may need to know. At least as far as the interviewing of political figures is concerned, the interview should represent a contribution towards the maintenance of a democratic society. It is a valuable element of broadcasting and care should be taken to ensure it is not damaged, least of all by casual abuse in the cult of personality on the part of broadcasters.

Types of interview

For the sake of simplicity three types of interview can be identified, although any one situation may involve all three categories to a greater or lesser extent. These are the informational, the interpretive and the emotional interview.

Obviously, the purpose of the *informational interview* is to impart information to the listener. The sequence in which this is done becomes important if the details are to be clear. There may be considerable discussion beforehand to clarify what information is required and to allow time for the interviewee to recall or check any statistics. Topics for this kind of interview include: the action surrounding a military operation, the events and decisions made at a union meeting, or the proposals contained in the city's newly announced development plan.

The *interpretive interview* has the interviewer supplying the facts and asking the interviewee either to comment on them or to explain them. The aim is to expose his reasoning and allow the listener to make a judgement on his sense of values or priorities. Replies to questions will almost certainly contain statements in justification of a particular course of action which should themselves also be questioned. The interviewer must be well briefed, alert, and attentive to pick up and challenge the opinions expressed. Examples in this category would be a government minister on his reasons for an already published economic policy, why the local council has decided on a particular route for a new road, or views of the clergy on proposals to amend the divorce laws. The essential point is that the interviewer is not asking for the facts of the matter, these will be generally known; rather he is investigating the interviewee's reaction to the facts. The discussion beforehand may be quite brief; the interviewer outlining the purpose of the interview and the limits of the subject he wishes to pursue. Since the content is reactive, it should on no account be rehearsed in its detail.

The aim of the *emotional interview* is to provide an insight into the interviewee's state of mind so that the listener may better understand what is involved in human terms. Specific examples would be the feelings of relatives of miners trapped underground in a pit accident, the euphoria surrounding the moment of supreme achievement for an athlete or successful entertainer, or the anger felt by people involved in an industrial dispute. It is the strength of feeling present rather than its rationality which is important and clearly the interviewer needs to be at his most sensitive in handling such situations. He will receive acclaim for asking the right question at the right time in order to illuminate a matter of public interest, even when the event itself is tragic. But he is quickly criticised for being too intrusive into private grief. It is in this respect that his manner of asking a question is as important as its content, possibly more so. Another difficulty which faces the interviewer is to reconcile his need to remain an impartial observer with his not appearing indifferent to the suffering. The amount of time taken in preliminary conversation will vary considerably depending on the circumstances. The interviewer should be prepared for a lengthy process establishing the necessary relationship and also be ready to begin at any time. Such a situation allows little opportunity for retakes.

Preparation before the interview

It is essential for the interviewer to know what he is trying to achieve. Is the interview to establish facts, or to discuss reasons? What are the main points which must be covered? Are there established arguments and counter arguments to the case? The interviewer must obviously know something of the subject and a briefing from the producer, combined with some research on his own part is highly desirable. An essential is absolute certainty of any names, dates, figures or other facts used within the questions. It is very embarrassing for the expert interviewee to correct even a trifling factual error in a question — it also represents a loss of control, for example:

"Why was it only 3 years ago that you began to introduce this new system?"

"Well actually it was 5 years ago now".

It is important, although easily capable of being overlooked, to know exactly who you are talking to:

"As the chairman of the company, how do you view the future?"

"No, I'm the managing director . . ."

It makes no difference whatsoever to the validity of the question but a lack of basic care undermines the questioner's credibility in the eyes of the interviewee, and even more important, in the ears of the listener.

Having decided what has to be discovered, the interviewer must then structure his questions accordingly. Question technique is dealt with in a later section but it should be remembered that what is actually asked is not necessarily formulated in precise detail beforehand. Such a procedure could easily be inflexible and the interviewer may then feel obliged to ask the list of questions irrespective of the response by the interviewee!

To summarise, an interviewer's normal starting point would be:

1. To obtain sufficient briefing and background information on the subject and the interviewee.
2. To have a detailed knowledge of what the interview should achieve.
3. To know what the key questions are.

The pre-interview discussion

The next stage, after the preparatory work, is to discuss the interview with the interviewee. The first few minutes are crucial. Each party is sizing up the other and the interviewer must decide how to proceed.

There is no standard approach, each occasion demands its own. The interviewee may respond to the broadcaster's brisk professionalism, or might better appreciate a more sympathetic attitude. He may need to feel important, or the opposite. The interviewee in a totally unfamiliar situation may be so nervous as to be unable to marshal his thoughts properly, his entire language structure and speed of delivery may alter in order to cope with what is for him a condition of some stress. The good interviewer will be aware of this and must work hard so that the interviewee's thinking and personality are given a chance to emerge. Whatever the circumstances, the interviewer has to get it right, and he has only a little time in which to form his judgements.

The interviewer indicates the subject areas to be covered but he is well advised to let the interviewee do most of the talking. This is an opportunity to confirm some of the facts, and it helps the interviewee to release his own tensions while allowing the interviewer to anticipate any problems of language, coherence or volume.

It is wrong for the interviewer to get drawn into a discussion of the matter, particularly if there is a danger that he might reveal his own personal attitude to the subject. Nor must he adopt a hostile manner or imply criticism. This may be appropriate during the interview but even so it is not the interviewer's job to conduct a judicial enquiry, nor to represent himself as prosecuting counsel, judge and jury.

The interviewer's prime task at this stage is to clarify what the interview is about and to create the degree of rapport which will produce the appropriate information in a logical sequence at the right length. He must obtain the confidence of the interviewee while establishing his means of control. A complex subject needs to be simplified, and distilled for the purposes of say a 2½ minute interview – there must be no technical or specialist jargon, and the intellectual and emotional level must be right for the programme. Above all, the end result should be interesting.

It is a common and useful practice to say beforehand what the first question will be, since in a 'live' situation it can help to prevent a total 'freeze' as the red light goes on. If the interview is to be recorded, such a question may serve as a 'dummy' to be edited off later. In any event it helps the interviewee to relax and to feel confident about starting. The interviewer should begin the actual interview with as little technical fuss as possible, the preliminary conversation proceeding into the interview with the minimum of discontinuity.

Question technique

An interview is a conversation with an aim. On the one hand the interviewer knows what that aim is and he knows something of the subject. On the other he is placing himself where the listener is and is asking questions in an attempt to discover more. This balance of knowledge and ignorance can be described as 'informed naivety'.

The question type will provide answer of a corresponding type. In their simplest form they are:

1. Who?   –   asks a fact. Answer – a person.
2. When?   –   asks a fact. Answer – a time.
3. Where?   –   asks a fact. Answer – a place.
4. What?   –   asks for fact or an interpretation of fact. Answer – a sequence of events.
5. How?   –   asks for fact or an interpretation of fact. Answer – a sequence of events.
6. Why?   –   asks for opinion or reason for a course of action.

These are the basic question types on which there are many variations. For example:

"How do you feel about . . .?"
"To what extent do you think that . . .?"

The best of all questions, and incidentally the one asked least, is 'why?' Indeed after an answer it may be unnecessary to ask anything other than "why is that?" The 'why' question is the most revealing of the interviewee since it leads to an explanation of his actions, judgements and values.

"Why did you decide to . . .?"
"Why do you believe it necessary to . . .?"

It is sometimes said that it is wrong to ask questions based on the 'reversed verb'.

Are you . . .?
Is it . . .?
Will they . . .?
Do you . . .?

What the interviewer is asking here is for either a confirmation or a denial; the answer to such a question is either yes or no. If this is really what the interviewer is after, then the question structure is a proper one. If however it is an attempt to introduce a new topic in the hope that the interviewee will continue to say something other than yes or no, it is an ill-defined question. As such it is likely to lead to the interviewer's loss of control, since it leaves the initiative completely with the interviewee.

In this respect the 'reversed verb' question is a poor substitute for a question which is specifically designed to point the interview in the desired direction. The 'reversed verb' question should therefore only be used when a yes/no answer is what is required – "Will there be a tax increase this year?"

Question 'width'

This introduces the concept of how much room for manoeuvre the interviewer is to give the interviewee. Clearly where a yes/no response is being sought, the interviewee is being tied down and there is little room for manoeuvre; the question is very narrow. On the other hand it is possible to ask a question which is so enormously wide that the interviewee is confused as to what is being asked – "You've just returned from a study tour of Europe, tell me about it". This is not of course a question at all, it is an order. Statements of this kind are made by inexperienced interviewers who think they are being helpful to a nervous interviewee. In fact the reverse is more likely with the interviewee baffled as to where to start.

Beware also the interviewer who has to clarify his own question – "How was it you embarked on such a course of events, I mean what made you decide to do this – after all at the time it wasn't the most obvious thing to do, was it?" Confusion upon confusion, and yet this kind of muddle can be heard on the air. If the purpose of the question is not clear in the interviewer's mind, it is unlikely to be understood by the interviewee – the listener's confusion is liable to degenerate into indifference and subsequent total disinterest.

Devil's advocate

If the interviewee is to express his own point of view fully and to answer his various critics, it will be necessary for those opposing views to be put to him. This gives him the opportunity of demolishing the arguments to the satisfaction, or otherwise, of the listener. In putting such views the interviewer must be careful not to associate himself with them, nor must he be associated in the listener's mind with the principle of opposition. His role is to present propositions which he knows to have been expressed elsewhere, or the doubts and arguments which he might reasonably expect to be in the listener's mind. In adopting

the 'devil's advocate' approach common forms of question
are:

> "On the other hand it has been said that . . ."
> "Some people would argue that . . ."
> "How do you react to people who say that . . ."
> "What would you say to the argument that . . ."

The first two examples as they stand are not questions but
statements and if left as such will bring the interview dangerously
close to being a discussion. The interviewer must ensure that the
point is put as an objective question.

It has been said in this context that 'you can't play good
tennis with a bad opponent.' The way in which broadcasters
present counter-argument needs care, but most interviewees
welcome it as a means of making their case more easily understood.

Multiple questions

A trap for the inexperienced interviewer, obsessed with the
fear that his interviewee will be lacking in response, is to ask
two questions at once:

> "Why was it that the meeting broke up in disorder, and
> how will you prevent this happening in future?"

The interviewee presented with two questions may answer
the first and then genuinely forget the second, or he may
exercise his apparent option to answer whichever one he prefers.
In either case there is a loss of control on the part of the interviewer as the initiative passes to the interviewee.

Questions should be kept short and simple. Long rambling
circumlocutory questions will get answers in a similar vein;
this is the way conversation works. The response tends to
reflect the stimulus – this underlines the fact that the interviewer's initial approach will set the tone for the whole interview.

Another type of multiple question, which on the face of it
seems helpful, is the 'either/or' question.

> "Did you introduce this type of engine because there is a
> new market for it, or because you were working on it anyway?"

The trouble here is that the question 'width' is so narrow that in
all probability the answer lies outside it so leaving the inter-

viewee little option but to say "Well neither, it was partly . . ." Things are seldom so clear cut as to fall exactly into one of two divisions. In any case it is not up to the interviewer to suggest answers; what he wanted to know was – "Why did you introduce this type of engine?"

Leading questions

Lazy, inexperienced or malicious questioning can appear to put the interviewee in a particular position before he begins.

"Why did you start your business with such shaky finances?"
"How do you justify such a high handed action?"

It is not up to the interviewer to suggest that finances are shaky or that action is high handed, unless this is a direct quote of what the interviewee has just said. Given the facts, the listener must be able to determine for himself from what the interviewee says whether the finances were sufficient or whether the action was unnecessarily autocratic. Adjectives which imply value judgements must be a warning signal, for interviewee and listener alike, that all is not quite what it appears to be. Here is an interviewer who has a point to make, and in this respect he may not be properly representing the listener. The questions can still be put in a perfectly acceptable form:

"How much did you start your business with?" (fact)
"At the time did you regard this as enough?" (yes/no)
"How do you view this now?" (judgement)
"What would you say to people who might regard this action as 'high handed?' " (This is the 'devil's advocate' approach already referred to).

It is surprising how one is able to ask very direct, personally revealing, 'hard' questions in a perfectly acceptable way by maintaining at the same time a calmly pleasant composure. When a broadcaster is criticised for being over-aggressive, it is his manner rather than what he says which is being questioned. Even persistence can be politely done:

"With respect, the question was *why* this had happened."

In asking *why* something happened it is not uncommon to get in effect *how* it happened, particularly if the interviewee wishes to be evasive. If he is evasive a second time, this will be obvious to the listener and there is no need for the interviewer to labour the point, it is already made.

Non-questions

Some interviewers delight in making statements instead of asking questions. The danger is that the interview may become a discussion. For example, an answer might be followed by the statement:

"This wouldn't happen normally."

Instead of with the question — "Is this normal?"
A further example is the statement:

"You don't appear to have taken that into account."

Instead of the question — "To what extent have you taken that into account?"

Again, the fault lies in the question not being put in a positive way; the interviewee can respond how he likes and the interviewer finds it more difficult to exercise control over both the subject matter and the timing.

Occasionally interviewers ask whether they can ask questions:

"Could I ask you if . . ."
"I wonder whether you could say why . . ."

This is unecessary of course since in the acceptance of the interview there is an agreement to answer questions. There may occasionally be justification for such an approach when dealing with a particularly sensitive area and the interviewer feels the need to proceed gently. This phraseology can be used to indicate that the interviewer recognises the difficulty inherent in the question. Much more likely however it is used by accident when the questioner is uncertain as to the direction of the interview and is 'padding' in order to provide himself with more thinking time. Such a device to gain time is likely to give the listener the feeling that his is being wasted.

Non-verbal communication

Throughout the interview the rapport established earlier must continue. This is chiefly done through eye contact and facial expression. Once the interviewer stops looking at his respondent, perhaps for a momentary glance at the machinery or at his notes, there is a danger of losing the thread of the interview. At worst, the interviewee will himself look away, and his thoughts as well as his eyes are then liable to wander. The concentration must be maintained. The eyes of the interviewer will express his interest in what is being said — the interviewer is never bored. He can express surprise, puzzlement or encouragement by nodding his head. In fact, it quickly becomes annoying to the listener to have these reactions in verbal form — "ah yes", "mm", "I see".

Eye contact is also the most frequent means of controlling the timing of the interview — of indicating that another question needs to be put. It may be necessary to make a gesture with the hand, but generally it is acceptable to butt-in with a further question. Of course the interviewer must be courteous and positive to the point of knowing exactly what it is he wants to say. Even the most talkative interviewee has to breathe and the signs of such small pauses should be noted beforehand so that the interviewer can use them effectively.

During the interview

The interviewer must be actively in control of four separate functions — the technical, the direction of the interview, the supplementary question, and the timing.

The technical aspects must be constantly monitored. Is the background noise altering so requiring a change to the microphone position? Is the position of the interviewee changing relative to the microphone, or have the voice levels altered? If the interview is being recorded, is the machine continuing to function correctly — the spools rotating and the meter or other indicator giving a proper reading?

The aims of the interview must always be kept in mind. Is the subject matter being covered in terms of the key questions decided beforehand? Sometimes it is possible for the interviewer to make a positive decision and change courses but in any event he must keep track of where he is going.

The supplementary question. It is vital that the interviewer is not so preoccupied with the next question that he fails to listen to what the interviewee is saying. The ability to listen and to think quickly are essential attributes of the interviewer. He must be able to ask the appropriate *supplementary question* for clarification of a technicality or piece of jargon, or to question further the reason for a particular answer. Where an answer is being given in an unnecessarily academic or abstract way, the interviewer must have it turned into a factual example.

The timing of the interview must be strictly adhered to. This is true whether the interview is to be of half an hour or 2½ minutes. If a short news interview is needed, there is little point in recording for 10 minutes with a view to cutting it to length later. There may be occasions when such a time-consuming process will be unavoidable, even desirable, but in general the preferred method must be 'to sharpen one's mind beforehand, rather than one's razor-blade afterwards'. Thus the interviewer when recording keeps a clock running in his head. It stops when it hears an answer which is known to be unusable but continues again on hearing an interesting response. He controls the flow of the material so that the subject is covered as required in the time available. This sense of time is invaluable when it comes to doing a 'live' interview when of course timing is paramount. Such a discipline is basic to the broadcaster's skills.

Winding up

The word 'finally' should only be used once. It may usefully precede the last question as a signal to the interviewee that time is running out and that anything important left unsaid should now be included. Other signals of this nature are words such as:

"Briefly, why . . ."
"In a word, how . . ."
"At its simplest, what . . ."

It is a great help in getting an interviewee to accept the constraint of timing if the interviewer has remembered to tell him beforehand the anticipated duration.

Occasionally an interviewer is tempted to sum up. This should be resisted since it is extremely difficult to do without some subjective evaluations being made by the interviewer. It must always be borne in mind that the broadcaster's greatest asset is his objective approach to facts and his impartial attitude to opinion. To go further is to forget the listener, or at least to underestimate the listener's ability to form a conclusion for himself. A properly structured interview should have no need of a summary, much less should it be necessary to impose on the listener a view of what has been said.

If the interview has been in any sense chronological, a final question looking to the future will provide an obvious place to stop. A positive convention as an ending is simply to thank the interviewee for taking part — "Mr. Jones, thank you very much." However, an interviewer quickly develops an ear for a good out cue and it is often sufficient to end with the words of the interviewee, particularly if he has made an amusing or strongly assertive point.

After the interview

The interviewer should feel that it has been an enlightening experience which has provided a contribution to the listener's understanding and appreciation of both the subject and the interviewee. If the interview has been recorded, it should be immediately checked by playing back the last 15 seconds or so. No more, otherwise the interviewee is sure to want to change something and one embarks on a lengthy process of explanation and reassurance. The editorial decision as to the content of the interview as well as the responsibility for its technical quality rests with the interviewer. If for any reason he wishes to retake parts of a recording, he would be wise to adopt an entirely fresh approach rather than attempt to re-create the original. Without making problems for the later editing, the questions should be differently phrased to avoid an unconscious effort to remember the previous answer. This amounts to having had a full rehearsal and will almost certainly provide a stale end-product. The interviewee who is losing track of what is going into the final tape is also liable to remark " . . . and as I've already explained . . ." or " . . . and as we were saying a moment ago . . ." Such references to material which has been edited out will naturally mystify the listener, possibly breaking his concentration on what is currently being said.

If the interview has been recorded, the interviewee will probably want to know the transmission details. If the material is specific to an already scheduled programme, this information can be given with some confidence. If however it is a news piece intended for the next bulletin or magazine, it is best not to be too positive lest it be overtaken by a more important story and consequently held over for later use. Tell the interviewee when you hope to broadcast it but if possible avoid total commitment.

Thank the interviewee for his time and trouble and for taking part in the programme. If he has come to the studio, it may be normal to offer his travelling expenses or a fee according to station policy. Irrespective of how the interview has gone, professional courtesy at the closing stage is important. After all, you may want to talk to him again tomorrow.

Location interviews

The businessman in his office, the star in her dressing room, the worker in the factory or out of doors; all are readily accessible with a portable tape recorder and provide credible programming with atmosphere. Yet all pose special problems of noise and interruption.

In any room other than a studio, the acoustics are likely to be poor with too much reflected sound. It is possible to over-

Traffic Islands   **Alcoves**

Tables   **Bathrooms**

Some interviewing situations to avoid. These would be noisy, acoustically poor, or at least asymmetrical, or physically awkward.

52

come this to an acceptable degree by avoiding hard, smooth surfaces such as windows, desk tops, linoleum floors or plastered walls. A carpeted room with curtains and other furnishings is generally satisfactory, but in unfavourable conditions the best course is to work closer to the microphone, while also reducing the level of input to the recorder.

The same applies to situations with a high level of background noise, nevertheless the machine shop or aeroplane cockpit need present no insuperable technical difficulty. The condition which can bring greater problems is where the noise is intermittent — aircraft passing overhead, a telephone ringing, or clock striking. At worst the sound may be so overwhelming as to prevent the interview from being audible but even if this is not the case, such sudden noises are a distraction for the listener which a constant level of background is not. Background sounds which

Gardens **Curtains**

Settees **Pedestrian Precincts**

Some good places for location interviews. These provide a low or at least a constant background noise, acoustically absorbent surroundings, or a comfortable symmetry.

vary in volume and quality can represent a considerable problem if the tape is to be edited later – a point interviewers should remember before beginning. The greatest difficulty in this respect arises when an interview has been recorded against a background of music.

It is generally desirable for location interviews to have some acoustic effect or background noise and only practical experience will indicate how to achieve the proper balance with a particular type of microphone. When in doubt, priority should be given to the clarity of the speech.

As with the studio interview, the discussion beforehand is aimed at putting the interviewee at his ease. When outside, using a portable recorder, part of this same process is to show how little equipment is involved. The microphone and machine should be assembled, made ready, and checked during this preliminary conversation. It is important to handle these items in front of the interviewee and not spring the technicalities on him at the last moment. Before starting it is advisable to make a final check by 'taking level', i.e. by recording some brief conversation to test the relative volume of the two voices. A satisfactory playback is the final stage before beginning the interview.

Some further rules in the use of portable recorders:
1. Always check the machine and its microphone before leaving base – record and replay.
2. Take with you spare batteries if there is any doubt about the machine's state of electrical charge.
3. Do not leave a recorder unattended, where it can be seen, even in a locked car.
4. Always use a microphone windshield when recording out of doors.

4

BEING INTERVIEWED

MESMERISED perhaps by the 'media moguls' who revel in the cut and thrust of the questioning which appears on the nation's television screens, standing in awe of the assumed omniscience of the interview barons who probe the judgements of the greatest in the land, some people are understandably a little fearful of being interviewed, even by their own local radio station. They may feel that they are at the mercy of the interviewer and let their minds go blank, hoping for the best. While the previous chapter insists that the overall initiative remains with the interviewer, there are processes which the interviewee must bear in mind — after all the reason for the broadcast lies within the interviewee, he is the expert.

The interviewee should not be nervous — after all, he is the one with the information — the expert! Note even this interviewer loops the microphone cable through his hand to prevent noise caused by cable movement.

Aims and attitudes

For someone about to be interviewed it is essential to recognise what an interview is and what opportunities it presents, and what it is not.

For example it is not a confrontation, which it is the interviewer's object to win. An interviewer whose attitude is one of battle, to whom the interviewee represents an opponent who has to be defeated, will almost inevitably alienate the audience. The listener quickly senses such hostility and the probability is that he will side with the underdog. It is easy to cause affront to the listener's sense of fair play and he generally feels that the balance of advantage already lies with the broadcaster. For an interviewer to be unduly aggressive therefore is counter-productive. Neither is an interview a 'point scoring' operation – this is best left to the debate and the discussion. A would-be interviewee therefore need not feel that he is going to be up against the views of someone else, other than in the indirect 'devils advocate' form referred to earlier.

On the other hand, an interview is not a platform for the totally free expression of opinion. The assertions made are open to challenge, if not within the interview itself, then possibly in an adjacent 'balancing' interview. The interviewee may not even know about this unless he remembers to ask, but it does illustrate the need for some preparation on his part. He needs particularly to realise that even if nothing positive is said, an impression will certainly have been made. Radio is to do with pictures and the listener will visualise some sort of image to accompany the broadcast. The most useful impression which an interviewee can convey is one of credibility. Only when the listener is prepared to believe in the interviewee, or for that matter any speaker, will he begin to pay much attention to what is being said.

What the interviewee should know

Since it is impossible to interview someone who does not want to be interviewed, it is reasonable to assume that the arrangement is mutually agreed. The broadcaster in contacting a potential interviewee asks whether an interview might take place. The information which the interviewee needs at this point is as follows:

56

1. What is it to be about? Not the exact questions but the general areas, and the limits of the subject.
2. Is it to be broadcast live or recorded?
3. How long is it to be? Is the broadcast a major programme or a short item? This sets the level at which the subject can be dealt with and helps to guard against the interviewee recording a long interview without his being aware that it must be edited to another length.
4. What is the context? Is the interview part of a wider treatment of the subject with contributions from others or a single item in a news or magazine programme?
5. For what audience? A local station, network use, for syndication?
6. Where? At the studio or elsewhere?
7. When? How long is there for preparation?

No potential interviewee need feel rushed into undertaking an interview and certainly not without establishing the basic information outlined above. Sometimes a fee is paid but this is unlikely in community radio; it is worth asking about.

Shall I be interviewed?

Having obtained an overall picture of what the broadcaster wants, the potential interviewee must ask himself whether he is the right person to be interviewed. Broadcasters will generally approach the person they believe to be most closely involved in the matter but their knowledge of contacts is not infallible. They may go to a company chairman when the PRO would be more appropriate, or they might approach the bishop when one of the lay workers is more informed on the factual detail as opposed to the policy involved.

In deciding whether to be interviewed or not, there may be considerations of possible repercussions at home or at work, the publicity value, or the personal satisfaction of broadcasting. It may also be necessary to ask what the broadcaster would do if there were a refusal to be interviewed. There are at least three courses open to him − to drop the subject altogether; to ask someone else; to broadcast the fact that 'no comment' was forthcoming. This last has the inevitable innuendo that there is something to hide; in this situation the listener should know why a full interview is not possible.

Making time for preparation

The broadcaster may telephone initially and on securing consent to an interview arrive with his portable recorder later that day. Alternatively, he may arrange a studio interview several days in advance. Here there is time for preparation by the interviewee. On the other hand, the interviewer may arrive equipped with his recorder and ask for an interview on the spot — or even telephone and tell the interviewee that he is already on the air! This last technique is bad practice, and besides contravenes the basic rights of an interviewee that his telephone conversation will not be broadcast or recorded without his consent. There can be no question of doing this without his knowledge. It should be a standard procedure amongst all broadcasters that in telephoning a potential interviewee nothing is begun, recorded or transmitted without the interviewee being in possession of all the information outlined earlier. Even so, to be rung up and asked for an interview there and then is asking a great deal and no one should feel obligated to accept this invitation. It is in no-one's interest, least of all the listener's to have an ill-thought out interview with incomplete replies and factual errors.

The broadcaster may ask for an immediate reaction to a news event and the interviewee may be perfectly prepared, indeed anxious to give it. It is however worth making sure that you are fully up-to-date on the news story before stating your views. It is likely to need thinking through, even briefly; there may be facts to check and other arguments to consider. The broadcaster has his deadline and is not in a position to wait indefinitely, but there may be good reasons why the potential interviewee suggests some slight delay, say ten minutes. This is not to remove the possibility of the immediate interview by telephone, the quick comment, the emotive 'gut' reaction.

Preparing for the interview

Knowing now the subject areas to be discussed, the interviewee needs to crystallise and hold in the front of his mind the *two* most important points he wants to put over. These are the *key points* which he believes should be made — irrespective of the questions he is asked! If he and the interviewer are of a similar mind, these points will be obvious and will occur naturally as the response to questions. If not, the interviewee should include them where he feels it is appropriate.

Recognising the interviewer's role as 'devil's advocate', the wise interviewee will prepare for the possible *counter-arguments* which might be put to him. He should realise that the listener is likely to identify more readily with reasoned argument, based on a capacity to appreciate both sides of a case, than with dogma and bigotry. Accepting the existence of an opposite view and logically explaining why you believe it to be wrong, is one of the best ways of sounding convincing on radio.

Whatever is said is enhanced by good *illustration* which underlines the point being made. Drawn from the interviewee's own experience and conjuring up the appropriate pictures, an illustration is a powerful aid to argument. It should be *brief, factual, recent* and *relevant* — that is both relevant to the case being put and to the experience of the listener. The intention is that there should be a point of contact, a means by which the listener can identify with the interviewee. For community radio this will almost certainly mean that the illustration is 'local'. For example in interviewing a police officer about vandalism, a question might be put about boredom as a possible cause. After answering the question, the interviewee might well illustrate his point with "For example only last week we had a case of two boys in the city centre who . . ." To be effective, illustrations have to be thought about in the interviewee's preparation time.

Check the *essential facts* of the interview — the amount of money committed, the name of the person involved, the tonnage of cargo exported, etc. It is important not to appear too glib, but an interviewee who is in possession of the facts is more likely to gain the respect of the listener.

The interviewee has now prepared his two key points, counter arguments, illustration and facts, and on meeting the interviewer he confirms with him the aim of the interview, its context and duration.

Nerves

It is not the slightest use telling anyone 'not to be nervous'. Nervousness is an emotional reaction to an unusual situation and as such it is inevitable. Indeed it is desirable in that it causes the adrenalin to flow and improves concentration —with experience it is possible to use such 'red light' tensions con-structively. On the other hand, if the interviewee is completely relaxed he may appear to be blasé about the subject and the listener may react against this approach. In practical terms he should listen hard to the interviewer and look at him, eye-contact is a great help to concentration.

Making an impression

In aural communication information is carried on two distinct channels — *content* (what is said) and *style* (how it is said). They should both be under the speaker's control and to be fully effective one must reinforce the other. Due however to stress, it is not always easy, for example, to make a light point lightly. Without intention, it is possible to sound serious, even urgent and the effect of making a light point in a serious way is to con-vey irony. The reverse, that of making light of something serious, can sound sarcastic. The problem therefore is how to appear natural in a tense situation. It may be useful to ask yourself 'how should I come over?'

In discussing the 'images' or impressions which people want to project, the same epithets invariably occur. Interviewees wish to be seen as friendly, sincere, human, competent, etc. The following list may be helpful:

1. To be *sincere* — say what you really feel and avoid acting.
2. To be *friendly* — use an ordinary tone of voice and be capable of talking with an audible smile. Avoid 'jargon' and specialist language.
3. To appear *human* — use normal conversational language and avoid artificial 'airs and graces' Admit when you do not know the answer.
4. To be *considerate* — demonstrate the capacity to under-stand views other than your own.
5. To be *helpful* — offer useful, constructive practical advice.
6. To appear *competent* — demonstrate an appreciation of the question and ensure accuracy of answers. Avoid 'waffle' and 'padding'.

This is of course no different from the ordinary personal contacts made hundreds of times each day without conscious thought. What is different for a broadcast interview is that the stress in the situation can swamp the normal human qualities, leaving the 'colder' professional ones to dominate. An official concerned to appear competent will all too easily sound efficient to the point of ruthlessness unless the warmer human characteristics are consciously allowed to surface.

The most valuable quality is the interviewee's credibility. It is only when the listener believes him as a person will he be prepared to take notice or act on what he is saying. For this reason, style is initially more important than content.

Non-answers

The *accidental evasion* of questions may be due to the interviewee genuinely misunderstanding the question, or the question may have been badly put; in either case the interview goes off on the wrong tack. When recording this is easily remedied, but if it happens on the air the listener may be unable to follow and lose interest, or he may think the interviewee stupid or the interviewer incompetent. One or other of the parties must bring the subject back to its proper logic.

The *deliberately evasive* technique often adopted by the non-answerer is to follow the interviewer's question with another question of his own:

"That certainly comes into it but I think the real question is whether . . ."

If the new question genuinely progresses the subject, the listener will accept it. If not, he will quickly detect evasion and will expect the interviewer to put the question again. Rightly or wrongly the listener will invariably believe that someone who does not answer has something to hide and is therefore suspect.

There may be genuine reasons why *"No comment"* is an acceptable answer to a question. The facts may not yet be known with sufficient certainty, there may be a legal process pending, a need to honour a guarantee given to a third party, or the answer should properly come from another quarter. It may be that an interviewee legitimately wishes to protect himself from his business competitors – a factor which occurs in the sporting as well as the commercial world.

Nevertheless, the interviewee must be seen to be honest and to say why an answer cannot be given.

"It would be wrong of me to anticipate the report . . ."
"I can't say yet until the enquiry is finished . . ."
"I'm sure you wouldn't expect me to give details but . . ."

Even if the inability to give a particular answer has been discussed beforehand, an interviewee should still expect to have the question put if it is likely to be in the listener's mind.

In an attempt to slow down the questioning rate or avoid the obvious next question, an interviewee may end his answer with a question back to the interviewer.

" . . . a lot of people are like that, don't you think?"
" . . . so that's what I did; how would you have gone about it?"

It is a golden rule that interviewers never answer questions and the interviewee will get himself ignored for trying to turn an interview into a discussion. The listener, however, may already have gained the impression that the interviewee is unwilling to be interviewed. As with all non-answers this damages his credibility.

The triangle of trust

The whole business of interviewing is founded on trust. It is a 3-way structure involving the interviewer, the interviewee, and the listener.

The interviewee trusts the interviewer to keep to the original statement of intent regarding the subject areas and the context of the interview, and also that he will maintain both the spirit and the content of the original in any subsequent editing. The interviewer trusts the interviewee to respond to his questions in an honest attempt to illuminate the subject. The listener trusts the interviewer to be acting fairly in his interests and believes there to be no secret collusion between the interviewer and the interviewee. The interviewee trusts the listener not to misrepresent what he is saying and to understand that within the limitations of time the answers are the truth of the matter.

This 'triangle of trust' is an important constituent not only of the media's credibility but of society's self-respect as a whole. Should one side of the triangle become damaged − for example listeners no longer trusting broadcasters, interviewees no longer trusting interviewers, or neither having sufficient regard for the listener – there is a danger that the process will be regarded simply as a propaganda exercise. Under these conditions it is no longer possible to distinguish between 'the truth as we see it' and 'what we think you ought to know'. Consequently, the underlying reason for communication begins to disappear, thereby reducing broadcasting's contribution to the maintenance of a democracy. Thus the fabric of society is affected. This is to take an extreme view, but every time a broadcaster misrepresents, every time an interviewee lies or a listener disbelieves, we have lost something of value.

5

WRITING

Writing for radio is the storage of talk. Presentation of a script at the microphone is the retrieval of that talk out of storage. The overall process should give the listener the impression that the broadcaster's *talking* to him rather than *reading* at him. It's prepared of course, but it should *sound* spontaneous.

This chapter's written in a quite different style from the rest of the book, — it'll contain things which are quite against the rules of 'literary' convention. It may even be difficult for some people to read; the point is, though, that it's in a style which is all right for me to *say*, — it's *spoken* English, — a personal talk set out in a way which I would find suitable as a script. Everyone of course has to find their own way, and a style such as this for a relaxed twenty minute talk certainly wouldn't do as a voice piece in the news, which would obviously have to be much more tightly written.

I mentioned that this might be difficult to read. There's good reason for this and it's important to realise that writing words on paper is a very crude form of storage. It doesn't give you half what you want in order to make unambiguous sense of it. It doesn't for example, give you any idea of where the emphasis should go. It's possible to underline certain words but this isn't the whole story by any means. The written word provides no indication of the vocal sounds intended, — the shape of the sentence as it's said. Yet quite a lot of the meaning of words and phrases is conveyed in the subtleties of their inflection. Neither does the page say how it should sound in terms of speed, or where the pauses should go. Yet all these qualities help to convey sense, — without them, the words on the paper can be virtually meaningless — or at least ambiguous. Take this sentence:

"You mean I have to be there at ten, tomorrow."

The words stay the same but the precise meaning can alter 8 ways depending where you put the emphasis.

Just try it out loud!

So writing is only one part of the communication process, and it isn't completed until the script is *said*, — and said properly. It's difficult enough to do well when you're writing something which you're going to read yourself, it's doubly so when writing for someone else to read.

Then why do we have a script at all? — Wouldn't it be better just to have notes to 'talk through' at the microphone? This is possible, but it's not always advisable — even when the writer is the same person as the broadcaster. No, there are good reasons for having a script, like:-

— making sure there's as little stress in the actual broadcast as possible. The script is a 'safety-net' — at least you know what you're going to say, even though the script won't tell you exactly *how* you're going to say it.

— other points are that a full script makes sure that nothing is left out, that it runs to time and all the information and arguments are presented in the right order. One of the most important things about the spoken word is that it must be *logical*. Try telling a joke and getting the information in the wrong order! It falls flat on its face of course. In print it's different because the whole thing is there in front of you, — you can look back at something again to make sense of it. With 'talk' — it has to make sense there and then, or it's likely not to make sense at all. And this point depends very largely on getting the material in a logical order.

— Finally, why we write a script, is obviously to enable other people to communicate our thoughts, — to give some permanent form to the otherwise very transient nature of speech.

Well, having established the reasons *'why'*, let's have a look at *'what'* we're going to write.

The first thing to do, and it applies to any piece of communication, is to decide what it is you want to say. What are the points you want to make, and what sort of impression do you want to leave behind? You can never be 100% successful in this, but at least it'll work a good deal better than if you have no aims at all. You know those times when you're doing a bit of writing and you stop because you somehow can't finish the sentence — you've written yourself into a corner. That's when you cross that sentence out, put your pen down and say to yourself, "What am I trying to say?" It's often a very good question!

So you list out your main points and make sure that you've got the necessary facts or illustrations to support them. Then in the cause of logic, you assemble these ideas to put them in the right order — the order which makes them most easily understood by your listener. And you can't do this without having the listener in mind, — a typical member of your target audience. A housewife at home, a child at school, or a man in his car. It's a great help actually to *visualise* your listener as you write, it helps to prevent it becoming patronising. We often say 'how can I put this *across*?' Across, — this implies a horizontal communication. Not 'how can I put it down?' which is the patronising attitude — or worse still 'how can I put it up?' which sounds servile — but 'across' — someone on the *same level* as yourself. That's where the writer should be with regard to his listener.

This approach also stops the writer from suffering the dread disease of 'difficult' words. We all like to impress, but if we want to communicate then what's important is not the impressive word, but the right word, — the one that's right for our audience I mean. After all, if we want to sound as though we're talking, we'll use the everyday language of our natural speech rather than the stilted 'officialese' or jargon that so often appears in print. And if we want to sound as though we're caring, — caring about our audience — then the impression we want to make won't be the broadcaster saying "aren't I clever!" I'll come back to this business of language in a moment.

A further point about visualising your listener is to think about broadcasting to *one* person. Radio is one of the 'mass media' and it goes to thousands, millions of people. Yet your message ends up in the mind of the individual listener. It's wrong to think of radio as a group experience — like an audience in a hall, — or to treat it as a massive public address system reaching out across the housetops and countryside. So avoid phrases like *"listeners* may like to know . . ."* or *"some of you* will have seen . . ."

Talking just to *one* person you'd say, — "you may like to know . . ." and "If you've seen . . ." It's a communication between you, the broadcaster, and the listener with his own thoughts. So write for the individual, — he'll feel that you're talking just to him and your words'll have much more impact.

So, having decided what we want to say, and in what order; and we know who we're talking to; let's set about the script itself.

Radio is an immensely 'switch-offable' medium, you're talking to a very non-captive audience, so the very first sentence must be interesting. Don't spend a long time 'getting into' the subject, start with an idea that's intriguing, relevant, or at least unusual. And follow it with something which tells me what you're on about, — don't leave me in doubt about that!

"The first sentence must interest, the second must inform". It's an over-simplified 'rule of thumb' but it's the right idea. Now you go through your list of points linking them together in a logical way, threading them in a sequence like beads on a string. And always make it quite clear what you're doing.

Let me explain. If you get to a difficult point, you might include the phrase, — "how can I explain that?" This is a signal that you're about to digress into an amplification of the point. Or you might finish a point and join it on to the next one by saying, — "Let's go on from there to see how this works in practice". This is a clear indication to your audience that you're introducing a new topic, — in this case turning from a theory to its practical application. Such 'indicators' are generally called 'signposts', and there are plenty in this script, — the trouble is, in the written word they can be rather tedious, since on a printed page they normally appear much more economically as paragraph headings. When spoken though, they generally sound alright, indeed without 'signposts', it's easy for the listener to lose your train of thought.

I said I'd come back to the actual use of language, and the point I want to make is this; that the overall style of broadcast talk should be conversational. I don't mean that it should be sloppy or casual, — some conversation can be quite formal; and in radio, writing 'the news' generally adopts a more 'careful' approach. But writing the links for a magazine programme, or compiling the weather forecast, a religious talk, book review — or any piece of *spoken* communication — it should sound colloquial, — like someone talking. This means that 'it is' becomes 'it's'; 'I would' sounds better as 'I'd'. You have splendid words like 'this'll' and 'shouldn't've'. They look terrible on the printed page because we're not used to seeing them, but listen to people talking, — they're the stuff of living language, — and good language at that.

There's a golden rule for getting the spoken word on to paper — and that's simply to speak it out loud as you go along, — and to write down what you hear. Don't write it in your head, but from the sounds you make as you talk. Once it's on the page you can always change it, re-arrange and polish it, but the basis of your script will be a spoken language — much easier to put across in the studio. How many times have you heard someone say — "as soon as I said it, I knew it was wrong"? Well then, as a broadcaster, don't let anything go down on to paper until you've actually heard it, and known it to be right.

Something else happens when you talk your sentences out loud, — they get shorter. And they're not necessarily the kind of sentences we were taught to write at school. But they have colour and life, and meaning — if you let them. Short sentences are easier to read, and easier for the listener to understand. You get away from the complexities of relative clauses, — this sort of thing:—

Jim who is just about to leave the school where he's been for five years, which included a time as head boy is looking for a job.

That's not much good on the air, and the three thoughts are much better written as three sentences:—

Jim has been at school for five years. This includes a time as head boy. He's now about to leave and is looking for a job.

A further point about saying your script out loud as you write it, is that it helps to avoid the tongue twister or the unintentional meaning. The following examples are quite genuine pieces of broadcast script. They may look alright on paper, but try them out loud:—

— Six Swedish fishing vessels sailed into the Skagerrak.

— This morning our reporter spoke to Mr . . . on the golf course, as he played a round with his wife.

— The Union said the report was wrong.

— At first, supplies of the new car would be restricted to the home market.

I'm still wondering about this last one. I think it means that the new car would only be sold at home. But couldn't it also mean that supplies to the home market would be restricted and that it was all going for export? It depends on the emphasis given to the word 'restricted'. The sentence itself is unclear.

Punctuation should help the reader extract the sense from the writing, but it's a very flimsy device when the whole meaning depends on a comma or two. Take that third example — The Union said the report was wrong, — as it stands, it's the report that was wrong and the Union that's saying so, — the Union said the report was wrong. Put in two commas and the situation is exactly reversed, — the Union, said the report, was wrong. Look hard at any sentence containing a dependent clause or a bracketed phrase, — is there an easier, a more natural way of saying it? In punctuating a script, I'm very fond of the 'comma dash', — you may have noticed! This joins phrases together yet shows me that there ought to be a small pause. Some people's scripts are covered with all sorts of marks, — arrows to indicate inflection, musical notation, even directions like *"smile"*, — everything designed to help the reader re-create the way he originally wanted it to sound.

Some points now on the mechanics of a script. If at all possible it should be typed, double or even triple spaced to make it easy to read — a large typeface rather than a small one, — and leave clear margins on both sides. This enables alterations and additions to be made without obliterating the part you want. If a script has to be written in longhand, make sure it's *totally* clear for the reader. Some people put handwritten scripts all in capital letters, but this reduces the amount of information on the page in terms of how you read it, — there's less warning for example about the start of a new sentence, or a 'proper' name.

Carbon copies can be typed on 'flimsy' paper, but the

top copy, actually used in the studio, should be a good quality paper, − the sheets are much quieter to handle. To avoid unnecessary turning of pages, scripts should be typed only on one side of the paper.

The page itself should be set out with clear paragraphs' indicating separate thoughts. A sentence shouldn't run over to another page but each sheet end with a full stop. Indeed, sometimes it may be desirable not to split an important phrase across two lines of the script, − after all you wouldn't do it if you were writing figures.

On the subject of numbers, there are three schools of thought, − writing them in figures, writing them in words, or putting it both ways. For example:−

The Ministry of Defence expenditure on this item would amount to one and a quarter million pounds.

The cost of the new engine, only came to $380.

Twenty-seven (27) people were injured in the accident. The only rule is that the meaning should be clear. The reader can always cross out the form he doesn't want.

What about speed and timing? Our reading speed varies, but a rate of 160 to 180 words a minute would be normal for a newscast. To give a quick reckoning on the time a script will take, a single typed line is 3 to 4 seconds, and a double-spaced page of A4, — 27 lines, say 270 words, about 1½ minutes. A certain amount of precision is wanted here, a thirty second voice report means about 85 words, a 2½ minute piece for the breakfast programme will be 400. It's a very great art, and a discipline, to get what you want to say to fit neatly into the time allowed, but the clock is a hard taskmaster.

Now, on finishing. We started with an interesting sentence, and it's often a good idea in a general talk to end up with a reference back to that same thought. It reinforces the point and ought to act as a 'trigger' for the later recall of what you said. Of course, if you want to leave your listener with a specific thought, or motivate him to a particular action, then these points must come right at the end. What I'm trying to say here is that there *must* be an end, — not a sudden stop, or a drifting away, — but a clear 'rounding off'. A resumé perhaps, or a provocative question to stimulate the listener to further thought. Openings and closings — without doubt the most difficult part of any broadcast, — but the final word is often how you'll be remembered.

And if, in between the beginning and the end, you've avoided the kind of convoluted literary prose which so often comes out when we put pen to paper, but instead have used words in a style which has the texture of a living, spoken language, — and if the listener can understand the language, he may understand the content. He may even have come closer to understanding *you*. In fact, you'll have communicated.

So to summarise on what's often called 'writing for the ear'. Here are 11 points.

— decide what you want to say.

— list your points in a logical order.

— the opening must interest and inform.

— write for the individual listener, — visualise him or her as you write.

— speak out loud what you want to say, then write it down.

— use 'signposts' to explain the structure of your talk.

— use ordinary conversational language.

— write in short sentences or phrases.

— use punctuation to aid clarity for the reader.

— type the script, double spaced, wide margins, with clear paragraphs.

— and when in doubt, keep it simple.

Having got our script on to paper, I'll be dealing later on with Presentation — the art of getting it off again.

6

CUE MATERIAL

THE paperwork which accompanies a recorded interview or other item such as a programme insert, has two quite separate functions. The first is to provide the studio staff with information. The second is to introduce the item for the listener so that it makes sense within the surroundings.

The general rules concerning cue material apply equally to the links between items in a magazine programme and to the introductions given to whole programmes.

Information for the broadcaster

Before a recorded programme or item can reach the air, the producer, presenter or studio operational staff require certain information about it. The way these details are laid out on a single page is standard and a sheet of cue material is recognisable as such in most radio stations round the world. It must indicate the following:

1. Name of the radio station.
2. Title of the programme.
3. Date of the intended transmission.
4. Reference title of the piece, a 'catch line'.
5. Suggested on-air introduction.
6. The 'in' and 'out' cues of the programme as they appear on the tape.
7. Precise duration of the material.
8. Suggested on-air 'back announcement'.
9. Any additional details of a technical or programme nature – editing requirements, unusual tape speed, mono/stereo etc.

The cue material sheet may also include a note of payment to be made to the contributor. Thus all the information about the programme or item is drawn together on one page, as shown by the following example:

1.	*Radio London* *Women Bus Drivers*
2.	Rush Hour
3.	27 June
5.	*Annct:*
	Are you one of those people who believe that women drivers are worse road users than men? London Transport certainly don't and they're recruiting members of the fair sex to drive their 10 ton double-deckers.
	The first of these trainee drivers has now arrived. She's Mrs. Freda Gibbs, a 29 year old housewife from Brixton. Down at the driving school, John Buckland asked her whether it was more difficult than she'd expected.
6.	Cue In: No, it's great . . .
	Cue Out: . . . not really different from our own mini.
	(Bus drives off. 10 sec.)
	Duration 2' 47"
8.	*Annct:*
	Mrs. Freda Gibbs, the first of London Transport's 'lady learners'.
	Payment
9.	7½ i.p.s. Ready for transmission
	Buckland £ . . . . .

Tapes may carry a recording number in which case this should appear at the bottom of the cue sheet. However, numbering systems can be time consuming to administer and no system should be introduced unless it saves effort and is actually useful. There is sufficient information on the example given here for the tape to be easily identified and many radio stations do without recording numbers, especially for insert tapes.

Some of the details will also appear on the outside of the tape box — station, programme and catch-line or title. The catch-line should be repeated on the spool itself — written on a small adhesive label rather than on the plastic.

The producer can often make his decisions based on the cue sheet information — whether in fact to use the item, or where to place it in the programme. If he knows his contributor well and is short of time, he can sometimes use the tape without hearing it first. This is not a recommended procedure, and the overall responsibility for the programme still rests with the producer.

The studio operator also has all the information he needs to ensure the tape gets safely on the air. Prior to transmission the tape is checked to 'take level' and to confirm the 'in' cue.

The studio presenter has a clear indication of how to introduce the tape. He may have to alter words to suit his own style, but the good cue writer will write in a way which fits the specific programme.

In the example here the interviewer's first question has been removed from the tape and transferred to the introduction, the tape then begins with the first answer. This is a very common form of cue but it is only one method of many and it should not be over used, particularly within a single programme. It is easy for cue material to become mechanical — to 'write in a rut' — it is important to search for fresh approaches.

Information for the listener

The actual piece of writing which introduces the tape has three functions for the listener. It must be interesting, act as a 'signpost' and be informative.

The information must be *interesting*. The first sentence should contain some point to which the listener can relate. It should be written in response to likely questions: 'What is the purpose of this interview?' 'Why am I broadcasting this piece?' Having found the most interesting facet – the 'angle' most relevant to the listener – the writer starts from that. A good opening line is worth thinking about. In the example of the 'women bus drivers', the introduction begins with a question. This is an attempt to involve the listener by eliciting a sub-conscious response.

Cue material is a *signpost* and should make a promise about what is to follow. Having gained the listener's interest, it is then important to satisfy his expectations.

The introduction must be *informative*. One purpose of an introduction is to provide the context within which the item may be properly understood. There may have to be:

1. A summary of the events leading up to or surrounding the story.
2. An indication of why the particular interviewee was chosen.
3. Additional facts to help the listener's understanding. It may be necessary to clarify technical terms and jargon, or to explain any background noise or sounds which would otherwise distract the listener.

Unless the interview or voice piece is very short, say less than a minute, it will be necessary to repeat after an interview the information about the interviewee. There is a high probability that the listener is not wholly committed to the programme and heard the introduction only superficially, despite a compellingly interesting opening line. The listener's full attention frequently becomes engaged only during the interview itself. Having become fascinated or outraged, it is afterwards that he wants to know the name of the interviewee and their qualification for speaking.

Radio is prone to fashion and there has been a tendency for the 'back announcement' to be omitted. It is said that it slows the programme down. It is true that a 'backward pointing' signpost may have such an effect, whereas introductions help to drive the programme forward. However the argument in favour of a back announcement puts listener information above programme pace. It also helps to give the impression that the presenter has been listening. Without some reference to the interview, the presenter who simply continues with the next item can sound extremely discourteous. Broadcasters should remember that to the listener, pre-recorded items are people rather than spools of magnetic tape. They should therefore be referred to as if they had actually taken part in the programme.

The practice of omitting the back announcement is probably an example of radio being influenced by television. In vision, it is possible to superimpose on an interview a caption giving the name and qualification of the interviewee. This can happen at any time throughout a piece and makes a back announcement unnecessary. The two channels of television information, sound and vision, can be used simultaneously for different purposes. This is not the case with radio where post hoc advice is often the simplest and most logical way of 're-informing' the listener.

Two further examples will illustrate the functions of cue material — that is to obtain the listener's interest, provide context, explain background noise, clarify technicalities and to 'back announce'.

Example one:

> *Annct.* The strike at Abbots Electrical is over. Involving 75 assembly workers and lasting nearly two weeks, the strike has meant a loss of production worth over £20,000.
>
> The dispute began when three men were sacked for what the management called, "persistent lateness affecting the productivity of other workers".
>
> The Union objected, saying that the men were being "unduly victimised".
>
> Two of the men have since been reinstated. Is such a stoppage worth it? On the now busy shop floor, our reporter spoke to the Union representative, Joe Frimley.

Cue In: (noise 3") No stoppage is ever . . .

Cue Out: . . . making up for lost time. (noise 2")

Duration 2' 08"

> *Annct:* Joe Frimley, the Union representative at Abbots Electrical.

85

When a recording is made against background noise, it is useful to begin the piece with two or three seconds of the sound alone. The insert tape can be started before the cue and faded up under speech so that its words begin neatly after the introduction. Similarly at the end of the insert, the background noise is faded down behind the presenter's back announcement. Such a technique is preferable to the jarring effect of 'cutting' on to noise.

In the interests of fairness and objectivity, such an item would invariably need to be followed and 'balanced' by a management view of the situation.

Example two:

    Annct.   Space research and your kitchen sink. It seems an unlikely combination but the same advanced technology which put man on the moon has also helped with the household chores.

              For example, the non-stick frying pan uses a chemical called – Poly–tetra–fluoro–ethylene (Pron: POLLY TETRA FLOOR-ERO ETH-A-LEEN). Fortunately it's called PTFE for short. Used now for kitchen pans, this PTFE was developed for the coating of hardware out in space.

              Dr. John Freeburg of the National Research Council explains.

    Cue In: We've known about PTFE for some time . . .

    Cue Out:. . . always looking to the future.

Duration 3' 17"

Annct: Dr. Freeburg.

7

NEWS AND CURRENT AFFAIRS

THE best short definition of news is 'that which is new, interesting, and true'.

'New' in that it is an account of events which the listener has not heard before – or an update of a story familiar to him. 'Interesting', in the sense of the material being relevant, or affecting him in some way. 'True', because the story as told is factually correct.

It is a useful definition not only because it is a reminder of three crucial aspects of a credible news service but because it leads to a consideration of its own omissions. If all news is to be really 'new' a story will be broadcast only once. Yet there is an obvious obligation to ensure that it is received by the widest possible audience. At what stage then can the news producer update a story, assuming that the listener already has the basic information? What do we mean by 'interesting' when we speak not of an individual but of a large, diversified group with various interests? Do we simply mean 'important'? In any case, how does the broadcaster balance the short-term interest with the long? And as for the *whole* truth – there simply is not time. So how should we decide out of all the important and interesting events which confront us, what to leave out? And concerning what is included, how much of the context should be given in order to give an event its proper perspective. And to what extent is it possible to do this without indicating a particular point of view? And if the broadcaster is to remain impartial, do we mean totally?

These are some of the questions involved in the editorial judgement of news. To begin with we need to consider not the practical solutions, but the criteria by which possible answers may be assessed.

Note: In America, the area of Current Affairs is known as Public Affairs.

Starting with the listener, what does he expect to hear? Certainly in a true democracy he has a general right to know and discuss what is going on around him. There will be imposed limitations which are defined and maintained by law — matters of national security, confidences of a business or private nature, to which the public does not have rightful access. Any of these reasons can be used to cloak the genuine interest of the individual. Caught in such a conflict, the broadcaster is faced with a moral problem — the not unfamiliar one of deciding the greater good between upholding the law and championing the rights and freedom of the individual. At such times, those involved in public responsibility should consider two separate propositions:

1. Broadcasters are not elected, they are not the government and as such are not in a position to take decisions affecting the interest of the state. If they go against the practice of the law they do so as private citizens, with no special privileges because they have access to a radio station.
2. Associated with the public right to know, is the private right not to divulge. A society which professes individual freedom does not compel or allow the media to extract that which a person wishes lawfully to keep to himself.

Thus the listener has a right to be informed; but although the constraints may be few and the breaches of it comparatively rare, the right is not total. Every broadcaster must know where he stands and on what basis his lines of editorial demarcation are drawn.

Item selection and treatment

From all the events and stories of the day how does the broadcaster decide what he will include in his news bulletin? His decision to cover, or not to cover, a particular story may itself be construed as bias. The producer's initial selection of an item on the basis of it being worthy of coverage is often referred to as 'the media's agenda-setting function'. The extent to which a producer allows his own judgement to select the items for broadcast is a subject for much debate. People will discuss what they hear on the radio and are less likely to be concerned with topics not already given wide currency. So is a radio station's judgement as to what is significant, worth having? If so, the process of selection, the reasons for rejection, and the weight accorded to each story (treatment, bulletin order and duration) are matters which deserve the utmost care.

The broadcaster's power to select the issues to be debated represents a considerable responsibility. Yet given a list of news stories a group of editors will each arrive at widely different running orders for a news bulletin. They may agree over their lead, and possibly second lead stories, but after that there is likely to be little agreement. Are there any objective criteria?

The first consideration is to produce a news package suited to the style of the programme within which it is broadcast. A five-minute bulletin can be a world view of twenty items, superficial but wide-ranging; or it can be a more detailed coverage of the four or five major stories. Both have their place, the first to set the scene at the beginning of the day, the second to highlight and update the development of certain stories as the day proceeds. The important point is that the shape and style of a bulletin should be matters of design and not of chance. Unlike a newspaper with its ability to vary the type size, radio can only emphasise the importance of a subject by its placing and treatment. A typical five-minute bulletin may consist of eight or nine items the first two or three stories dealt with at one minute's length, the remainder decreasing to thirty seconds each or less. The point was made earlier that compared with a newspaper this represents a very severe limitation on *total* coverage.

Having decided the number and the length of items, the news producer has to select what is important as opposed to what is of passing interest. When short of time it is easier to gain the interest of the listener with an item on the Miss World contest than with one on the state of the economy. The second item is more significant for everyone in the long term, but requires more contextual information. The news producer however must not be put off by such difficulties, for it is the temptation of the easy option which leads to some justification in the charge that 'the media tends to trivialise'. An effect of the policy that news must always be available at a moment's notice is that stories of long term significance do not find a place in the bulletin. It is after all easier to report the blowing up of an aircraft than the development of one.

A second criterion for selection is to favour items to do with people rather than things. The threat of an industrial dispute affecting hundreds of jobs will rate higher than a world record price paid for a painting. 'How could this event affect my listeners?' is a reasonable question to ask. For the listener to a local station in Britain, fifty deaths following an outbreak of typhoid in Hong Kong would probably be regarded with less significance than a road accident in his own area in which no one was hurt. But should it? Particularly in local radio there is a tendency to run a story because of its association with mayhem and disaster rather than its relevance. A preoccupation with house fires and traffic accidents, called 'the journalists's predilection for ambulance chasing', is to be discouraged.

By definition, news is to do with the unusual and abnormal but the basis of news selection must not be whether a story is simply interesting or spectacular, but whether it is significant and relevant. This certainly does not mean adopting a loftily worthy approach – dullness is the enemy of interest – it is to find the right point of human contact in a story. This may mean translating an obscure but important event into the listener's own understanding. The job of news is not to shock but to inform. A broadcasting service will be judged as much by what it omits as what it includes.

Objectivity

Some declare it to be impossible, others that it is unnecessary but the basis of news and current affairs broadcasting in the BBC has always been and still is – firstly to separate the reporting of events (news) from the discussion of issues and comment (current affairs), and secondly to give both sides of an argument. Arising from the broadcaster's privileged position as the custodian of this form of public debate, the role of a radio service, even one under government or commercial control, is to allow expression to the various components of controversy but not to engage itself in the argument nor to lend its support to a particular view.* What the producer must not do is to introduce a partiality as a result of his own conscious but undisclosed personal convictions and motivation. Even for the best of reasons he must avoid decisions based on his own

* This policy of impartiality is by no means universal and in some countries stations are encouraged to take an editorial line. In Britain, radio was for many years the monopoly of the BBC, it had to be as objective as possible. Where there are several broadcasting sources, each may develop its own attitude to political and other controversial issues and like a newspaper attempt to sway public opinion.

religious, political or commercial views — since this is putting himself before his listener. The impartiality of chairmanship is an ideal to which the producer must adhere; any bias will seriously damage his credibility for honest reporting. Yet in a world when one man's 'terrorist' is another man's 'freedom fighter, the very language we use in imparting the facts is itself a matter of dispute and allegiance.

Objectivity becomes more difficult and more crucial as society becomes less ordered in its deliberations and more torn with its own divisions. This is something which many countries have witnessed in recent years. The crumbling of an established code of behaviour alters the precepts for making decisions — it may be possible to act impartially in a discussion on, say the permissive society, but the rest of the station's output is likely to indicate clearly the broadcaster's viewpoint. What is the meaning of impartiality when covering a complex industrial dispute involving official and unofficial representatives, break-away groups, vocally militant individuals and separate employers' and government views and solutions?

Even more difficult situations are those such as Northern Ireland where there is a 'limited' civil war. Do we give equal time for those who would uproot society — for those who oppose the rule of law? These are not easy questions since there is a limit to the extent to which anyone may be impartial. While society may be divided and changing in its regard for what is right and wrong, it is less so in its more fundamental approach to good and evil. No public medium of communication can function properly and without critical dissent unless society is agreed within itself on what is lawful and unlawful. It is possible to be impartial in a peaceful discussion on attempts to bring about changes in the existing law, but such impartiality is not possible in reporting attempts to overthrow it by force. One can be objective in reporting the activities of the man with the gun, but not in deciding whether to propagate his views.

A former Director General of the BBC, Sir Hugh Greene, said in the sixties, "I do not mean to imply that a broadcasting system should be neutral in clear issues of right and wrong, even though it should be between Right and Left. I should not for a moment admit that a man who wanted to speak in favour of racial intolerance had the same rights as a man who wanted to condemn it. There are some questions on which one should not be impartial".

There are those who disagree that race relations is a proper area for showing partiality just as there are those who oppose the underlying acceptance of the Christian faith as a basis for conducting public affairs. This is not an abstract or purely academic issue, it is one which constantly faces the individual producer. He must decide whether it is in the public interest to give voice to those who would challenge the very system of democracy which enables him to provide that freedom of expression. On the one hand to give them a wider currency may be interpreted as a form of public endorsement, on the other to expose them for what they are may result in their total censure. What is important is the maintenance of the freedom to exercise that choice, and ultimately to be account-able for it to an elected authority. Sir Geoffrey Cox, former Chief Executive of ITN (Independent Television News), has said of the broadcaster's function, "It is not his duty, or his right, to editorialise on the question of democracy, to advocate its virtues or attack its detractors. But he has a firm duty to see that society is not endangered either because it is inadequately informed, or because the crucial issues of the day have not been so probed and debated as to establish their truth. A good broad-cast news service is essential to the functioning of democracy. It is as necessary to the political health of society as a good water supply is to its physical health".

Democracy cannot be exercised within a society unless its individual members are given a choice on which to make their own moral, political, and social decisions. That choice does not exist unless the alternatives are presented in an atmosphere of free discussion. This in turn cannot exist without freedom — under the law — of the press and broadcasting. The key to objectivity lies in the avoidance of secret motivation and the broadcaster's willingness to be part of the total freedom of discussion — to know that even his editorial judgement, the very basis of his programme making, is open to challenge. Keep the listener informed about what you are doing and why you are doing it — that is the public interest.

The reporting function

The reporter out on the street and the sub-editor at his desk are the people who make the decisions about news. Their concern is accuracy, intelligibility, legality, impartiality and good taste.

Accuracy

A reporter's first duty is to get the facts right. Names, initials, titles, times, places, financial figures, percentages, the sequence of events – all must be accurate. Nothing is broadcast without the facts being double checked, not by hearsay or suggestion but by thorough reliability. 'Return to the source' is a standard maxim. If it is not possible to check the fact itself, at least attribute the source declaring it to be a fact. Under pressure from a tight deadline, it is tempting to allow the shortage of time to serve as an excuse for lack of verification. But such is the way of the slipshod to their ultimate discredit. Even in a competitive situation, the listener's right to be correctly informed stands above the broadcaster's desire to be first. The radio medium, after all, offers sufficient flexibility to allow opportunity for continuing intermittent follow-up. Indeed, it is ideally suited to the running story.

Sometimes accuracy by itself is not enough. With statistics the story may be not in their telling but in their interpretation. For instance, according to the traffic accident figures the safest age group of motorbike users is the 'over 80's' – not one was injured last year! So a story concerning a 20% increase in the radioactivity level of cows' milk over two years may be perfectly true, but is it significant? How has it varied at other times? Was the level two years ago unusually low? Were the measurements on precisely the same basis? And so on. Statistical claims need care.

Accuracy is required too in the sounds which accompany a report. The reporter working in radio knows how atmosphere is conveyed by 'actuality' – the noise of a building site, the shouts of a demonstration. It is important in achieving impact and establishing credibility to use these sounds, but not to make them 'bigger' than they really are. The accurate reporter, as opposed to a merely sensationalist one, will need a great deal of judgement if he is to excite and interest, but not mislead.

Intelligibility

Conveying immediate meaning with clarity and brevity is a task which requires refinement of thought and a facility with words. The first requisite is to understand the story so that it can be told without recourse to scientific, commercial, legal, governmental or social gobbledegook which so often surrounds the official giving of information. A reporter determined to show that he is at home with such technicalities through their frequent application has little use as a communicator. He must be the translator of jargon not its disseminator.

In recognising where to start he must have an insight into how much the listener already knows and how ideas are expressed in everyday speech. In being understood, the reporter's second requirement is therefore a knowledge of his audience — it is unwise of him to deal only with colleagues and professional sources for he will find himself subconsciously broadcasting only to them.

The third element in telling a story is that it should be logically expressed. This means that it should be chronological and sequential — cause comes before effect.

> *Not*: A reduction in the permitted level of cigarette advertising is recommended in a Department of Health report out today.
>
> *But*: In a report out today The Department of Health recommends a reduction in the permitted level of cigarette advertising.

The key to intelligibility therefore is in the reporter's own understanding of the story, of the listener, and of the language of communication.

Legality

To stay within the law demands a knowledge of the legal process and of the constraints which the law imposes on anyone, individual or radio station, to say what they like. In Britain no-one for example is allowed to pre-judge a case, to interfere with a trial, influence a jury or anticipate the findings. Thus there are considerable restrictions on what can be reported while a matter is sub-judice. To exceed the defined limits is to run the very severe risk of being held in contempt of court — an offence which is viewed with the utmost seriousness since it is the law's own credibility which is at threat.

Under present British law the outline of what is permissible in reporting a crime falls under four distinct stages:

94

1. *Before a charge is made* it is permissible to give the *facts* of the crime but the description of a death as 'murder' should only be used if the police have made a statement to that effect. Witnesses to the crime may be interviewed but they must not attempt to describe the identity of anyone they saw or speculate on the motive.
2. After a charge is made and *while the trial is in progress* it is not permissible to report on committal proceedings in a magistrates' court, other than by giving the names and addresses of the parties involved, the names of counsel and solicitors, and the decision of the Court. The reporting of subsequent proceedings in the higher court is permitted but no comment is allowed.
3. Responsible comment is permissible *after the conviction and sentence is announced*, so long as the judge is not criticised for the severity or otherwise of the sentence, and there is no allegation of bias or prejudice.
4. *If an appeal is lodged*, then the matter again becomes sub-judice. No comment or speculation is allowed and only factual court reports should be broadcast.

Complications can arise after an arrest has been made but before the person has been charged. There are special rules too which apply to the reporting of the juvenile and matrimonial courts. The key question throughout is whether what is broadcast is likely to help or hinder the police in their investigation or undermine the authority of the judicial process.

Such matters are the stock in trade of the journalist, and producers unacquainted with the courts are advised to proceed carefully and to seek expert advice.

The second great area of the law of which all programme makers must be aware is that of libel. The broadcaster enjoys no special rights over the individual and he is not entitled to say anything which would 'expose a person to hatred, ridicule or contempt, cause him to be shunned or avoided, or tend to injure him in his office, profession or trade'. To be upheld, a libel can only be committed against an identifiable individual. In law, it is not possible to defame the dead. The most damaging accusation that can be brought against a broadcaster standing under the threat of a libel action is that he acted out of malice. This is not an unknown hazard for the investigative journalist working for example on a story involving the possibility of corruption or dubious practice involving well-known public figures. The broadcaster's only real defence against a charge of libel is that what he said was true. Again, we have the absolute necessity of checking the facts and using words with a precision which precludes a possibly deliberate misconstruction.

To repeat a libellous statement made by someone else is no defence unless that person enjoys 'absolute privilege', as in a court of law or in Parliament. Even so, reports of such proceedings have to be fair as well as accurate and if the statement made turns out to be wrong and an apology or correction is issued, this too is bound to be reported. Where no 'privilege' exists, the broadcaster is as guilty as the actual perpetrator of the libel. Producers and presenters of the phone-in should be constantly on their guard for the caller who complains of shoddy workmanship, professional incompetence, or worse on the part of an identifiable individual. An immediate reference by the presenter to the fact that 'well, that's only your view' may be regarded as a mitigation of the offence, but the broadcaster can nevertheless be held to have published the libel.

The law also impinges directly on the broadcaster in matters concerning 'official' secrets, elections, consumer programmes, race relations, gaming and lotteries, reporting from foreign courts, and copyright.

The individual producer should remain aware of the major legal pitfalls and must have a reliable source of legal advice. Without it he is likely, sooner or later, to need the services of a good defence lawyer.

Impartiality

The reporter does not select 'victims' and hound them — he does not ignore those whose views he dislikes — he does not pursue vendettas, nor have favourites. He does not promote the policies of sectarian interests and he resists the persuasions of those seeking free publicity. He is fair. Having no editorial opinion of his own, he seeks to tell the news without making moral judgements about it. He is the servant of his listener. Broadcasting is a general dissemination and no view that he initiates is likely to be universally accepted. 'Good news' of a pay rise for miners is bad news for consumers affected by an increase in the price of coal. 'Good news' of another sunny day is bad news for farmers anxiously waiting for rain. The key is a careful watch on the adjectives, both in value and in size. Superlatives may have impact but are they fair? He may report an industrial dispute but what right does he have to describe it as 'a *serious* industrial dispute'? On what grounds may he refer to a company's '*poor* record', or a medical research team's '*dramatic* breakthrough'? Much better to leave the qualifying adjectives to the actual participants and for the newswriter to let the facts speak for themselves.

Reporters are occasionally concerned that they may not be able to be totally objective since they have received certain inbuilt values from their upbringing and education. While it may be true that broadcasting has more of its fair share of people from middle-class families and with a college education, any imbalance or restriction which results is the problem not of the reporter but the editor in chief. The reporter need not be unduly concerned with his own unconscious motivations of background and experience, but only with any conscious desire he may have to persuade others to think the same way. It may be sensible to ensure that any significantly large ethnic group in the community is represented in the broadcasting staff.

Unlike the junior newspaper journalist where every last adjective and comma can be checked before publication, the broadcast reporter is frequently in front of the microphone on his own. To help guard against the temptation to insert his own views, reporters should not be recruited straight from school, but have as wide and varied a background as possible and preferably bring to the job some experience of work outside broadcasting.

Good taste

As with all broadcasting, news programmes have a responsibility to abide by the generally accepted standards of what listeners would regard as 'good taste'. There are two areas which can create special problems – giving offence and causing distress.

In avoiding needless offence there must first be a professional care in the choice of words. People are particularly sensitive, and rightly so, about descriptions of themselves. The word 'immigrant' means someone who entered a country from elsewhere, yet it tends to be applied quite incorrectly to people whose parents or even grandparents were immigrants. Human labels pertaining to race, religion or political affiliations must be used with especial care and never as a social shorthand to convey anything other than their literal meaning. Examples are 'black', 'coloured', 'muslim', 'guerilla', 'southern', 'jewish', 'communist', etc. − used loosely as adjectives they tend to be more dangerous than as specific nouns.

The matter of giving offence must be considered in the reporting of sexual and other crimes. News is not to be suppressed on moral or social grounds but the desire to shock must be subordinate to the need to inform. The journalist must find a form of words which when spoken will provide the facts without causing embarrassment, for example in homes where children are listening. With print, parents may divert their children from the unsavoury and squalid, in radio an immediate general care must be exercised at the studio end. A useful guideline is for the broadcaster to consider how he would actually express the news to, say, the man in his local supermarket with other people gathered round.

More difficult is the assessment of what is good taste in the broadcasting of 'live' or recorded actuality. Reporting an angry demonstration or confrontation at the dock gates when tempers arc frayed is likely to result in the broadcasting of 'bad' language. What should be permitted? Should it be edited out of the recording? To what extent should it be deliberately used to indicate the strength of feeling aroused? There are no set answers, the context of the event and the situation of the listener are both pertinent to what is acceptable. However in using such material as news, the broadcaster must ensure that his motive is really to inform and not simply to sensationalise. It may be 'good copy', but does it genuinely help the listener in his understanding of the subject? If so it may be valid but the listener retains his right to react as he likes to the broadcaster's decision.

News of an accident can cause undue distress. It is necessary only to mention the words 'air crash' to cause immediate anxiety among the friends and relatives of anyone who boarded a 'plane in the previous 24 hours. The broadcaster's responsibility is to contain the alarm to the smallest possible group by identifying the time and location of the accident, the airline, flight number, departure point and destination of the aircraft concerned. The item will go on to give details of the damage and the possibility of survivors, but by then the great majority of air travellers will be outside the scope of the story. In the case of accidents involving casualties, for example a bus crash, it is helpful for listeners to know to which hospital the injured have been taken or to have a telephone number where they can obtain further information. The names of those killed or injured should not normally be broadcast until it is known that the next-of-kin have been informed.

A small but not unimportant point in bulletin compilation is the need to watch for the unintended and possibly unfortunate association of individual items. It could appear altogether too callous to follow a murder item with a report on 'a new deal for butchers'. Common sense and an awareness of the listener's sensitivities will normally meet the requirements of good taste but it is precisely in a multi-source and time constrained process, which news represents, that the niceties tend to be overlooked.

The newsroom operation

Almost every broadcasting station ultimately stands or falls by the quality of its news and information service. Its ability to respond quickly and to report accurately the events of the day extends beyond just news bulletins. The newsroom is likely to represent the greatest area of 'input' to a station and as such it is the one source capable of contributing to the whole of the output. Unlike a newspaper which directs its energies towards one or two specific deadlines, a radio newsroom is involved in a continuous process. The main sources of news coverage can be listed as:

1. *Professional*: Staff Reporters and Specialist Correspondents e.g. crime; local government; freelances and 'stringers'; teleprinter and wire services; news agencies; syndicating sources including other broadcasting stations; newspapers.
2. *Official*: Government sources both national and local; emergency services such as police, fire and hospitals; military and service organisations; public transport authorities.
3. *Commercial*: Business and commercial P.R. departments; entertainment interests.
4. *Public*: Information from listeners, taxi drivers, etc; voluntary organisations, societies and clubs.

The heart of the newsroom is its diary. As much information as possible is gleaned in advance so that the likely stories of the day can be covered within the resources available. Reporters will be allocated to the opening of a new trunk road, the controversial public meeting, the press conference, the arrival of an international pop star, or the publication of an important report. But the news editor must always consider how he would deal with the unforseen — an explosion at the chemical works, a surprise announcement by an important political figure. A newsroom however cannot wait for things to happen, it must pursue its own lines of enquiry, to investigate issues as well as report events.

It is not uncommon for a newsroom to think of its bulletins in terms of 'coverage' — to attempt 20 stories geographically representative of its area, instead of 10 items likely to be of more universal interest. This difference of approach should be resolved in the form of a stated policy — that is the extent to which a newsroom regards itself as serving several minorities as opposed to one audience of collective interest. The first is certainly true of a newspaper where each reader selects his own item for consumption, the second is more appropriate to radio where the selection is done for him. Given considerably less 'space' the fewer stories have to be of interest to everyone.

The competent newsroom must be organised in its copy flow. There should be one place which receives the input of letters, press releases, teleprint material and other written data. A reporter making 'routine' calls to the emergency services or other regular contacts collects the verbal information so that, after consulting the diary, the news editor can decide which stories to cover. He may call a meeting of all the staff on duty to discuss the likely prospects. One person will be allocated to write the actual bulletins — a task not to be regarded as a committee job. If possible a second writer is put on the shorter bulletins and summaries. Working from the same material a quite different approach is needed when producing a two minute summary. Omitting the last three sentences of each story in a five minute bulletin will not do!

Reporters and freelances are allocated to the stories selected, each one is briefed on the implications and possible 'angles' of approach, together with suggestions for its treatment, and given a deadline for completion. Elsewhere in the room or nearby, tapes are edited, cue material written, recordings made of interviews over the phone, and previous copy 'subbed', updated or otherwise refreshed for further use. The mechanical detail

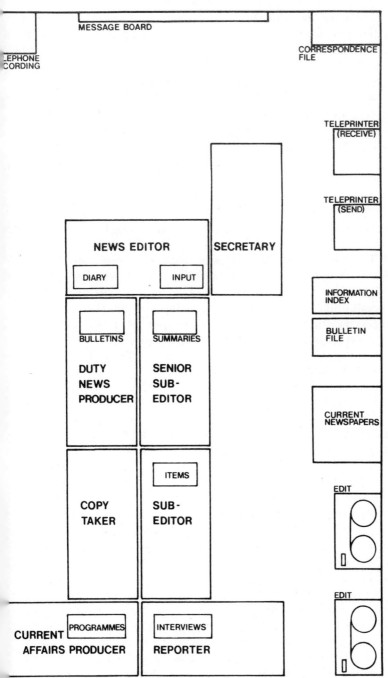

atures of a newsroom. A possible layout involving 8 job functions.

will depend on the degree of sophistication enjoyed by the individual newsroom — the availability of a radio car or other mobile direct inject equipment, O.B. and other 'remote' facilities, electronic data processes, off-air or closed circuit television, intercom to other parts of the building etc.

A newsroom also requires systems for the speedy retrieval of information from a central index. This will take the form of a file containing the names, addresses and telephone numbers of useful contacts, plus newspaper cuttings, scripts or other items relating to running stories or future events. These can be arranged either alphabetically or in date order but in such a way that everyone has access and understands the system. For the short term retention of information, the urgent telephone number or message to a colleague on another shift, a blackboard or similar device is simple and effective.

The important principle is that everyone should know exactly what they have to do to what timescale, and to whom they should turn in difficulty. The news editor or director in overall charge must be in possession of all the information necessary for him to control the output. He must also be clear, as must everyone else, on the extent to which the minute by minute operation is delegated to others. There is no place or time for confusion or conflict.

8

NEWSREADING AND PRESENTATION

PRESENTATION is radio's packaging. It hardly matters how good a programme's content, how well written or how excellent its interviews; it comes to nothing if it is poorly presented. It is like taking a beautiful perfume and marketing it in a medicine bottle. Good presentation stems from an understanding of the medium and a basically caring attitude towards the listener. A broadcaster at the microphone ought consciously to care whether or not the listener can follow and understand what he is saying. By 'thinking outwards', away from himself, he is less prone to the destructive effects of studio nerves; or for that matter the complacency of over-familiarity, and more likely to communicate his meaning. Since he does not know the listener personally he adopts the relationship of an acquaintance rather than that of a friend. He is friendly, respectful, informative and helpful. He has something to offer the listener, but does not use this to gain advantage either by exercising a knowledgeable superiority or by assuming any special authority. The relationship is a horizontal one, he refers to his 'putting something across', not down or up. He does not make undue assumptions about his acquaintance, or presume on the relationship, but works at it always taking the trouble to make what he is saying interesting.

Of course newsreading tends to be more formal than a record programme but there is room for a variety of approaches. Whatever the overall style of the station, governed by its basic attitude to the listener, it should be fairly consistent. While the sociologist may regard radio as a mass-medium, the man at the microphone sees it as an individual communication, he is talking to some*one*. Thinking of his listener as one person he says, "If you're travelling south today, . . ." not "Anyone travelling south . . ." The presenter does not shout. If he is two feet from

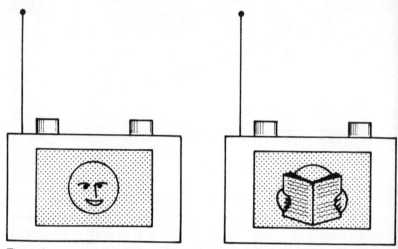

The script must not come between the broadcaster and the listener. The listener should feel that he is being spoken to — not read to. The script needs to be written for talking aloud and the vocal inflections and stresses kept as natural as the broadcaster's own speech.

the microphone and his listener is four feet from the radio, the total distance between them is six feet. What is required is not volume but an ordinary clarity. Too much projection causes the listener psychologically to 'back off' — it distances the relationship. Conversely by dropping his voice the presenter adopts the confidential or intimate style more appropriate to the closeness of late night listening.

The rate of delivery depends on the style of the station and the material being broadcast. Inter-programme or continuity announcements should be at the presenter's own conversational speed, for example newsreading at 160 – 200 words per minute but slower if for short wave transmission. Commentary should be at a rate to suit the action. If a reader is going too fast it may not help simply to ask him to slow down, this is likely to make him sound stilted and over-careful. What is required is that he leaves more pause between the sentences — that is when the understanding takes place. It is not so much the speed of the words which can confuse, but the lack of sufficient time to make sense of them.

The simplest way of getting the style, projection and speed right, is to visualise the listener sitting in the studio a little way beyond the microphone. The presenter is not by himself reading, he is talking with the listener. This small exercise in imagination is the key to good presentation.

Newsreading

The first demand placed on the newsreader is that he understands what he is reading. He cannot be expected to communicate sensibly if he has not fully grasped the sense of it himself. With the reservations expressed later about 'rip 'n' read' material, there is little place for the newsreader who picks up a bulletin with thirty seconds to go and hopes to read it 'word perfect'. He must be better than punctual, he must be early. Neither is technically faultless reading the same thing as communicating sense. A newsreader should be well informed and have an excellent background knowledge of current affairs so that he can cope when changes occur just before bulletins. He should take time to read it out loud beforehand — this gives him a chance to understand the content and be aware of pitfalls. There may be problems of pronunciation over a visiting Chinese trade mission or statement by an African foreign minister. There may be a phrase which is awkward to say, an ambiguous construction, or typing error. The pages should be verbally checked by the person who, in the listener's mind, is responsible for disseminating them. While a newsroom may like to give the impression that its material is the latest 'hot off the press' rush, it is seldom impossible for the reader to go through all the pages as a bulletin is being put together. Thorough preparation should be the rule, with reading at sight reserved for emergencies.

Of course in practice this is often a counsel of perfection. In a small station where the newsreader may be working single-handed, the news can arrive on the teleprinter within seconds of its deadline. It has to be read at sight. This is not the best practice and runs a considerable risk of error. It places on the central news service, and on the transmitting keyboard operator, a high responsibility for total accuracy. The reason for poor broadcasting of 'rip 'n' read' material may lie with the station management for insufficient staffing, or with the news agency for less than professional standards. The fact of the matter is that in the event of a mistake on the air, from whatever cause, the listener blames the newsreader.

The man at the microphone therefore has the right to expect a certain level of service. This means a well written and properly set out bulletin, accurately typed, arriving on a well maintained machine a few minutes before it is needed. He can then check to see if the lead story has changed and scan it quickly for any unfamiliar names. He picks out figures and dates to make sure he understands them. In the actual reading, his eyes are a little ahead of his speech, enabling him to take in groups of words, understanding them before passing on their sense to the listener.

The idea of 'rip'n' read' is excellent but it should not become the cause nor be made the excuse for poor microphone delivery;

In the studio the newsreader sits himself comfortably but not indulgently, feeling relaxed but not complacent, breathing normally and taking a couple of extra deep breaths before he begins.

Pronunciation

A station should as far as possible be consistent over its use of a particular name. Problems arise when its output comprises several sources, e.g. syndicated material, a live audio news feed, a sustaining service. What must be avoided is one pronunciation in a nationally syndicated bulletin, followed a few minutes later by a different treatment in a locally read teleprint text or 'rip 'n' read'. The newsroom must listen to the whole of the station's news output, from whatever source, and advise the newsreader accordingly. Secondly, listeners are extremely sensitive to the incorrect pronunciation of names with which they are associated. The station which gets a local place name wrong loses credibility, one which mispronounces a personal name is regarded as either ignorant or rude. The difficulty is that listeners themselves may not agree on the correct form. Nevertheless a station must make strenuous efforts to ensure a consistent treatment of place names within its area. A pronunciation list based on 'educated local knowledge' must be adopted as a matter of policy and a new broadcaster joining the staff should acquaint himself with it at the earliest possible time.

Vocal stressing

An important aspect of conveying meaning about which a script gives no clue is that of stress — the degree of emphasis laid on a word. Take the phrase:

"What do you want me to do about that?"

Put the stress on the 'you', it is a very direct question. On the 'me' it is more personal to the questioner; on the 'do' it is a practical rather than a theoretical matter; on the 'that' it is different again. Its meaning changes with the emphasis. In reading news such subtleties can be crucial. For example we may have in a story on Arab/Israeli affairs the following two statements:

Mr. Radim is visiting Washington where he is due to see the President this afternoon. Meanwhile the Israeli Foreign Minister is in Paris.

The name is fictional but the example real. Put the emphasis on the word 'Israeli', and Mr. Radim is probably an Arab foreign minister. Put it on 'Foreign', and he becomes the Israeli Prime Minister. Listening to newsreaders it is possible to discern a widespread belief that there is a universal news style, where speed and urgency have priority over meaning, where the emphasis is either on every word or scattered in a random fashion, but always on the last word in every sentence. Does it stem from the journalist's need for clarity when dictating copy over the 'phone? The fact is that many sentences have a central 'pivot', or are counter-balanced about each other: 'While *this* is happening over *here*, *that* is taking place over *there*'. Many sentences contain a counter-balance of event, geography, person or time: 'Mr *Smith* said an election should take place *now*, *before* the issue came up. Mr. *Jones* thought it should wait at least until *after* the matter had been debated'.

A misplaced emphasis will cloud the meaning, possibly alter it. The only way of achieving correct stressing is by fully understanding the implications as well as the 'face value' of the material. This must be a conscious awareness during the preparatory read-through. As has been rightly observed, 'take care of the sense and the sounds will take care of themselves'.

Inflection

The monotonous reader either has no inflection in his voice at all, or the rise and fall in pitch becomes regular and repetitive. It is the predictability of the vocal pattern which becomes boring. A too typical sentence 'shape' starts at a low pitch, quickly rises to the top and gradually descends, arriving at the bottom again by the final full stop. Placed end to end, such sentences quickly establish a rhythm which, if it does not mesmerize will confuse because with their beginning and ending on the same 'note', the joins are scarcely perceptible.

Meaning begins to evaporate as the structure disappears. Without sounding artificial or contrived, sentences normally start on a higher pitch than the one on which the previous one ended – a new paragraph certainly should. There can often be a natural rise and fall within a sentence, particularly if it contains more than one phrase. Meaningful stressing rather than random patterning will help.

A newsreader is well advised occasionally to record his work for his own analysis – is it too rhythmic, dull or aggressive? In the matter of inflection he should experiment off the air, putting a greater rise and fall into his voice than usual to see whether the result is more acceptable. Very often when he may feel he is really 'hamming it up', the playback sounds perfectly normal and only a shade more lively. Even experienced readers can become stale and fall into the traps of meachnical reading, and a little non-obsessive self-analysis and experimentation is very healthy.

Quotation marks

Reading quotes is a minor art on its own. It is easy to sound as though the comment is that of the newsreader although the writing should avoid this construction. Some examples:

> While an early bulletin described his condition as 'comfortable', by this afternoon he was 'weaker'. (This should be rewritten to attribute both quotes.)
> The opposition leader described the statement as "a complete fabrication designed to mislead".
> He later argued that he had "never seen" the witness.

To make someone else's words stand out as separate from the newsreader's own, there is a small pause and a change in voice pitch and speed for the quote.

Alterations

Last minute hand written changes to the typed page should be made with as much clarity as possible. Crossings out should be done in blocks rather than on each individual word. Lines and arrows indicating a different order of the material need to be bold enough to follow quickly and any new lines written clearly at the bottom of the page. To avoid confusion a 'unity of change' should be the aim. It is amazing how often a reader will find his way skilfully through a maze of alterations only to stumble when his concentration relaxes on the next perfectly clear page.

Corrections

But what happens when a mistake is made? Continue and ignore it or go back and correct it? When is an apology called for? It depends of course on the type of error. There is the verbal slip which it is quite unnecessary to do anything about, a misplaced emphasis, a wrong inflection, a word which comes out in an unintended way. The key question is 'could the listener have misconstrued my meaning?' If so, it must be put right. If there is a persistent error, or a refusal of a word to be pronounced at all, it is better to restart the whole sentence. Since "I'm sorry I'll read that again" is the title of a BBC programme, something else might be preferred – "I'm sorry, I'll repeat that", or "Let me take that again". It is whatever comes most naturally to the unflustered reader. To the broadcaster it can seem like the end of the world; it is not. Even if the listener has noticed it he simply wants a correction with as little fuss as possible.

Lists and numbers

The reading of a list can create a problem. A table of sports results, stock market shares, fatstock prices or a shipping forecast; these can sound very dull. Again, the first job for the reader is to understand his material, to take an interest in it so that he can communicate it. Secondly the inexperienced reader must listen to others, not to copy them, but to pick up the points in their style which seem right for himself. There are particular inflections in reading this material which reinforce the information content. With football results, for example, the voice indicates the result as it gives the score.

In passing, it is worth noting that sport has a good deal of its own jargon which looks the same on the printed page, for instance the figure '0'. The newsreader should know when this should be interpreted as 'nought', 'love', 'zero', 'oh', or 'nil' – the listener will certainly know what is correct. Unless it is automatic, it is well worth writing the appropriate word on the script. Whenever figures appear in a script, the reader should sort out the hundreds from the thousands and if necessary write the number on the page in words.

If it has been correctly written, a script consists of short unambiguous sentences or phrases, easily taken in by the eye and delivered vocally well within a single breath. The sense is contained not in the single words but in their grouping. To begin with we learn to read letter by letter, then word by word. The intelligent newsreader delivers his material phrase by phrase, taking in and giving out whole groups of words at a time, leaving little pauses between them to let their meaning sink in. The overall style is not one of 'reading' – it is much more akin to 'telling'.

In summary, the 'rules' of newsreading are:

1. Understand the content by preparation.
2. Visualise the listener by imagination.
3. Communicate the sense by telling.

Continuity presentation

Presenting a sequence of programmes, giving them continuity, acting as the voice of the station, is very similar to being the host of a magazine programme responsible for linking different items. The job is to provide a continuous thread of interest even though there are contrasts of content and mood. The presenter makes the transition by picking up in the style of the programme that is finishing so that by the time he has done the back announcements and given incidental information, station identification and time check, he is ready to introduce the next programme in perhaps a quite different manner. Naturally to judge the mood correctly he has to do some listening. It is no good coming into a studio with under a minute to go, hoping to find the right piece of paper so as to get into the next programme, without sounding detached from the whole proceedings. A station like this might as well be automated.

Continuity presentation requires a sensitivity to the way a programme ends, to leave just the right pause, to continue with a smile in the voice or whatever is needed. He has to develop a precise sense of timing, the ability to talk rather than 'waffle', for exactly fifteen seconds, or a minute and a half. A good presenter knows it is not enough just to get the programmes on the air, his concern is the person at the end of the system.

What about emergencies? The cartridge fails to 'fire', the machine does not start or having given an introduction there is silence when the fader is opened. Firstly, no oaths or exclamations! The microphone may still be 'live' and this is the time when one problem can lead to another. Secondly, look hard to see that there has not been a simple operational error. Are all the signal lights showing correctly? Is there an equipment fault which can be put right quickly? Can a tape be transferred to another machine? If by taking action the programme can continue with only a slight pause, five seconds or so, then no further announcement is necessary. If it takes longer to put right, ten seconds or more, something should be said to keep the listener informed:

> "I'm sorry about the delay, we seem to have lost that report for a moment . . ."

Then if action is assured it is possible to continue:

> "We'll have it for you shortly . . ."

The presenter may assume personal or collective responsibility for the problem but what he must not do is to blame someone else:

> "Sorry about that, the man through the glass window here pressed the wrong button"!

The same goes for tapes or discs played at the wrong speed, the wrong item following a particular cue, or pages read in the wrong order. The professional does not become self-indulgent, saying how complicated his job is, he simply puts it right, with everybody else's help, in a natural manner and with the minimum of bother. His job is to expect the unexpected.

Sooner or later a more serious situation will occur which demands that the presenter 'fills' for a considerable time. Standby announcements of a public service type – an appeal for blood donors, safety in the home, code for drivers, procedure for contacting the police or hospital service. Also programme trails and other promotional material can be used. These 'fills' should always be available to cover the odd twenty seconds, and changed once they have been used.

A box of standby records is an essential part of the emergency procedure. Something for every occasion – a break in the relay of a church service, the loss of Saturday football, an under-run of a children's programme. To avoid confusion the music chosen should not be identical to anything it replaces, simply of a sympathetic mood. Once a record is on there is a breathing space to attempt to get the problem sorted out. The principle is to return to the original programme as quickly as possible. Very occasionally it may be necessary to abandon a fault-prone programme and some stations keep a 'timeless talk' or fifteen minute feature permanently on standby to cover such an eventuality.

A vocal performer can sometimes become obsessed with the sound of his own voice. The warning signs include a tendency to listen to himself continuously on headphones. The purpose of headphone monitoring is essentially to provide talkback communication, or an outside source or cue programme feed. Only if it is unavoidable should both ears be covered, otherwise the presenter begins to live in a world of his own, out of touch with others in the studio. If he has a great deal of routine work, the same announcements, station identifications, time checks and introductions, it is easy not to try very hard to find appropriate variations. Like the newsreader he should occasionally listen to himself recorded off-air, checking a repetitive vocabulary, use of cliché or monotony of style.

Trails and promos

Part of a station's total presentation 'sound' is the way it sells itself. Promotional activity should not be left to chance but be carefully designed to accord with an overall sense of style. 'Selling' one's own programmes on the air is like marketing any other product, except that the appeal can only be directed to those people who are already listening. The task is therefore to describe a future programme as so interesting and attractive that the listener is bound to tune in again. The qualities which people enjoy and which will attract them to a particular pro-gramme are:

1. Humour that appeals.
2. Originality that is intriguing.
3. An interest that is relevant.
4. A cleverness which can be appreciated.
5. Musical content.

112

6. Simplicity – a non-confusing message.

7. A good sound quality.

If one or more of these attributes is presented in a style to which he can relate, the listener will almost certainly come back for more. The station is all the time attempting to develop a rapport with the listener, and the programme trailer is an opportunity to do just this. It is saying of a future programme, "this is for *you*".

Having obtained the listener's interest, a trail must provide some information on content – what the programme is trying to do, who is taking part, and what form (quiz, discussion, phone-in etc) it will take. All this must be in line with the same list of attractive qualities. But this is far from easy – to be humorous *and* original, to be clever as well as simple. The final stage is to be sure that the listener is left with clear transmission details, the day and time of the broadcast. This information is best repeated:

"... You can hear the show on this station tomorrow at six p.m. Just the thing for early evening – the 'Kate Greenhouse Saga', on 251 – six o'clock, tomorrow".

Trails are often wrapped around with music which reflects something of the style of the programme, or at least the style of the programme in which the trail is inserted. It should start and finish clearly, rather than on a fade; this is achieved by pre-fading the end music to time and editing it to the opening music so that the join is covered by speech.

At its simplest, a trail lasting 30 seconds looks like this:

Music	Bright, faded on musical phrase, held under speech.	5"
Speech	Obtains interest.	10"
	Provides information on content. (Music edit at low level.)	5"
	Gives transmission details.	5"
Music	Faded up to end.	5"

There is little point in ordering a listener to switch on (buy some today!), the effect is better achieved by convincing him that he will be deprived if he does not. And of course if that is the station's promise then it must later be fulfilled. Trails should not be too mandatory, and above all they should be memorable.

9

THE RADIO PRESS RELEASE

PRESS releases, publicity handouts, notices and letters rain down on the news editor's desk in considerable quantities. Although a conscientious newsroom looks at everything that comes in, most of them will end up on the spike, unused. In order to get the material read fully, and acted upon, there are some simple rules for those issuing releases about how the information should be set out.

The editor is short of time and is not able to sift through a mass of verbiage. A press release is simply an indication that something is happening and not a total account of it from every conceivable angle. It should therefore be as brief as possible — preferably on one side of a single sheet of paper.

A standard size of paper is generally preferred, such as A4, but it should be of distinctive appearance. A printed letterhead, identifying logo or trademark, or simply a coloured paper is a help in finding the material for later reference.

A release must be immediately intelligible. Handwritten information is discouraged as more difficult to read than printed or typed copy. It should be double spaced with well separated paragraphs and broad margins.

It should begin with a descriptive title or headline which identifies the news story or event.

The purpose of a press release is to create interest in its subject and to encourage further action by the radio station. The copy should quickly get to the heart of the matter providing only sufficient context to highlight the significance of the event. The material should be 'new', 'interesting', and 'true' within the terms of the earlier chapter on News and Current Affairs. This means that it should be relevant to the target audience.

The writing style should be more conversational than formal.

This enables it to be readily visualised in script or interview form. Technical or legal jargon and other specialist professional language must be avoided.

All pertinent facts should be included, having been double checked. An error in a press release will seriously undermine the credibility of the sender. Names of people should include at least the first Christian name and not merely the initials. The information given must be totally correct – personal qualifications, titles, business occupations, ages, addresses, dates, times, places, sums of money, percentages etc. Any detail about which there may be the slightest doubt should be omitted. If an error is subsequently discovered, the recipients should be immediately informed.

A press release must clearly indicate its writer or office of origin together with its date, and if necessary its time of issue. The point of reference for further contact should be given, including the appropriate business and home telephone numbers.

Having produced a press release it should be made available as soon as possible – hours or even minutes may be significant in deciding if or how it should be used. Unlike a newspaper, most of which have a single daily deadline, a radio newsroom has a series of deadlines throughout its broadcasting day. New material can therefore be assimilated at almost any time and the perceptive issuer of press releases will provide information at those times when the newsroom is not already swamped with good material. There may be advantages in delivering a press release by hand rather than have it arrive with the rest of the mail.

An embargo should only be placed on a press release if there is an obvious reason – for example in the case of an advance summary of a speech, or where it is sensible to allow time to digest or analyse a complex issue before general publication. Once suitable information is in the broadcaster's hands, he would obviously like to use it straightaway. Radio is an immediate medium and newsmen in particular have no natural inclination to wait around observing an embargo placed simply to provide a simultaneity of announcement with their competitors. Embargoed releases should carry a word of explanation and be rare. The observation of an embargo is in any case a voluntary matter and not a formal or legal obligation imposed on the recipient.

If a release is not particularly suitable for inclusion in a news

116

bulletin, the well organised radio station will redirect it internally to the appropriate programme department. However this introduces delay and there is no guarantee that the information will end up in the right place. It may be useful, particularly when dealing with a large station, to send more than one copy — for example to the news editor, the programme organiser or controller and the appropriate specialist producer. It is a question of the sender knowing his market.

To avoid subsequent duplication of action, it is important when sending several copies to indicate the fact on the press release.

A final word of warning. A radio station does not exist purely as an outlet for those seeking publicity; As has been indicated earlier there may be many and complex reasons why a piece of information is or is not broadcast. The use made of a release is a matter which must be left to the judgement of the station. It is wise not to 'over-sell' a contribution and not to be discouraged if it is not used.

Overleaf are examples of how a press release might be set out:

MINISTRY OF DEFENCE NEWS RELEASE

Royal Marines in European Infantry Competition

Two teams of Royal Marines from 42 Commando will be taking part in the tenth annual Northern European Command Infantry Competition to be held at Plon, Schleswig-Holstein, West Germany from 11 to 15 September.

See list of names attached.

In competition with squads from Norway, Denmark, Germany, Netherlands and Canada, the eight-man teams will be tested in various infantry skills including shooting, map-reading, obstacle crossing and field craft.

The aim of the competition is to improve the professional standards of infantry units within the Northern European Command of NATO and to improve mutual understanding of the troops taking part through friendly competition.

Issued by: Public Relations (Royal Navy)
             Ministry of Defence,
             Main Building,
             Whitehall, London S.W.1.
             021-218-3257/3258

AMPERSAND
CROYDON ARTS ASSOCIATION
Civic Centre Croydon
PRESS NOTICE
Date

TO: News Editor,
and Producer, "Music Box"

CROYDON SYMPHONY ORCHESTRA — NEW CONDUCTOR

JOHN THORNEHILL is to join the Croydon Symphony
Orchestra as its resident conductor on a 3-year contract from
1st January 1979. He is currently musical director of The
Music Group of New York.

Born in Philadelphia in 1945, he studied the piano and violin
at Columbia University and won a 2 year scholarship in composition at the Paris Conservatoire.

He visited Britain in 1975 with the Lincoln Youth Orchestra
during which tour he gave a concert at the Croydon Civic
Hall. He also met his wife, Julia, from Cambridge.

He is particularly interested in the training of young musicians
and for 3 years has been involved in the summer school at
Tanglewood, Massachusetts.

The composer of several published works for string orchestra,
he hopes to have more time for composition.

Note to the Editor: Mr & Mrs Thornehill are visiting Croydon on
November 18-19th and will be available for interview.

Details of press conference to be announced.

Further information from: Gavin Watson,
Croydon 4411 ext 671 (office)
Westerham 55931 (home)

119

10

THE DISCUSSION PROGRAMME

THE topic for a broadcast debate should be a matter in which there is genuine public interest or concern. The aim is for the

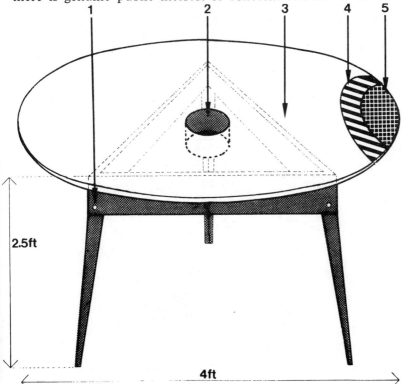

A talks/discussion table. Designed for studio use the table has 3 legs to reduce obstruction and to prevent it wobbling on an uneven floor. 1. Headphone Jack carrying a programme feed with or without additional talkback. 2. Centre hole to take the microphone either placed on a special carrier fitting, or on a floor stand. 3. Acoustically transparent table top consisting of a loose weave cloth surface, 4 a layer of padding, and 5 a steel mesh base. (Courtesy BBC Engineering Information Department.)

listener to hear argument and counter-argument expressed in conversational form by people actually holding those views with conviction. The broadcaster can then remain independent.

Format

In its simplest form there will be two speakers representing opposing views together with an impartial chairman. The producer may of course decide that such an arrangement would not do justice to the subject, that it is not as clear cut as the bi-directional discussion will allow and it might therefore be better to include a range of views — the 'multi-facet' discussion.

In this respect the 'blindness' of radio imposes its own limitations and four or five speakers should be regarded as the maximum. Even then it is preferable that there is a mix of male and female voices.

Under the heading of the discussion programme should also come what is often referred to as 'the chat show'. Here, a well known radio personality introduces a guest and talks with him. It may incorrectly be described as an interview but since 'personalities' have views of their own which they are generally

A discussion can become confusing if it contains too many different points of view.

only too ready to express, the result is likely to be a discussion. The 'chairman plus one' formula can be a satisfactory approach to a discussion, particularly with the more lightweight entertainment, the non current-affairs type of subjects. It works less well in the controversial, political, current-affairs field since it is more difficult for the chairman to retain his neutrality if he is part of the discussion. In any case the danger for the broadcaster is that in order to draw out his guest contributor, he is always acting as 'the opposition' and becomes identified as 'anti everything'. In such cases the more acceptable format is that of the interview.

Selection of participants

It is possible to 'load' a discussion so that it is favourable to a particular point of view but since the listener must make up his mind by hearing different views adequately expressed, the producer should look for balance — of ability as well as opinion. Often there are on the one hand the 'official spokesmen', and on the other the good broadcasters! Sometimes they combine in the same person but not everyone, in the circumstances of the broadcast debate, is quick thinking, articulate and convincing — however worthy they may be in other respects. In selecting the

Mr. A. Spokesman   **SMOOTHIE (PR) LTD**

Do all participants start equal? A discussion tends to favour the articulate and well organised. The chairman may have to create opportunities for others to make their case.

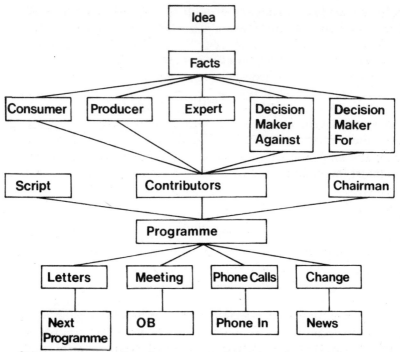

Stages is producing a discussion programme. Select the topic — research the information — choose the participants — co-ordinate the contributors — broadcast the programme — deal with the response — evaluate the possibility of follow-up.

spokesman for one political party it is virtually obligatory also to include his 'shadow' opposite number — whatever the quality of his radio performance.

There will obviously be times when it is necessary to choose the leader of the party, the council member, the chairman of the company or the official spokesman; but there will also be occasions when the choice is more open to the broadcaster and in the multi-faceted discussion it is important to include as diverse a range of interests as is appropriate.

In general terms these can be summarised as: power-holders and decision makers, legal representation and 'watch dog' organisations, producers of goods and services, and consumers of goods and services. These categories will apply whether the issue is the flooding of a valley for a proposed hydro-electric scheme, a change in the abortion law, or an increase in the price of food.

The listener should also be regarded as a participant and the topic should at least be one which involves him. If the listener is directly affected he can be invited to take part in a follow-up programme either by letter or by phone. In the event of a public meeting on the subject it may be that the broadcaster can arrange to cover it with an outside broadcast.

The chairman

Having selected the topic and the team, the programme will need a chairman. The ideal is knowledgeable, firm, sensitive, quick thinking, impartial, and courteous. He will be interested in almost everything and will need a sense of humour – no mean task!

Preparation

Having obtained this paragon of human virtue who also possesses a good radio voice and an acute sense of timing, there are several points which need his attention before the broadcast.

The subject must be researched and the essential background information gathered and checked. Appropriate reference material may be found in libraries, files of newspaper cuttings, and in the radio station's own newsroom. The chairman must have the facts at his fingertips and have a note of the views already expressed so that he understands the points of controversy. He can then prepare a basic 'plot' of the discussion outlining the main areas to be covered. This is in no sense a script, it is a reminder of the essential issues in case they should get sidetracked in the debate.

It is important that the speakers are properly briefed beforehand making sure that they understand the purpose, range *and limitations* of the discussion. They should each know who is to take part and the duration of the programme. It is not necessary for them to meet before the broadcast but they should be given the opportunity to do their own preparation.

Starting the programme

At the start of the broadcast the chairman introduces the subject making it interesting and relevant to the listener. This is often done by putting a series of questions on the central issues, or by quoting remarks already made publicly.

The chairman should have everyone's name, and his or her designation, written down in front of him. He then introduces them, making sure that all their voices are heard as early as possible in the programme. During the discussion he should continue to address them by name, at least for the first two 'rounds' of conversation. Their names should be used again at intervals throughout. It is essential that the start of the programme is factual in content and positive in presentation. Such an approach will be helpful to the less confident members of the team and will reassure the listener that the subject is in good hands. It also enables the participants to have something 'to bite on' immediately so that the discussion can begin without a lengthy warming up period.

Speaker control

In the rather special conditions of a studio discussion, some people become highly talkative believing that they have failed unless they have put their whole case in the first five minutes. On the other hand there are the nervously diffident. The chairman cannot make a poor speaker appear brilliant, but there is an important difference between someone with poor delivery and someone with little to say. The chairman must draw out the former and curb the latter. Even the most voluble have to breathe – a factor which the chairman must observe closely! The chairman's main task is to provide equal opportunity of expression for all participants. To do this he will have to suppress as well as to encourage and such disciplines as are required should be communicated – probably non-verbally.

After having an opinion strongly expressed, that speaker should not be allowed to continue for too long before another view of the matter is introduced. The chairman can interrupt, particularly if he does so constructively . . . "That's an important point, before we go on, how do others react to that? – Mrs. Jones?" The chairman must in these cases give a positive indication by voice, facial expressions and possibly hand signal as well, of who is to speak. He should prevent two voices from speaking at once, other than for a brief interjection, by a decisive and clear indication of 'who holds the floor'. It is not a disaster when there are two or more voices, indeed it may be a useful indicator of the strength of feeling. It has to be remembered however, particularly when broadcasting monophonically, that when voices overlay each other, the listener is unlikely to make much sense of the actual content.

Subject control

The chairman has to obtain clarification of any technical jargon or specialist language which a contributor may use. Abbreviations, particularly of organisations, are generally far less well understood by the listener than people sitting round a studio table would like to think.

With one eye on his prepared 'plot' and the other on the clock, the chairman steers the subject through its essential areas. However he must remain reasonably flexible and if one particular aspect is proving especially interesting, the chairman may decide to depart from his original outline.

Above all, he must be able to spot and deal with red herrings and digressions. To do this he must know where the discussion should be going and have the appropriate question phrased so that he can interrupt positively, constructively and courteously.

In a lengthy programme it may be useful to introduce a device which creates variety and helps the discussion to change direction. Examples are a letter from a listener, or quote from an article read by the chairman, a pre-recorded interview, a piece of actuality, or a phone call. If the chairman is to retain his impartiality such an insert should not be used to make a specific point but simply to raise questions on which the participants may then comment.

Technical control

The chairman has to watch for, and correct, alterations in the balance of voices which was obtained before the programme began. This may be due to a speaker moving back 'off-mic', turning directly to address his neighbour or leaning in too close. There may be wide variations in individual voice levels as the participants get annoyed, excited, discomfited or subdued. And he has to be aware of any extraneous noise such as paper rustle, matches being struck or fingers tapping the table. Non-verbal signals should suffice to prevent them becoming too intrusive.

As an aid in judging the effect of any movement, changes in voice level or unwanted sounds, the chairman will often wear headphones. These should be on one ear only to avoid his being isolated acoustically from the actual discussion. This will also enable him to hear talkback from the producer so that

TIME GONE - TIME TO GO

HOW LONG HAS HE HAD?

IS IT IRRELEVANT?

IS IT BORING?

IS IT INCOMPREHENSIBLE?

NEXT QUESTION

WHO NEXT?

Questions in the chairman's mind.

Voice levels must be watched throughout. A person with a quiet voice will have to sit close in to the table and the discussion chairman must prevent too much movement.

he can be fed with additional ideas — for example on a point of the discussion which might otherwise be overlooked. On occasions, everyone in the studio will require headphones. This is likely if the programme is to include phone calls from listeners, or when members of the discussion group are not

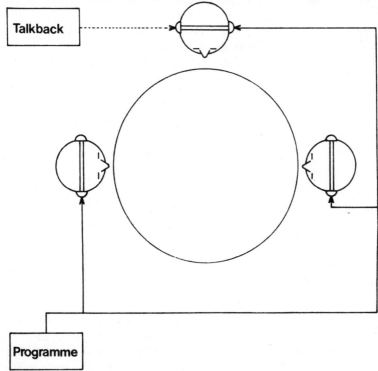

Talkback from the producer goes only to the discussion chairman. The other participants may also have to wear head-phones, carrying the programme feed only, in order to hear a remote contributor or phone call.

physically present in the same studio but are talking together over links between separate studios. In these circumstances, the talkback arrangements have to be such that the producer's editorial comments are confined only to the headphones worn by the chairman. To avoid embarrassment and confusion such a system must be checked before the programme begins.

An important part of the technical control of the programme is its overall timing. The chairman must never forget the clock.

Ending the programme

It is rarely desirable for the chairman to attempt a summing up. If the discussion has gone well, the listener will already have recognised the main points being made and the arguments which support them. If a summary *is* required, it is often better to invite each speaker to have a 'last word'. Alternatively, the chairman may put a key question to the group which points the subject forward to the next step — "Finally, what do you think should happen now?" This should be timed to allow for sufficient answering discussion.

Many a good programme is spoiled by an untidy ending. The chairman should avoid giving the impression that the programme simply ran out of time:

> "Well, I'm afraid we'll have to stop there . . ."
> "Once again the old clock has beaten us . . ."
> "What a pity there's no time to explore that last point . . ."

The programme should cover the material which it intended, in the time it was allowed. With a minute or less to go, the chairman should thank his contributors by name, giving any other credits due and referring to further programmes or public events related to the subject.

After the broadcast comes the time when the participants think of the remarks they should have made. An opportunity for them to relax and 'unwind' is important, and this is preferably done as a group, assuming they are still speaking to each other. They are at this stage probably feeling vulnerable and exposed, wondering if they have done justice to the arguments they represent. They should be warmly thanked and allowed to talk informally if they wish. The provision of some refreshment or hospitality is often appropriate.

It is not the broadcaster's job to create confrontation and

dissent where none exists. But genuine differences of opinion on matters of public interest offer absorbing broadcasting since the listener may feel a personal involvement in the arguments expressed and in their outcome. The discussion programme is a contribution to the wider area of public debate and may be regarded as part of the broadcaster's positive role in a democratic society.

11

THE PHONE-IN PROGRAMME

CRITICS of the phone-in describe it as no more than a cheap way of filling air-time and undoubtedly it is sometimes used as such. But like anything else, the priority it is accorded and the production methods applied to it will decide whether it is simply transmitter fodder or whether it can be useful and interesting to the listener.

Through public participation its aim is to allow a democratic expression of view and to create the possibility of community action. An important question therefore is to what extent such a programme excludes those listeners who are without a telephone? Telephone ownership can vary widely between regions of the same country, and the cities are generally far better served than the rural areas. Per head of population North America has more telephones than anywhere else in the world. It follows that to base programmes simply on the American or Canadian practice may be misleading.

In Britain, telephone ownership by households is less than 50% and this has to be taken into account in two ways. First, it is possible to be over-glib with the invitation – " . . . if you want to take part in the programme just give us a ring on . . ." Cannot someone take part simply by listening? Or to go further, if the aim is public participation, will the programme also accept letters, or people who actually arrive on the station's doorstep?

Secondly, it is especially gratifying to have someone, without a phone at home, go to the trouble of phoning from a public call box. To avoid losing the call when the money runs out, the station should always take the number and initiate such calls as are broadcast on a phone-back basis.

Technical facilities

When inviting listeners to phone the programme it is best to have a special number rather than take the calls through the normal station telephone number. Otherwise the programme can bring the general telephone traffic to a halt. The technical means of taking calls have almost infinite variation but the facilities should include:

1. Off-air answering of calls.
2. Acceptance of several calls – say four or five simultaneously.
3. Holding a call until required, sending it a feed of cue programme.
4. The ability to take two calls simultaneously on the air.
5. Origination of calls from the studio.
6. Picking up a call by the answering position after its on-air use.

Programme classification

The producer of a phone-in must decide the aim of his programme and design it so that it achieves a particular object-ive. If he simply throws the phone-lines open to listeners, the result can be a hopeless muddle. There are always cranks and exhibitionisis ready to talk without saying anything, and there are the lonely with a real need to talk. Inexpert advice given in the studio will annoy those listeners who know more about the subject than the presenter, and may actually be harmful to the person putting the question. It is essential that the producer knows what he is trying to do and by an adequate screening of the incoming calls, limits the public participation to the central purpose of the programme.

Types of phone-in include:

1. The open line – discussion with the studio presenter.
2. The specific subject – expert advice on a chosen topic.
3. Consumer affairs – a series providing 'action' advice on detailed cases.

Staffing a phone-in. 1. The total self-op. The presenter takes his own calls. 2. A 'Call taker' screens the calls and provides information to the presenter in advance of each call. 3. Operator to control all technical operation e.g. discs, tapes, levels etc., while producer/presenter concentrates on programme content. 4. Separate producer in control area to make programme decisions e.g. to initiate 'phone-out' calls. 5. Guest 'experts' in the studio with research support available.

Ops. Room | **Studio**

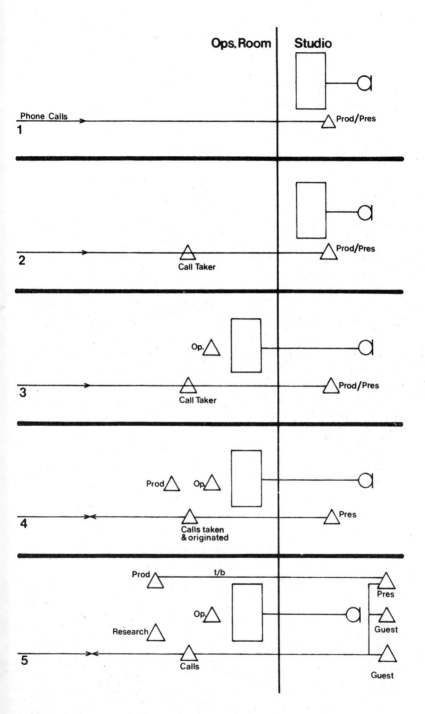

Phone Calls →

1 △ Prod/Pres

2 △ Call Taker △ Prod/Pres

3 Op.△ △ Call Taker △ Prod/Pres

4 Prod△ Op△ △ Calls taken & originated △ Pres

5 Prod△ t/b △ Pres
Op.△ △ Guest
Research△ △ Calls △ Guest

135

4. Personal counselling — problems discussed for the individual rather than the audience.

The open line

A general programme where topics of a non-specific nature are discussed with the host in the studio. There need be no theme or continuity between the calls but often a discussion will develop on a matter of topical interest.

Support staff

There are several variations on the basic format in which the presenter himself simply takes the calls as they come in. The first of these is that the lines are answered by a programme assistant or secretary who ensures that the caller is sensible and has something interesting to say. She will outline the procedure — "please make sure your radio set is not turned on in the background" (to avoid acoustic 'howl-round') — "you'll hear the programme on this phone-line and in a moment Mr. X (the presenter) will be talking to you". The call is held until the presenter wants to take it. Meanwhile the secretary has written down the details of the caller's name and the point he wishes to make and this is passed to the presenter. Since they are in separate rooms studio talkback will be used or, better, a third person involved to pass this information. This person is often the producer who will decide whether or not to reject the call on editorial or other grounds, to take calls in a particular order, or to advise the presenter on how individual calls should be handled. If the staffing of the programme is limited to two, the producer should take the calls since this is where the first editorial judgement is made.

The role of the presenter

The primary purpose of the programme is democratic — to let people have their say and express their views on matters which concern them. It is equivalent to the 'letter to the editor' column of a newspaper or the soap-box orator stand in the city square. The role of the presenter or host is not to take sides — although some radio stations may adopt a positive editorial policy — it is to stimulate conversation so that the matter is made interesting for the listener. He must be well versed in the law of libel and defamation and be ready to terminate a caller who becomes obscene, overtly political, commercial or illegal in accordance with the programme policy.

Very often such a programme succeeds or fails by the personality of the host presenter — quick thinking with a broad general knowledge, interested in people, well versed in current affairs, wise, witty, and by turn as the occasion demands genial, sharp, gentle, possibly even rude. All this combined with a good characteristic radio voice, the presenter is a paragon of broadcasting virtue!

Reference material

The presenter may be faced with a caller actually seeking practical advice and it is important for the producer to know in advance how far the programme should go in this direction, otherwise it may assume expectations for the listener which cannot be fulfilled. Broadcasters are seldom recruited for their practical expertise outside the medium and there is no reason why they should be expected spontaneously to answer specialist questions. However the availability in the studio of suitable reference material will enable the presenter to direct the caller to the appropriate source of advice or information. Reference sources may include telephone directories, names and addresses of local councillors, members of parliament or other elected representatives, government offices, public utilities, social services, welfare organisations and commercial PR departments. This information is usually given on the air; but it is a matter of discretion. In certain cases it may be preferable for the presenter to hand the caller back to the secretary who will provide the appropriate information individually. If there is a great deal of factual material needed then a fourth person will be required to do the immediate research.

Studio operation

At the basic level it is possible for the presenter himself to undertake the operation of the studio control desk. But as facilities are added, it becomes necessary to have a specialist panel operator, particularly where there is no automatic equipment to control the sound levels of the different sources. In this respect an automatic 'voice over' unit for the presenter is

137

particularly useful, so that when he speaks the level of the incoming call is decreased. It must however be used with care if he is to avoid sounding too dominating.

Additional telephone facilities

If the equipment allows, the presenter may be able to take two calls simultaneously so setting up a discussion between callers as well as with himself. The advice and co-operation of the telephone service is required prior to the initiation of any phone programme. This is because there may well have to be safeguards taken to prevent the broadcasting function from interfering with the smooth running of the telephone service. These may take the form of limitations imposed on the broadcaster in how he may use the public telephone in programmes, or possibly the installation of special equipment either at the telephone exchange or at the radio station.

Use of 'delay'

The listening interest of this type of programme depends to an extent on the random nature of the topics discussed and the consequent possibility of the unexpected or outrageous. There is a vicarious pleasure to be obtained from a programme not wholly designed in advance. But it is up to the presenter to ensure that there is reasonable control. However as an additional safeguard, it is possible to introduce a delay time between the programme and the transmission – indeed some radio stations and broadcasting authorities insist on it. Should any caller become libellous, abusive or obscene a delay device, of say ten seconds, enables that part of the programme to be deleted before it goes on the air. The programme, usually a short term recording off magnetic tape, is faded out and is replaced by the 'live' presenter's voice. With a good operator, this substitution can be made without it being apparent to the listener. Returning from the 'live' to the 'delayed' programme is more difficult and it is useful to have on hand news, music or other breaks to allow the presenter time to return to another call. If the caller is occasionally using words which the producer regards as offensive these can be 'bleeped out' by replacing them with a tone source as they reach the air. Again, good operation is essential. Overall however, a radio station gets the calls it

138

deserves and given an adequate but not oppressive screening process, the calls will in general reflect the level of responsibility at which the programme itself is conducted.

The specific subject

The subject of the programme is selected in advance so that the appropriate guest expert, or panel of experts, can be invited to take part. It may be that the subject lends itself to the giving of factual advice to individual questions, for example child care, motoring, medical problems, gardening, cooking, citizens' rights. Or the programme may be used as an opportunity to develop a public discussion of a more philosophical nature, for instance the state of the economy, political attitudes, education or religious matters.

'Early lines'

In order to obtain questions of the right type and quality, the phone lines to the programme may be opened some time before the start of the transmission — say half an hour. The calls are taken by a secretary or programme assistant who notes the necessary details and passes the information to the producer who can then select the calls he wants for the programme. For the broadcast these are originated by the studio on a phone-back basis.

The combination of 'early' lines and 'phone-back' gives the programme the following advantages:

1. The calls used are not random but are selected to develop the chosen theme at a level appropriate to the answering panel and the aim of the programme.
2. The order in which the calls are broadcast is under the control of the producer and so can represent a logical progression of the subject.
3. The studio expert, or panel, has advance warning of the questions and can prepare more substantial replies.
4. The phone-back principle helps to establish the credentials of the caller and serves as a deterrent to irresponsible calls. The programme itself may therefore be broadcast 'live' without the use of any delay device.
5. At the beginning of the programme there is no waiting for

the first calls to come in, it can start with a call of strong general interest already established.

Consumer affairs

The consumer phone-in is related to the 'specific subject' but its range of content is so wide that any single panel or expert is unlikely to provide detailed advice in response to every enquiry. As the range of programme content increases, the type of advice given tends to become more general, dealing with matters of principle rather than the action to be taken in a specific case. For example, a caller complains that an electrical appliance bought recently has given persistent trouble — what should they do about it? An expert on consumer legislation in the studio will be able to help distinguish between the manufacturer's and the retailer's responsibility, or whether the matter should be taken up with a particular complaints council, electricity authority or local government department. To provide a detailed answer specific to this case requires more information. What were the exact conditions of sale? Is there a guarantee period? Is there a servicing contract? Is the appliance being used correctly?

The need to be fair

Consumer affairs programmes rightly tend to be on the side of the complainant, but it should never be forgotten that a large number of complaints disintegrate under scrutiny and it is possible that such fault as there is lies with the user. Championing 'the little man' is all very well, but the community radio station has a responsibility to shopkeepers and manufacturers too. Once involved in a specific case the programme must be fair, and be seen to be fair. Two further variations on the

---

The use of delay in a phone-in. 1. The presenter P is fed directly to the transmitter. 2. To introduce a delay the presenter is recorded and held on a short term — 10 sec — tape loop. The programme output is maintained for this duration by an identification cartridge. 3. As the cartridge ends, the programme continues using the output of the tape delay. The transmission is now 10 seconds behind 'reality'. 4. If a caller says something which has to be cut, the delayed tape output is replaced by the presenter 'live'. 5. To reinstate the delay the procedure is as 2 but using a different cartridge. 6. The programme continues through the delay device. 7. The presenter brings the programme to an end allowing the delay device to finish the transmission. 8. Normal 'live' presentation.

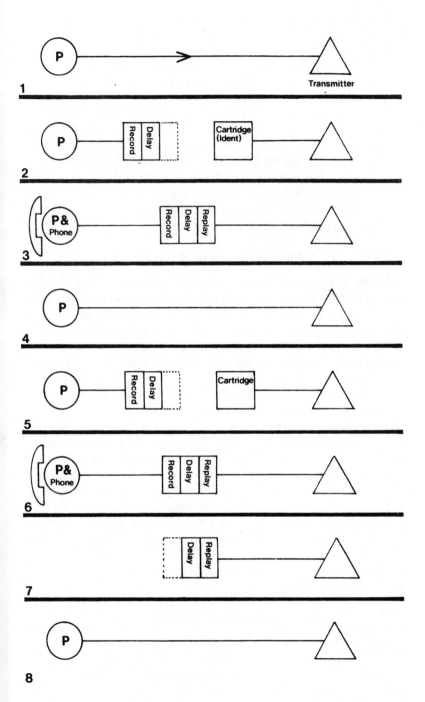

1   Transmitter

2

3

4

5

6

7

8

141

phone-in help to provide this balance:

1. *The phone-out.* A useful facility while taking a call is to be able to originate a second call and have them both on the air simultaneously. In response to a particular enquiry, the studio rings the appropriate head of sales, PR department, or council official to obtain a detailed answer, or at least an undertaking that the matter will be looked into.
2. *The running story.* The responsibility to be fair often needs more information than the original caller can give or than is immediately available and an enquiry may need further investigation outside the programme. While the problem can be posed and discussed initially, it may be that the subject is one which has to be followed up later.

Linking programmes together

Unlike the 'specific subject' programme which is an individual 'one-off', the broad consumer affairs programme may run in series – weekly, daily or even morning and afternoon. A complex enquiry may run over several programmes and while it can be expensive of the station's resources, it can also be excellent for retaining and increasing the audience. For the long term benefit of the community, and the radio station, the broadcaster must assure himself that such an investigation is performing a genuine public service

As with all phone-in programmes consideration must be given to recording the broadcast output in its entirety as a check on what was said – indeed this may be a statutory requirement imposed on the broadcaster. People connected with a firm which was mentioned but who heard of the broadcast at second hand may have been given an exaggerated account of what transpired. An ROT (recording off transmission) enables the station to provide a transcript of the programme and is a wise precaution against allegations of unfair treatment or threat of legal proceedings – always assuming of course that the station has been fair and responsible!

Personal counselling

With all phone-in programmes, the studio presenter is talking to the individual caller but has constantly to bear in mind the needs of the general listener. The material discussed has to be of interest to the very much wider audience who might never

142

phone the station but who will identify with the points raised by those who do. This is the nature of broadcasting. However once the broadcaster declares that he will tackle personal problems, sometimes at a deeply psychological and emotionally disturbing level, he cannot afford to be other than totally concerned for the welfare of the individual caller. For the duration, his responsibilities to the one exceed those to the many. Certainly, the presenter cannot terminate a conversation simply because it has ceased to be interesting or because it has become too difficult. Once a radio service says 'bring your problems here', it must be prepared to supply the answers.

This raises important questions for the broadcaster. Is he exploiting individual problems for public entertainment? Is the radio station simply providing the opportunities for the aural equivalent of the voyeur? Or is there sufficient justification in the assumption that without even considering the general audience, at least some people will identify with any given problem and so be helped by the discussion intended for the individual? It depends of course on how the programme is handled, the level of advice offered, and whether there is a genuine attempt at 'caring'.

To what extent will the programme provide help outside its own air time? The broadcaster cannot say 'only bring your depressive states to me between the transmission times of 9 to 11 at night'. Having offered help, what happens if the station gets a call of desperation during a record request show? The radio station has become more than simply a means of putting out programmes, it has developed into a community focus to which people turn in times of personal trouble. The station must not undertake such a role lightly, and it must have sufficient contacts with the various community services so that it can call on specialist help to take over a problem which it cannot deal with itself.

How can he ensure the giving of responsible advice? Of all the types of programme which a station puts out, this is the one where real damage may be done if the broadcaster gets it wrong. Discussing problems of loneliness, marriage, and sex, or the despair of a would-be suicide, has to be taken seriously. It is important to get the caller to talk and to enlist his support for the advice given.

The presenter as listener

As with all phone-in programmes the presenter in the studio cannot see the caller. He is denied all the usual non-verbal indicators of communication — facial expression, gesture, etc. This becomes particularly important in a counselling programme when the caller's reaction to the advice given is crucial. The person offering the advice must therefore be a perceptive listener — a pause, a slight hesitation in what the caller is saying may be enough to indicate whether he is describing a symptom or a cause, or whether he has yet got to the real problem at all. For this reason many such programmes will have two people in the studio — the presenter, who will take the call initially and discuss the nature of the problem — and the specialist counsellor who has been listening carefully and who takes over the discussion at whatever stage he feels necessary. Such a specialist may be an expert on marriage guidance, a psychiatrist, a minister of religion, or doctor.

Non-broadcasting effort

It is important that the programme also has off-air support — someone to talk further with the caller or to give names, addresses or phone numbers which are required to be kept confidential. The giving of a phone number over the air is always a signal for some people to call it, so blocking it as an effective source for the one person the programme is trying to help. Again, the broadcaster needs to be able to pass the problem back into the community for the appropriate follow-up.

The time of day for a broadcast of this type seems to be especially critical. It is particularly adult in its approach and is probably best at a time when it may be reasonably assumed that few children will be listening. This indicates a late evening slot — but not so late as to prevent the availability of unsuspected practical help arising from the audience.

Anonymity

Often a programme of this type allows the caller to remain unidentified. His name is not given over the air, the studio counsellor referring to him by his Christian name only or by an agreed pseudonym. This convention preserves what most callers need – privacy. It is perhaps surprising that people will call a radio station for advice, rather than ask their family, friends or specialist, simply because they do not have to meet anyone. It can be done from a position of security, perhaps in familiar surroundings where they do not feel threatened.

People with a real problem seldom ring the station in order to parade it publicly – such exhibitionists should be weeded out in the off-air screening and helped in some other way. The genuine seeker of help calls the station because he already knows it as a friend and as a source of unbiased personal and private advice. He knows he need not act on that advice unless he agrees with it. This is a function unique to radio broadcasting. It is perhaps a sad comment when a caller says "I've rung you because I can't talk to anyone about this", but it is in a sense a great compliment to the radio station to be regarded in this way. As such it must be accepted with responsibility and humility.

Phone-in checklist

The following list gives a quick 'run-down' of what is needed for a phone-in programme:

1. Discuss the programme with the telephone service and resolve any problems caused by the additional traffic which the programme could generate.
2. Decide the aim and type of the programme.
3. Decide the level of support staff required in the studio. This may involve a screening process, phone-back, immediate research, operational control and phone-out.
4. Engage guest speakers.
5. Assemble reference material.
6. Decide if 'delay' is to be used.
7. Arrange for 'Recording Off Transmission'.
8. Establish appropriate 'follow-up' links with community agencies.

12

THE VOX POP

'VOX POPULI' is the voice of the people, or 'man in the street' interview. The use of the opinions of 'ordinary' members of the public adds a useful dimension to the coverage of a topic which might otherwise be limited to a straight bulletin report or a studio discussion among officials or experts. The principle is for the broadcaster using a portable tape recorder to put one, possibly two specific questions on a matter of public interest to people selected by chance; and to edit together their replies to form a distillation of the overall response. While the aim is to present a sample of public opinion, the broadcaster must never claim it to be statistically valid, or even properly representative. It can never be anything more than – "the opinions of some of the people we spoke to this afternoon". This is because gathering material out on the streets for an afternoon magazine programme will almost certainly over-represent shoppers, tourists and the unemployed; and be low on business-men, motorists, night shift workers and farmers! Since the interviewing is done at a specific time and generally at a single site, the sample is not really even random – it is merely unstructured and no-one can tell what the views obtained actually represent. So no great claim can be made for the simple 'vox pop' on the basis of its being truly 'the voice of the people'.

It is easier to select a specific grouping appropriate to a particular topic – for example early risers, commuters, children or lorry drivers. If the question is to do with an increase in petrol prices, one will find motorists, together with some fairly predictable comment, on any garage forecourt. Similarly, a question on medical care might be addressed to people coming out of the city hospital. Incidentally, many apparently public places are in fact private property and the broadcaster must remember that he has no prescriptive right to work there without permission.

As the question to which reaction is required becomes more specific, the group among which the interviews are carried out may be said to be more representative. Views on a particular industrial dispute can be canvassed among the pickets at the factory gate, opinions on a new show sought among the first night audience. Nevertheless it is important in the presentation of 'vox pop' material that the listener is told where and when it was gathered. There must be no weighting of the interview sample of which the listener is unaware. Thus the introductory sentence — "We asked the strikers themselves what they thought" may mislead by being more comprehensive than the actual truth; A more accurate statement would be — "We asked some of the strikers assembled at the factory gate this morning what they thought". It is longer, but brevity is no virtue at the cost of accuracy.

Phrasing the question

Having decided to include a 'vox pop' in his programme the producer, or the reporter working to him, must decide carefully the exact form of words to be used. The question is going to be addressed to someone with little preparation or 'warm-up' and so must be relatively simple and unambiguous. Since the object is to obtain opinions rather than a succession of 'yes/no' answers, the question form must be carefully constructed. Once decided, the same question is put each time otherwise the answers cannot sensibly be edited together. A useful question form in this context is — "What do you think of . . .". This will elicit an opinion which can if necessary be followed with the interviewer asking 'why' — this supplementary to disappear in the editing.

An example

What do you think of the proposal to raise the school leaving age?

It sounds all right but who's going to pay for it?

I think it's a good idea, it'll keep the youngsters out of mischief.

It'll not do *me* any good, will it?

Bad in the short term, good in the long.

(Why?)

(Well) it'll cause an enormous upheaval over teachers' jobs and classrooms and things like that, but it's bound to raise standards overall eventually.

I've not heard anything about it.

The cost! — and that means higher taxes all round.

I don't think it'll make much difference.

(Why?)

Because for those children who want to leave and get a job it'll be a waste and the brighter ones would have stayed on anyway.

I think it's a load of rubbish, there's too much education and not enough work.

It is important that the question is phrased so that it contains the point to which reaction is required. In this example reference is made to the proposal to raise the school leaving age to which people can respond even if they had not heard about it. This is so much better than asking — "What do you think of the Government's new education policy?"

In addition to testing opinion, the 'vox pop' can be used to canvass actual suggestions or collect facts, but where the initial response is likely to be short, a follow-up is essential. This question can be subsequently edited out. For example — Who is your favourite TV personality? The answer is followed by asking, — Why? Another example — How often do you go to the cinema? — and then, — Is this less often than you used to go? — or, — Why would you say this is?

It is undoubtedly true that the more complex and varied the questioning, the more difficult will be the subsequent editing. The 'vox pop' producer must remember that he is not conducting an opinion poll or assembling data, he is making interesting radio which has to make sense in its limited context. The second example here may be useful in allowing the listener to compare his frequency of cinema-going with that of other people. But the producer must ask himself whether his intention would be equally well met, and more simply obtained, by the question — "What do you think of the cinema these days?"

A characteristic of the 'vox pop' is that in the final result, the interviewer's voice does not appear. The replies must be such that they can be joined together without further explanation to the listener and hence the technique is distinguished from simply a succession of interviews. The conversations should not be so complex that the interviewee's contribution cannot stand on its own.

Choosing the site

If the questioning is to be carried out amongst a specific group, this may itself dictate the place – on the docks, children leaving school, at the airport, etc. If the material is to be gathered generally, the site or sites chosen will be limited by technical factors, so as to permit easy editing at a later stage. These are to do with a reasonably low but essentially constant background noise level.

The listener expects to hear some background actuality and it would be undesirable to exclude it altogether. However, in essence, the broadcast is to consist of snatches of conversation in the form of remarks made off-the-cuff in a public place, and under these conditions immediate intelligibility is more difficult to obtain than in the studio. A side street will be quieter than a main road but a constant traffic background is preferable to intermittent noise. For this reason the interviewing site should not be near a bus stop, traffic lights or other road junction – the editing process becomes intrusively obvious if buses are made to disappear into thin air and lorries arrive from nowhere. For a similar reason, the site should be free from any sound which has a pattern of its own, such as music, public address announcements, or a chiming clock. Editing the speech so that it makes sense will be difficult enough without having to consider the effect of chopping up the background. A traffic-free pedestrian precinct or shopping arcade is often suitable, but a producer should avoid always returning to the same place – one of the attractions of the 'vox pop', in the general form as well as in the individual item, is its variety.

The tape machine

Since the recording is to be heavily edited, a reel to reel machine is preferable although the cassette type is generally smaller, lighter and easier to carry. Recordings made on a cassette obviously need to be copied on the the open reel format to permit the subsequent editing.

The machine and its microphone are tested before leaving

base and on site, a further check made to ensure an adequate speech level against the background noise. Some ten seconds of general atmosphere should be recorded to provide spare background for the fades in and out. From here on, the recording level control should not be altered otherwise the level of the background noise will vary. In order to maintain the same background level it is preferable to use a machine with a manual rather than an automatic recording control. Different speech volumes are compensated for by the positioning of the microphone relative to the speaker, and of course the normal working distance will be considerably less than in a studio.

To simplify the editing, only the actual replies need be recorded; any preamble and the questions themselves result in wasted tape. A machine with a rapid and unobtrusive means of starting is a considerable asset — some types may be kept running but held on a 'pause' key until required, others may be started by a switch on the microphone.

Putting the question

It is normal for the novice reporter to feel shy about his first 'vox pop' but cases of assault on broadcasters are relatively rare. It may be helpful to remember that the passer-by is being asked to enter the situation without the benefit of any prior knowledge and is probably far more nervous. However, the initiative lies with the interviewer and he needs to adopt a positive technique. He should explain quickly who he is and what he wants, put the question, and record the reaction.

First, the reporter should be obvious rather than secretive. He stands in the middle of the pavement with his machine over his shoulder holding the microphone for all to see. It is most useful for the microphone to carry an identifying badge so that the approaching pedestrian can already guess at the situation, and if necessary take avoiding action. No-one should be, or for that matter can be, interviewed against their will. Any potential but unwilling contributors should not be pursued or in any way harrassed. In this sense, although the interviewer may receive the occasional rebuff, the contributors are only those who agree to stop and talk.

Seeing a prospective interviewee, the reporter approaches and says pleasantly — "Good morning, I'm from Radio XYZ". At this the passer-by will either continue, protesting at how busy

he is, or he will stop, being reassured by the truth of the statement since it confirms what the station identification badge
states. He may possibly also be interested at the prospect of
being on the radio. The reporter continues – "Can I ask you
what you think of the proposal to keep all traffic out of the
city centre" – at which point he moves the microphone to
within a foot or so of the contributor and switches on the
recorder. In the chapter on 'Interviewing', questions which
began with 'Can I ask you' or 'Could you tell me', were generally
disallowed on the grounds that they were superfluous; permission
for the interview having already been granted, and that being
unnecessary they were a waste of the listener's time. In the
context of the 'vox pop' such a preamble is acceptable since it
allows someone the courtesy of non co-operation, and in any
case the phrase will disappear in the editing.

The normal reaction of the 'man in the street' will vary from
total ignorance of the subject, through embarrassed laughter
and a collecting of thoughts, to a detailed or impassioned reply
from someone who knows the subject well. All of this can be
useful but there is likely to be a wastage rate of at least 50%.
If about ten replies are to be used, then twenty should be
recorded. If the final tape is to be around two minutes – and a
'vox pop' would seldom if ever exceed this – a total of four or
five minutes of response should be recorded. A visual check on
the take-up spool will indicate when sufficient material has
been gathered, by which time the interviewer will hope to have
a diversity of views and some well made argument.

Occasionally a group of people will gather round and begin
a discussion. This may be useful although inevitably, some of
it will be 'off mic'. A developing conversation will be more
difficult to edit and the 'one at a time' approach is to be preferred; although particularly with children more revealing
comment is often obtained if they are within a group talking
among themselves.

Whatever the individual response, the interviewer remains
friendly and courteous. He will obviously want to give a good
impression of the radio station he represents and will avoid
becoming sidetracked into a discussion of the subject itself,
station policy or last night's programme. He thanks each contributor for taking the trouble to stop and talk, remembering
that it is they who have done him a favour.

The editing

Spontaneity, variety, insight and humour — these are the hall-marks of the good 'vox pop'. Listening to the material back at the base studio, the first step is to remove anything which is not totally intelligible. This must be done immediately, before the editor's ear becomes attuned to the sound. It is a great temptation to include a prize remark however imperfectly recorded on the basis of its being intelligible after a few playings under studio conditions! The rejection of material which is not of first class technical quality is the first prerequisite to preventing the finished tape from becoming a confusing jumble. If two tape machines are available, editing by dubbing rather than cutting will often be the quicker method of removing unwanted

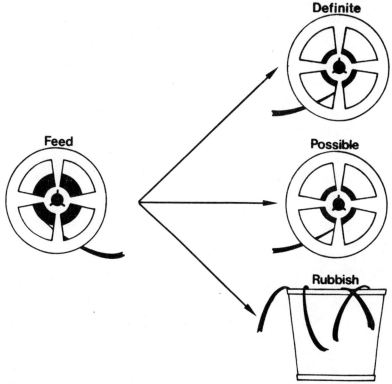

Vox pop editing. The feed spool of the original recordings is sorted into three categories. Definite material of positive and interesting replies — 'possible' material of less good but usable replies — and the distorted or incomprehensible which is discarded. 'Possible' material is transferred to the 'definite' reel to adjust the balance of the final tape.

material and rearranging the remainder into the desired order.

The first piece of the finished vox-pop needs to be a straight-forward, clearly understood response to the question that will appear in the introductory cue material. The subsequent comments are placed to contrast with each other, either in the opinions expressed or their style. Men's voices will alternate with those of women, the young with the old, the local accent with the 'foreign', the 'pros' with the 'antis'. The interviewer's voice is not used, except that occasionally it may be useful to be reminded of the question half way through. What must be avoided of course is its continual repetition. Sometimes the answers themselves are similar in which case sufficient should be used to indicate a concensus but not to become boringly repetitious. A problem can arise over the well argued but lengthy reply which would be likely to distort the shape of the vox pop if used in its entirety. A permissible technique here is to cut it into two or three sections placing them separately within the final tape.

The editor needs a good comment to end on. Its nature will depend on the subject but it might be a view forcefully expressed, a humorous remark, or the kind of plain truth which often comes from a child. Good closing comments are not difficult to identify and the interviewer, when he has finished collecting his material, generally knows how his vox pop will end. The spare background noise is used as required to separate replies, with a few seconds at the beginning and at the end as a 'fade up' and 'fade down' under speech — so much better than 'banging it in' and 'chopping it off' on the air.

It should go without saying that the finished vox pop will broadly reflect the public response found by the interviewer. It is possible of course for the editing to remove all views of a particular kind so giving the impression that they do not exist. It may be that a producer would set out with the deliberate intention of demonstrating the overwhelming popularity of certain public attitudes — presumably those which accord with his own. Such manipulation, apart from betraying the trust which hopefully the listener has in him, is ultimately self-defeating. The listener does his own vox pops every day of his life — he will know whether or not the radio station is biased in its reflection of public opinion. Probably more than the broadcaster, the listener knows his own reality when he hears it.

Used properly the vox pop represents another colour in the

broadcaster's palette. It provides contrast with studio material and in reflecting accurately what people are saying, it helps the listener to identify with the station and so enhance its credibility.

13

RECORD PROGRAMMES

THE filling of programme hours with records is a universal characteristic of radio stations around the world. This is hardly surprising in view of the advantages discs have for the broadcaster. They represent a readily available and inexhaustible supply of high quality material of enormous variety that is relatively inexpensive, easy to use and enjoyable to listen to. Before looking in detail at some of the possible formats and what makes for a successful programme, there are three important preliminaries to consider.

Firstly, the matter of music copyright. Virtually every record label carries the words, "all rights of the manufacturer and of the owner of the recorded work reserved. Unauthorised public performance, broadcasting and copying of this record prohibited". This is to protect the separate rights of the composer, publisher, performers and the record company, who together enabled the disc to be made. The statement is generally backed by law — in Britain the Copyright Act of 1956. It would obviously be unfair on the original artists if there were no legal sanctions against the copying of their work by someone else and its subsequent remarketing on another label. Similarly, broadcasters who in part earn their living through the effort of recording artists and others, must ensure that the proper payments are made regarding their use of records. As part of a 'blanket' agreement giving 'authorised broadcasting use', most radio stations are required to make some form of return to the societies representing the music publishers and record manufacturers, indicating what has been played. It is the producer's responsibility to see that any such system is carefully followed.

Secondly, it must be said that in using records, broadcasters are apt to forget their obligation to 'live' music. Whatever the

157

constraints on the individual station, some attempt should be made to encourage performers by providing opportunities for them to broadcast. Many recording artists owe their early encouragement to radio, and broadcasting must regard itself as part of the process which enables the first class to emerge. Having reached the top, performers should be given the fresh challenge which radio brings.

Thirdly, top flight material deserves the best handling. It is easy to regard a record simply as a piece of plastic but on the air someone's reputation may be at stake. Basic operational technique must be faultless – levels, accurate talk-overs, fades etc. Most important is that music should be handled with respect to its phrasing. These points are enlarged upon in Chapter 2, Operational Techniques.

The programme areas now discussed in detail are: record requests, guest programmes, and the DJ show.

Record requests

In presenting a request show it is all too easy to forget that the purpose is still to do with *broad*casting. There is a temptation to think only of those who have written in, rather than of the audience at large. Until the basic approach is clarified, it is impossible to answer the practical questions which face the producer. For example, to what extent should the same record be played in successive programmes because someone has asked for it again? Is there sufficient justification in reading out a lengthy list of names simply because this is what appears on the request card? While the basis of the programme is clearly dependent on the initiative of the individual listener who requests a record, the broadcaster has a responsibility to all listeners, not least the great majority who do not write in. The programme aims may be summarised:

1. To entertain the general audience.
2. To give especial pleasure to those who have taken the trouble to send a request.
3. To foster goodwill by public involvement.

Format

Programmes can be given additional objectives, and a good

deal of individual character by the presenter who states his own guidelines. He may deal only in requests related to birthdays, weddings or anniversaries, or he may insist that each request is accompanied by a personal anecdote, joke or reminiscence to do with the music requested. References to other people's nostalgia can certainly add to the general entertainment value of the programme. The presenter should be consistent about this and it is important that style does not take over from content. The declared intention of the programme is to play records and it is therefore music rather than speech which remains the central ingredient.

A further variation is to make a point of including dedications as well as requests, i.e. cards not related to a specific piece of music but which can be associated with any record already included in the programme. By encouraging 'open' cards of this type, the programme can carry more names and, as can be pointed out, listeners have a greater chance of hearing themselves mentioned.

Having decided the character and format of the programme there are essential elements in its preparation.

Choosing the music

With music items of 2½ minutes each, there will be some eight or nine requests in each half hour of air time. This allows for about a minute of introduction, signature tunes etc. Given the volume of letters and cards received, it soon becomes clear to what extent the actual requests can be met. The proportion which can be dealt with may be quite small and assuming that their number exceeds the capacity to play them, a selection process is necessary.

The criteria of selection will include the presenter's desire to offer an attractive programme overall, with a variety of music consistent with the programme policy. It may be limited to the current 'Top 40' records, to pop music, or it may specifically deal with one area, for example religious music. On the other hand, the choice may be much wider to include popular standards, light classical music or excerpts from symphonic works. The potential requester should know what kind of music a particular programme offers.

Another principle of selection is to choose requests that are likely to suit the presenter's remarks. Those which will make for an interesting introduction, an important or unusual event, an amusing remark or a particularly topical reference. It is frequently possible to combine requests using comments from a number of cards in order to introduce a single piece of music. The danger here is to become involved in several lists of names which may delight those who like hearing themselves referred to on the air, but which can become boring to the general listener. It is however a useful method of including a name check while avoiding a particular choice of music either because to do so would be repetitious, or because it is out of keeping with the programme – or of course because the station does not have the record.

Item order

After selecting the music, a decision has to be made about its sequence. This should not be a matter of chance since experience has shown that there are positive guidelines in building an attractive programme. 'Start bright, finish strong' is an old music hall maxim and it applies here. A tuneful or rhythmic familiar up-tempo 'opener' with only a brief speech introduction will provide a good start with which the general listener can identify. A slower piece should follow and thereafter the music can be contrasted in a number of ways: vocal/non vocal, female vocal/male vocal, group vocal/solo vocal, instrumental/orchestral, slow/fast, familiar/unfamiliar, and so on.

Having chosen the discs, many presenters will lay them out physically on a table to see the programme overall and so determine the order which provides the most satisfactory arrangement. It is sensible to scatter the very popular items throughout the programme and to limit the material which may be entirely new. Careful placing is required with slow numbers which need to be followed by something brighter. The order in which music is played of course affects all music programmes whether or not they are based on the use of records.

Prefading to time

The last piece of music can be chosen to provide 'the big finish' and a suitable finale will often be a non-vocal item. This allows it to be faded-in under the presenter's introduction. It should have been timed to end one minute before the close of the programme, so leaving room for the final announcements and signature tune. This is called 'prefading to time' (not to be confused with 'prefade' — audition or pre-hear) and is the most common device for ensuring that record programmes run to time. The closing signature tune will almost certainly be prefaded to time. In a similar way items within a programme, particularly a long one, can be subject to this technique to provide fixed points and to prevent the overall timing drifting.

Preparation of letters and cards

Requests as received are not always legible and so cannot be used in the studio without some form of preparation. This, the presenter should do himself. Some will type out the basic information to ensure clarity, others prefer to work directly from the original cards and letters. It is important that names and addresses are legible so that the presenter is not constantly stumbling, or sounding as though the problem of deciphering his correspondent's handwriting is virtually insurmountable. In reality, this may often be the case, but a little preparation will avoid needlessly offending the people who have taken the trouble to write and on whom the programme depends. In this respect, particular care has to be taken over personal information such as names and ages, and it goes without saying that such things should be correctly pronounced. This also applies to streets, districts, hospitals, wards, schools and churches where an incorrect pronunciation — even though it be caused by illegible handwriting — immediately labels the presenter as a 'foreigner' and so hinders listener identification. Such mispronunciations should be strenuously avoided, particularly for the community broadcasting station, and prior reference to telephone directories, maps, and other local guides is essential. This is not an immense task for with conscious effort one quickly becomes acquainted with the great majority of the 'non obvious' names.

Reading through the cards beforehand enables the presenter to spot dates, such as anniversaries, which will be passed by the time of the broadcast. This can then be the subject of a suitable apology coupled with a message of goodwill, or alternatively the request can be omitted. What should not happen is for the presenter to realise on-air during his introduction that the event which the writer in anticipating has already happened. Not only does this sound non-professional, but it gives the impression that the presenter does not really know what he is talking about, and worse, he does not care. Anything which hinders the rapport between listener and presenter will detract from the programme.

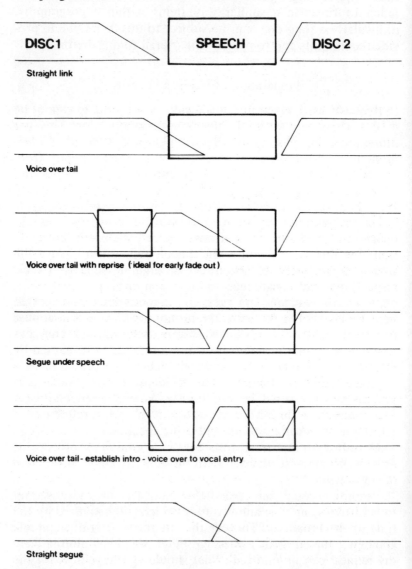

Six ways of going from one record to the next, with or without a speech link. The use of several different methods helps to maintain programme variety and interest.

162

In order to accommodate more requests, cards can be group-ed together, sharing a single piece of music. The music need not necessarily be precisely what was asked for, providing that the presenter makes it quite clear what he is doing. The piece should however be of a similar type to that requested for ex-ample by the same artist.

Such preparation of the spoken material makes an important contribution to the presenter's familiarity with the programme content. While it may be his intention to appear to be speaking informally 'off the cuff', matters such as pronunciation, accu-racy of information, relevance of content, and timing need to be worked on in advance. The art is to do all this and still retain a fresh, 'live', ad-lib sound. However, the experienced presenter knows that the best spontaneity contains an element of plan-ning.

Programme technique

On the air, each presenter must find his own style and be consistent to it. No one person or programme will appeal to everyone but a loyal following can be built up through main-taining a similarity of approach. A number of general tech-niques are worth mentioning.

Never talk over vocals. Given adequate preparation, it is often very pleasing to make an accurate 'talk over' of the non-vocal introduction to a record. But talking over the singer himself can be muddling, and to the listener may sound little different from interference from another station.

Avoid implied *criticism of the listener's choice* of music. The records may not coincide with your taste but they represent the broadcaster's intention to encourage public involvement. If a request is unsuitable, it is best left out.

Do not play less than one minute of anyone's request, the sender will feel cheated. If the programme timing goes adrift it is generally better to drop a whole item than to compress. If the last item, or the closing signature tune, or both are 'pre-faded to time' the programme duration will look after itself.

If by grouping requests together, there are several names and addresses for a single record, prevent the information from *sounding like a roll call.* Break up the list and intersperse the names with other remarks.

Develop the habit of talking *alternately* to the *general listener* and to the *individual listener* who asked for the record. For example:

"Now here's a card from someone about to celebrate 50 years of married bliss – that's what it says here and she's Mrs. Jane Smith, of Highfield Road, Mapperley. Congratulations Mrs. Smith on your half century, you'd like to dedicate this record with all your love to your husband John. What an example to the rest of us, – congratulations to you too, John. The record is from one of the most successful shows of the thirties . . . . . . "

Avoid remarks which combined with the address, may pose any kind of *risk to the individual.*
" . . . I'm asked not to play it before six o'clock because there's nobody at home 'till then . . ."
" . . . she says she's living on her own but doesn't hear too well . . ."
" . . . please play the record before Sunday the 18th because we'll all be away on holiday after that . . ."
" . . . he says his favourite hobby is collecting rare silver . . ."

To reduce such risks, some presenters omit the house detail, referring only to the street and town. However house numbers can generally be discovered by reference to voters' lists and other directories. Broadcasters must always be aware of the possible illegal use of personal information.

It is often a wise precaution to keep the cards and letters used in a programme for at least a week afterwards in order to deal with music enquiries or other follow-up which may be required.

Guest programmes

Here, the regular presenter invites a well known personality, not necessarily a musician, to the programme and plays his choice of music. The attraction of hearing artists and performers talk about music is obvious but it is also of considerable interest to have the lives of others, such as politicians, sportsmen and businessmen, illuminated in this way.

The production decisions generally centre on the ratio of music to speech. Is the programme really an excuse for playing a wide range of records or primarily a discussion with the guest but with musical punctuation? Certainly it is easy to irritate the listener by breaking off an interesting conversation for no better purpose than to have a musical interlude, but equally a tiny fragment only of a Beethoven symphony can be very unsatisfying. The presenter, through his combination of interview style and links into and out of the music, must ensure an overall cohesiveness to prevent the programme sounding 'bitty'. While it may be necessary to arrive at a roughly half and half formula, the answer could be to concentrate on the music where the guest has a real musical interest but to increase the speech content where this is not the case, using fewer but perhaps slightly longer music inserts.

Once again the resolution of such questions lies in the early identification of a programme aim appropriate to the target audience.

DJ programmes

The radio disc jockey defies detailed categorisation. His task is to be unique, to find and establish a distinctive formula different from all other DJs. The music content may vary little between two competing record programmes and in order to create a preference the attraction must lie in the way it is presented. If he is to be successful therefore, the DJ's personality and programme style must not only make contact with the individual listener, but in themselves be the essential reason for the listener's attention. His style may be elegant or earthy, raucous or restrained, but for any one DJ it should be consistent and the operational technique first class.

The same rules of item selection and order apply as those identified for request programmes. The music should be sufficiently varied and balanced within its own terms of reference to maintain interest and form an attractive whole. Even a tightly formated programme, such as a 'top 40' show will yield in all sorts of ways to imaginative treatment. The personal approach to this type of broadcasting differs widely and can be looked at under three broad headings.

The low profile DJ

Here the music is paramount and the presenter has little to say. His job is to be unobtrusive. The purpose of the programme

165

may be to provide background listening and all that is required is the occasional station identification or time check. In the case of a classical music programme the speech/music ratio should obviously be low. The listener is easily irritated by a presenter who tries to take over the show from Beethoven and Bach. The low profile DJ has to be just as careful over what he says as his more voluble colleagues.

The specialist DJ

Experts in their own field of music can make excellent presenters. They spice their introduction with anecdotes about the artists and stories of happenings at recording sessions, as well as informed comment on performance comparisons and the music itself. Jazz, rock, opera and folk all lend themselves to this treatment. Often analytical in approach, the DJ's job is to bring alive the human interest inherent in all music. The listener should obviously enjoy the records played but half the value of the programme is derived from hearing authoritative, possibly provocative, comment from someone who knows the field well.

The personality DJ

This is the most common of all DJ types. He must do more than just play records with some spontaneous ad-libs in between. However popular the music, this simple form of presentation soon palls. The DJ must communicate his own personality, creating a sense of friendship with his audience. He must entertain. To do this well, programme after programme, requires two kinds of preparation.

The first is in deciding what to say and when. This means listening to at least some of the records beforehand to decide the appropriate places for a response to the words of a song, a jokey remark or other comment, where to place a listener's letter, quiz question or phone call. The chat between the records should be thought about in advance so that it does not sound pedestrian, becoming simply a repetitive patter. All broadcast talk needs some real substance containing interest and variety. This is not to rule out entirely the advantages of spontaneity and the 'fly by the seat of your pants' approach. The self-operating DJ, with or without a producer, is often capable of creating an entertaining programme, making it up as he goes along. Undoubtedly though, such a broadcaster is even better given some preparation time.

The programme may also contain identifications, weather and traffic information, commercials, time checks, trails for other programmes and news. The DJ should therefore never be at a loss as to what to do next. He must know in advance what he wants to say, and be constantly replenishing his stock of anecdotes. Where possible these should be drawn from his own observation of the daily scene. Certainly for the local radio DJ, the more he can develop a rapport with his own area, the more his listeners will identify with him. The preparation of the programme's speech content will also include the timing of accurate talkovers and any research.

When a DJ is criticised for talking too much, what is often meant is that he is not interesting enough, i.e. there are too many words for what he has to convey. It is possible to correct this by talking less, but similarly the criticism will disappear if the same amount of speech is used to carry less waffle and more substance.

The second kind of preparation for a DJ, and where appropriate his producer, is in actually making additional bits and pieces of programme material which will help to bring the show alive. Probably recorded on tape, using cartridges for accurate cueing, these may consist of snatches of records, sound effects, funny voices on echo, chords of music, half or double speed tape and so on. Disc jockeys may even create extra 'people', playing the roles themselves on the air, talking 'live' to their own recordings. Such characters and voices can develop their own personalities appearing in successive programmes to become very much part of the show. Only the amount of time which is set aside for preparation and the DJ's own imagination, set limits on what can be achieved in this way.

For the most part such inserts are very brief but they enliven a DJ's normal speech material adding an element of unpredictability and increasing the programme's entertainment value.

Whether the programme is complex or simple, the personality DJ should, above all, be fun to listen to. But while the show may give the impression of a spontaneous happening, sustained success is seldom a matter of chance. It is more likely to be found in a carefully devised formula and a good deal of preparation and hard work.

14

THE MAGAZINE PROGRAMME

OF all programme types, it is the regular magazine, or sequence, which can so easily become boring or trivial by simply degenerating into a ragbag of items loosely strung together. The major problem for the producer is how best to balance the need for consistency with that of variety. Clearly there has to be a recognisable structure to the programme – after all, this is probably why the listener switched on in the first place. An obvious policy of marketing, which applies to radio no less than to any other products, is to build a regular audience by creating positive listener expectations, and then to fulfil, or better still, exceed them. The most potent reason for tuning in to a particular programme is that the listener liked what he heard last time. This time, therefore, the programme must be of a similar mould, not too much must be changed. It is equally obvious however that the programme must be *new* in the sense that it must have fresh and updated content and contain the element of surprise. The programme becomes boring when its content is too predictable, and it fails as a magazine if its structure is obscure. Yet it is not enough simply to offer the advice – 'keep the format consistent but vary the content'. Certainly this is important but there must be consistencies too in the intellectual level and emotional appeal of the material. From edition to edition there must be the same overall sense of style.

Since we have so far borrowed a number of terms from the world of print, it might be useful to draw the analogy more closely.

The newspapers and magazines we buy are largely determined by how we reacted to the previous issue. To a large extent purchases are a matter of habit and although some are bought on impulse, or by accident, changes in readership occur relatively slowly. Having adopted our favourite periodical, we do not care to have it tampered with in an unconsidered way. We develop a personal interest in the typography, page layout, length of feature article or use of pictures. We know exactly where to find the sports page, crossword or favourite cartoon. We take a paper which appeals to us as individuals; there is an emotional link and we can feel distinctly annoyed should a new editor change the typeface, or start moving things around when, from the fact that we bought it, it was all right as it was. In other words the consistency of a perceived structure is important since it leads to a reassurance of being able to find your way around, of being able to use the medium fully. Add a familiar style of language, words that are neither too difficult nor too puerile, sentences which avoid both the pompous and the servile, captions which illuminate and not duplicate; and it is possible to create a trusting bond between the communicator and the reader, or in our case the listener. Different magazines will each decide their own style and market. It is possible for a single publisher, as it is for the manager of a radio station, to create an output with a total range aimed at the aggregate market of the individual products.

For the individual producer, his crucial decision is to set the emotional and intellectual 'width' of his programme and to recognise when he is in danger of straying outside it.

To maintain programme consistency then several factors must remain constant. A number of these are now mentioned.

Programme title

This is the obvious signpost indicating the station's output, it should both trigger memories of the previous edition and provide a clue to content for the uninitiated. Titles such as 'Farm', 'Today', 'Sports Weekly', and 'Woman's Hour' are obviously self-explanatory. 'Roundabout', 'Kaleidoscope', 'Miscellany', and 'Scrapbook' are less helpful except that they do indicate a programme containing a number of different but not necessarily related items. With a title like 'Contact', 'The Jack Richards Show', or 'Horizon', there is little information on content, and a subtitle is often used to describe the general subject area. The title should stem directly from the programme aims and the extent to which the target audience is limited to a specialist group.

Signature tune

This is an optional additional signpost designed to cause the listener to turn up the volume. It should also convey something of the style of the programme — lighthearted, urgent, serious, or in some way evocative of the content. Fifteen seconds of the right music can be a useful way of quickly establishing the mood. Producers however should avoid the musical cliche. While 'Nature Notebook' may require a pastoral introduction, the religious magazine will often make strenuous efforts not to use opening music that is too churchy. If the aim is to attract an audience which already identifies with institutionalised religion, some kind of church music may be fine. If on the other hand, the idea is to reach an audience which is wider than the church-going or sympathetic group, it may be better to avoid too strong a church connotation at the outset. After all, the religious magazine is by no means the same as the Christian magazine, or the church programme.

Transmission time

There have been magazines which have tried to build an audience on the basis of a shifting start time. While it can be an understandable scheduling necessity, for example in following regular coverage of a 'live' event such as boxing, it is almost impossible to achieve successfully. Regular programmes must be at regular times and regular items within programmes given the same predictable placing in each programme. This rule has to be applied even more rigorously as the specialisation of the programme increases.

For example a half hour farming magazine may contain a regular three minute item on local market prices. The listener who is committed to this item will tune in especially to hear it even though he may not bother with the rest of the programme. A magazine having a wider brief, designed to appeal to the more general audience, is more likely to be on in the background and it is therefore possible to announce changes in timing. Even so, the housewife listening to the mid-morning magazine wants her serial instalment, item on current affairs, or recipe spot at the same time as yesterday since it helps to orientate her day.

The presenter

Perhaps the most important single factor in creating a consistent style, the presenter regulates the tone of the programme by his approach to the listener. He or she can be outgoing and friendly, quietly companionable, informal or briskly businesslike, or knowledgeable and authoritative. It is a consistent combination of characteristics, perhaps with two presenters, which allows the listener to build a relationship with the programme based on 'liking' and 'trusting'. Networks and stations which frequently change their presenters, or programmes which 'rotate' their front men are simply not giving themselves a chance. Occasionally you hear the justification of such practice as the need 'to prevent people from becoming stale', or worse, 'to be fair to everyone working on the programme'. Most programme controllers would recommend a six month period as the minimum for a presenter on a weekly programme, and three months for a daily show. Less than this and he may hardly have registered at all.

In selecting a presenter for a specialist magazine, the producer may find himself with a choice of either a good broadcaster, or an expert in the subject. Obviously the ideal is to find both in the same person, or through training to turn one into the other — the easier course is often to enable the latter to become the former. If this is not possible, an alternative is to use both. Given a strict choice the man who knows his material is generally preferable. Credibility is a key factor in whether or not a specialist programme is listened to, and expert knowledge is the foundation, even though it may not be perfectly expressed. In other words, if we have a doctor for the medical programme and a gardener for the gardening programme, should there be children for the children's show, and a disabled person introducing a programme for the handicapped? In a magazine programme for the blind — a group for whom radio obviously has a special affinity — there may be a bit more paper shuffling 'off mic', and the Braille reading may not be as fluent as with a sighted reader, but the result is likely to have much more impact and be far more acceptable to the target audience.

Linking style

Having established the presenter and assuming he will write, or at least rewrite, much of his own script, the linking material will have its own consistent style. The way in which items are introduced, the amount and type of humour used, the number of time checks, and the level at which the whole programme is pitched will remain constant. The links of course refer to the various items, as discussed under the heading of 'Cue Material', but they also enable the presenter to give additional information, personalised comment or humour. The 'link-man' is much more than a reader of cue material — announcements between items should extend beyond the simple 'this is' and 'that was'. It is interesting to speculate on the function of mortar in the building of a house. Does it keep the bricks apart or hold them together? It does both of course, and so it is with the magazine presenter. Through his handling of the links he separates and delineates while at the same time creating a cohesive sense of style.

Information content

The more local a magazine becomes, the more specific and practical can be the information it gives. It may be carried either in the form of regular spots at known times or simply included in the links. If a programme sets out with the intention of becoming known for its information content, the spots must be totally consistent in timing, duration and style. Their 'signposting' should be unchanging using the same form of words, introductory signature tune, musical identification or sound effect. It will not be adequate to have information standing by with a view to using it as filler material according to the time available.

The types of useful information will naturally depend on the particular needs of the audience in the locality covered by the station. The list is wide ranging and typical examples for inclusion in the general magazine are:

News reports	Time checks
Weather	River conditions (for anglers)
Traffic information	Mobile library services
Sports results	Tide times
Tonight's TV	Changes to ferry times
Late night chemists	Sea state — coastal waters
Road works for	Shipping movements
motorists	Lighting up times

Pollen count	Racing information
Pavement works for	What's on — entertainment
the blind	Top Twenty chart
Rail delays	Club meetings
Local flying conditions	Fatstock prices for farmers
Shopping prices	Blood donor sessions
Financial market trends	Station identification

Programme construction

The overall shape of the programme will remain reasonably constant. The proportion of music to speech should stay roughly the same between editions, and if the content normally comprises items of from three to five minutes duration ending with a featurette of eight minutes, this structure should become the established pattern. This is not to say that a half-hour magazine could not spend fifteen minutes on a single item given sufficient notification by the presenter. But it is worth pointing out that by giving the whole, or most of a programme, over to one subject, it ceases to be a magazine and instead becomes a documentary or feature. There is an argument to be made in the case of a specialist programme for occasionally suspending the magazine format and running a one-off 'special' instead, in which case this should of course be aimed at the same audience as the magazine it replaces. Another permissible variation in structure is where every item has a similar 'flavour' — as in a 'Christmas edition', or where a farming magazine is done entirely at an agricultural show.

Such exceptions are only possible where a standard practice has become established for it is only by having 'norms' that one is able to introduce the variety of departing from them.

Programme variety

Each programme must create fresh interest and contain surprise. Firstly, the subject matter of the individual items should itself be relevant and new to the listener. Secondly, the treatment and order of the items need to highlight the differences between them and maintain a lively approach to the listener's ear. It is easy for a daily magazine, particularly the news magazine, to become nothing more than a succession of taped interviews. Each may be good enough in its own right, but heard in the context of other similar material, the total effect may be worthy but dull.

Programme ideas

Producing a good magazine programme is one thing, sustaining it day after day or week after week for years is quite another. How can a producer, with little if any staff assistance, set about the task of finding the items necessary to keep his programme going? Firstly, he is never off duty but is always wondering if anything he sees or hears will make an item. He records even the passing thought or brief impression, probably in a small notebook. It is surprising how the act of writing down even a flimsy idea can help it to crystallise into something more substantial. Secondly, through a diary and other sources he has advance information on anniversaries and other future events. Thirdly he cultivates a wide range of contacts. This means that he reads, or at least scans, as much as he can; newspapers, children's comics, trade journals, parish magazines, the small ads, poster hoardings — anything which experience has shown can be a source of ideas.

He gets out of the studio and walks through his territory — easier for a local radio man than for a national broadcaster! He is a good listener, both to the media and in personal conversation. He is aware of people's problems and concerns, and of what makes them laugh. He encourages his contributors to come up with ideas and if he has little money to pay them, at least he makes sure they get the credit for something good. He welcomes correspondence. It is hard work but the magazine producer soon develops a flair for knowing which of a number of slender leads is likely to develop into something for his programme.

Having decided to include an item on a particular subject, the producer has several options on the treatment he can employ. A little imagination will prevent his programme from sounding 'samey' and he should consider the extent to which he can increase the variety of his programme by the use of the following radio forms.

Voice piece

A single voice giving information as with a news bulletin,

175

situation report, or events diary. This form can also be used to provide eye-witness commentary, or tell a story of the 'I Was There' type of personal reminiscence.

Interview

The types of interview (see Chapter 3) include those which challenge reasons, discover facts, or explore emotions. This sub-heading also includes the vox pop or 'man in the street' opinion interview.

Discussion

Exploration of a topic in this form within a magazine programme will generally be of the bi-directional type consisting of two people with opposing views. To attempt in a relatively brief item to present a range of views, as in the 'multi-facet' discussion, will often lead to a superficial and unsatisfactory result. If a subject is big enough or important enough to be dealt with in this way, the producer should ask himself whether it does not warrant a special programme.

Music

An important ingredient in achieving variety, it can be used in a number of ways:

1. A musical item, concert performance or record featured in its own right.
2. A new item reviewed.
3. Music which follows naturally upon the previous item. For example an interview with a pianist about to make his concert debut followed by an illustration of his work.
4. Where there is a complete change of subject, music can act as a link — a brief music 'bridge' may be permissible. This is particularly useful to give 'thinking time' after a thoughtful or emotional item where a change of mood is required.

Music should be used as a positive asset to the programme and not merely to fill time between items. It can be used to supply humour or provide wry comment on the previous item, e.g. one of the songs from 'My Fair Lady' could be a legitimate

176

illustration after a discussion on the pros and cons of speech training. Its use however should not be contrived or forced in to the programme merely because its title has a superficial relevance to the item. It would be wrong for example to follow a piece about an expedition to the Himalayas with 'Climb Every Mountain' from the Sound of Music. For someone who looks no further than the recording sleeve there appears to be a connection, but the discontinuity of context would lead to accusations of poor judgement.

One of the most difficult production points in the use of the medium is the successful combination of speech and music. Music is much more divisive of the audience since listeners generally have positive musical likes and dislikes. It is also very easy to create the wrong associations. However it remains a valuable part of the magazine producer's armoury so long as real care is exercised in its selection.

Sound effects

Like music, effects or actuality noises can add enormously to what might otherwise be a succession of speech items. They arouse the memory and paint pictures. An interview on the restoration of an old car would surely be accompanied by the sound of its engine and an item on new dental techniques by the buzzing of the drill. The scene for a discussion on education could be set by some actuality of playground or classroom activity, and a voice piece on road accident figures would catch the attention with the squeal of brakes. These things take time and effort to prepare and overdone, the programme suffers as it will from any other cliché. But used occasionally, appropriately and with imagination, the programme will be lifted from the mundane to the memorable. You do not have to be a drama producer to remember that one of the strengths of the medium is the vividness of impression which can be conveyed by simple sounds.

Listener participation

Magazine programmes often like to stimulate a degree of audience involvement. Again, the producer has several ways of achieving this:

1. *Requests* for music or for a particular subject to be discussed, or asking for a favourite item to be repeated.
2. *Letters spot* which acts as a follow-up to the previous programme, or a general correspondence column of the air.
3. *Competitions* are a good method of soliciting response. These could be in reply to quizzes and on-air games with prizes offered, or simply for the fun of it.
4. A *phone-in* spot in a 'live' magazine helps the sense of immediacy and can provide feedback on a particular item. Placed at the end, it can allow listeners the opportunity of saying what they thought of the programme as a whole. Used in conjunction with a quiz competition it obviously allows for answers to be given and a result declared within the programme.
5. Casual visitors to the radio station may be persuaded to *become broadcasters* for a short while and take part in a special spot, either 'live' or by editing recorded comments accumulated since the previous programme. Alternatively using a mobile facility such as a radio car, the programme can visit its listeners by 'dropping in' on a home discussion group or factory canteen.

Listener participation elements need proper planning but part of their attraction lies in their 'live' unpredictability. The confident producer or presenter will know when to stay with an unpremeditated turn of events and extend an item which is developing unexpectedly well. He will have also determined beforehand the most likely way of altering the running order to bring him back on schedule. In other words in live broadcasting the unexpected always needs to be considered.

Features

A magazine will frequently include a place for a package of material dealing with a subject in greater depth than might be possible in a single interview. Often referred to as a featurette, the variety of possibility defies detailed description here, but the general form is either person centred – 'our guest this week is . . .'; or place centred – 'this week we visit . . .'; or topic centred – 'this week our subject is . . .'

Even the topical news magazine, in which variety of item

treatment is particularly difficult to apply, will be able to consider putting together a featurette comprising interview, voice piece, archive material, actuality and links, even possibly music. For instance a report on the scrapping of an old wartime submarine could be run together with the reminiscences of its former skipper, describing some perilous exploit, with the appropriate sound effects in the background. Crossfade to breaker's yard and the sound of lapping water. This would be far more interesting than a straight report.

The featurette is a good means of distilling a complex subject and presenting its essential components. The honest reporter will take the crux of an argument, possibly from different recorded interviews, and so present them in the context of his own links. They should then form a logical, accurate and understandable picture on which the listener can base an opinion.

Drama

The weekly or daily serial has an established place in many magazine programmes. By itself it displays several characteristics which the magazine producer is attempting to embody — the same placing and introductory music, a consistent structure, familiar characters, and a single sense of style. On the other hand it needs a variety of new events, some fresh situations and people, and the occasional surprise. But drama can also be used in the one-off situation to make a specific point, for example in describing how a shopper should compare two supermarket products in order to arrive at a best buy. It will be far more effective than a talk by an official, however expert he might be.

Dialogue in a dramatised form can be an excellent vehicle for explaining legislation affecting citizen rights or simply for providing background on current affairs. Scriptwriters however will recognise in the listener an immediate rejection of any expository material which has about it the feel of propaganda. The most useful ingredients would appear to be: ordinary everyday humour, credible characters with whom the listener can identify, profound scepticism and demonstrable truth.

Magazine programmes for children will use drama to tell stories or explain a point in the educational sense. The use of this form may involve separate complex production effort,

179

but it can be none the less effective by being limited to the dramatised reading of a book, poem or historical document.

Item order

Having established the programme structure, set the overall style and decided on the treatment of each individual item, the actual order of the items can detract from or enhance the final programme.

In the case of a traditional circus or variety performance in a theatre, the best item − the top of the bill − is kept until last. It is safe to use this method of maintaining interest through the show since the audience is largely captive and it underwrites the belief that whatever the audience reaction, things can only get better. With radio, the audience is anything but captive and needs a strong item at the beginning to attract the listener to the start of the show, thereafter using a number of devices to hold his interest through to the end.

The news magazine will probably start with its lead story and gradually work through to the less important. However if this structure is rigidly applied the programme becomes less and less interesting − what has been called a 'tadpole' shape. News programmes are therefore likely to keep items of known interest until the end, e.g. sport, stock markets and weather, or at least end with a summary for listeners who missed the opening headlines. Throughout the programme as much use as possible will be made of phrases like, "more about that later". Some broadcasters deliberately avoid putting items in descending order of importance in order to keep 'good stuff for the second half'; a dubious practice if the listener is to accept that the station's editorial judgement is in itself something worth having.

The news magazine item order will be dictated very largely by the editor's judgement of the importance of the material, while in the tightly structured general magazine the format itself may leave little room for manoeuvre. In the more open magazine other considerations apply and it is worth noting once again the practice of the variety music bill. If there are two comedians they appear in separate halves of the show, something breathtakingly exciting is followed by something beautiful and charming, the uproariously funny is complemented by the serious or sad, the small by the visually spectacular. In other words, items are not allowed simply to stand on their own but through the contrast of their own juxtaposition and the skill of the compère they enhance each other so that the total effect is greater than the sum of the individual parts.

So it should be with the radio magazine. Two interviews involving men's voices are best separated. An urgently important item can be heightened by something of a lighter nature. A long item needs to be followed by a short one. Women's voices, contributions by children or old people, should be consciously used to provide contrast and variety. Tense, heated or other deeply felt situations need special care, for to follow with something too light or relaxed can give rise to accusations of trivialisation or superficiality. This is where the skill of the presenter counts for it is his choice of words and tone of voice which must adequately cope with the change of emotional level.

Variations in item style combined with a range of item treatment create endless possibilities for the imaginative producer. A programme which is becoming dull can be given a 'lift' with a piece of music half way through, some humour in the links, or an audience participation spot towards the end. For a magazine in danger of 'seizing up' because the items are too long, the effect of a brief snippet of information in another voice is almost magical. And all the time the presenter keeps us informed on what is happening in the programme, what we are listening to and where we are going to next, and later. The successful magazine will run for years on the right mixture of consistency of style and unpredictability of content. It could be that apart from its presenter the only consistent characteristic is its unpredictability.

Examples

The following examples of the magazine format are not given as ideals but as working illustrations of the production principle. Commercial advertising has been omitted in order to show the programme structure more clearly but the commercial station should be able to use its breaks to advantage, providing an even greater variety of content.

Example 1: Fortnightly Half-Hour Industrial Magazine

Structure	Running Order	Actual Timing
Standard Opening (1' 10'')	Signature tune	0 15
	Introduction	10
	Menu of content	15
	Follow-up to previous programmes	35
News (5 mins)	News round-up	5 05
	Link	15
Item	Interview on lead news story	3 08
	Link — information	30
Item	Voice piece on new process	1 52
	LInk	15
Item	Vox Pop — workers' views of safety rules	1 15
	Link	20
Trades Council Spot (2½ mins)	Union affairs — spokesman	2 20
	Link	20
Participation Spot (3 mins)	Listeners' letters	2 45
	Link — introduction	20
Discussion	Three speakers join presenter for discussion of current issue — variable length item to allow programme to run to time.	6 20
Financial news (3 mins)	Market trends	3 00
Standard Closing (50 secs)	Coming Events	30
	Expectations for next programme	10
	Signature tune	10
		29'50''

In this example, the programme structure allows 1' 10" for the opening and 50" for the closing. Other fixed items are a total of 8' 0" for news, 3' 0" for letters and 2' 30" for the Union spot. About 2' 0" are taken for the links. This means that just over half the programme runs to a set format leaving about 13' 0" for the two or three topical items at the front and the discussion towards the end.

So long as the subject is well chosen the discussion is useful for maintaining interest through the early part of the programme since it preserves at least the possibility of controversy, interest and surprise. With a 'live' broadcast it is used as the buffer to keep things on time since the presenter knows he must bring it to an end and get into the 'Market trends' four minutes before the end of the programme. The signature tune is 'prefaded to time' to make the timing exact. With a recorded programme the discussion is easily dropped in favour of a featurette which in this case might be a factory visit.

Example 2: Weekly 25-minute Religious Current Affairs Magazine

Structure	Running Order	Timing
Standard	Introduction	0 05
Opening (15")	Menu of content	0 10
Item	Interview — main topical interest	3 20
	Link	30
Item	Interview — woman missionary	2 05
	Link	10
Music (3 mins)	Review of gospel record release	2 40
	Link — information	55
Item	Interview — forthcoming convention	2 30
	Link	05
Featurette	Personality — faith and work	7 10
(7 mins)	Link	15
News (5 mins)	News round-up and What's On events	4 45
Standard		
Closing (15")	Closing credits	15
		24'55"

Notes:

With no signature tune, the presenter quickly gets to the main item. Although in this edition all the items are interviews, they are kept different in character and music is deliberately introduced at the mid point. The opening and closing take half a minute and the other fixed spots are allocated another fifteen minutes. If the programme is too long, adjustment can be made either by dropping some stories from the news or by shortening the music review. If it under-runs, a repeat of some of the record release can make a useful reprise at the end.

Example 3: Outline for a Daily 2-hour Afternoon Magazine

Fixed Times	Running Order	Approximate Durations
2.00	Sig. Tune/Intro — Programme information/Sig. Tune	1 min
	Music —	2
	Item — human interest interview	3
	Quiz competition (inc. yesterday's result)	3
	Music —	3
2.15	Listener's letters	5
	Music —	3
	Voice piece — background to current affairs	2
	Music —	2
	Leisure Spot — home improvements, gardening	3
	Humour on record	2
	Studio discussion — topical talking point	10
	Music —	3

	"Out and About" spot — visit to place of interest	5
	Music — (non vocal)	2
3.00	News Summary, sport and weather	2
	Phone-in spot	15
	Music —	3
	Film/Theatre/TV review — coming events voice piece	4
	Music —	3
3.30	Special Guest — interview	10
	Music — (illustrative)	2
	Item — child care or medical interview	3
	Quiz result	2
	Music — (non vocal)	2
3.50	Serial story — dramatised reading	9
	Closing sequence; items for tomorrow, production credits, sig. tune.	1

Notes:
In this example the speech/music ratio is regulated to about 3:1. A general pattern has been adopted that items become longer as the programme proceeds. Each half of the programme contains a 'live' item which can be 'backtimed' to ensure the time-keeping of the fixed spots. These are respectively the studio discussion and the special guest interview. Nevertheless the fixed spots are preceded by non-vocal music prefaded to time for absolute accuracy. Fifteen minutes is allowed for links.

Production method

A regular magazine programme has to be organised on two distinct levels — the long term and the immediate. Long term planning allows for 'one-off editions', the booking of guests reflecting special events, or the running of related spots to form a series across several programmes. On the immediate timescale, detailed arrangements have to be finalised for the next programme.

In the case of the fortnightly or weekly specialist magazine of the type represented in examples 1 and 2, it is a fairly straightforward task for the producer to make all the necessary arrangements in association with the presenter and a small group of contributors acting as reporters or interviewers. The newsroom or sources of specialist information will also be asked for a specific commitment. The important thing is that everyone knows his brief and his deadline. It is essential too that while the producer will make the final editorial decisions, all the contributors feel able to suggest ideas. Good ideas are invariably 'honed up', polished and made better by the process of discussion. Suggestions are progressed further and more quickly when there is more than one mind at work on them. Almost all ideas benefit from the process of counter-suggestion, development and resolution. This should be the pattern encouraged by the producer at his weekly planning meeting, by the end of which everyone should know what he has to do and what resources have been allocated to him.

The daily magazine indicated in example 3 is more complex and such a broadcast will require a larger production team. Typically, the main items such as the serial story and special guest in the second half will have been decided well in advance but the subject of the discussion in the first may well be left until a day or two beforehand in order to reflect a topical issue. Responsibility for collating the listeners' letters, organising the quiz, and producing the 'Out and about' spot will be delegated to specific individuals, and the newsroom will be made responsible for the current affairs voice piece, the news, sport and weather package, and perhaps one of the other interviews. The presenter will write his own links and probably choose his own music to a general brief from the producer. The detail is regulated at a morning planning meeting, the final running order being decided against the format structure which serves as the guideline.

At less frequent intervals, say once a month, the opportunity should be taken to stand back to review the programme and take stock of the long term options. In this way it may be possible to prevent the onset of the most prevalent disease of the regular programme — 'rut running' — while at the same time avoiding the disruptive restlessness which results from an obsession with change.

15

OUTSIDE BROADCASTS (REMOTES)

AS has been noted elsewhere, there is a tendency for broadcasters to shut themselves away in studios being enormously busy making programmes which do not originate from a direct contact with the audience. The outside broadcast, or 'remote', represents more than a desire to include in the schedule, coverage of outside events in which there is public interest. It is a positive need for the broadcaster to escape from the confines of his building into the world which is both the source and the target for all his enterprise. The concert, church service, exhibition, civic ceremony, sporting event, public meeting, conference or demonstration; these demand the broadcaster's attention. But it is not only good for radio to reflect what is going on, it is necessary for the stations's credibility to be involved in such things. Radio must not only go to where people are, it must come from the interests and activities of many people. If its sources are too few, it is in danger of appearing detached, sectional, elitist or out of touch. Thus the OB is essential to broadcasting's health.

Planning

The producer in charge, together with the appropriate engineering staff must first decide how much coverage is required of a specific event. The programme requirement must be established and the technical means of achieving it costed. Is it to be 'live', or recorded on site? What duration is expected? Once there is a definite plan, the resources can be allocated — people, facilities, money and time.

It is also at this first stage that discussions must take place with the event organiser to establish the right to broadcast. It may be necessary to negotiate over any fees payable, or conditions or limitations which he may wish to impose.

Visiting the site

A reconnaissance is essential, but it may take considerable imagination to anticipate what the actual conditions will be like 'on the day'. There are a number of questions which must be answered:

1. Where and of what type are the mains electricity supply points? Is the supply correctly earthed?
2. Where is the best vantage point to see the most action? Will there have to be more than one?
3. Will the sound mixing be done in the building, or in a

it's-a-beautiful-day

The radio station must involve itself in its own community, otherwise it will appear irrelevant and out of touch.

190

radio OB vehicle outside?

4. What on-site communications are required?
5. How many microphones and what type will be needed?
6. How long are the cable runs?

Site Plan

Location THE CHURCH HALL, HIGH STREET, EXLEY

Contact: Name JOHN SMITH **Post** CARETAKER **Phone** 135531

Transmission/~~Recording~~   **Date** 1 JULY **Time** 1900-2000

Rehearsal   **Date** 29 JUNE **Time** 2000-2230

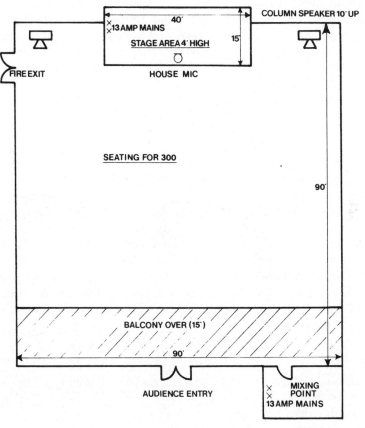

A sketch plan drawn up during the site visit is an invaluable aid to further planning.

191

7. Will a public address system be in use? If so, where are the speakers?
8. What else will be present on the day? e.g. flags which obscure the view, vehicles or generators which might cause electrical interference, background music, other broadcasters.

Communications to base

If the programme is 'live', how is the signal to be sent to the controlling studio? What radio links are required? Is the site within available radio car range? Are land lines available? They may be expensive but will additional programme or control circuits need to be ordered from the Post Office? If so will the quality be good enough for music — or will the programme circuit have to be 'equalised'? These questions need to be discussed at an early stage, for, amongst other things, the answers will have a direct bearing on the cost of the programme.

Sooner or later an OB will be required from a hall, or from the middle of a field, where no lines exist. Such conditions are best realised well in advance so that the telephone authority can make the appropriate connections, and if necessary actually build a suitable route; A decision has to be made as to whether only a one-way programme circuit is required — the broadcaster at the site must then be able to obtain his cue to go ahead by listening off-air — or whether a second two-way telephone or control line is also needed. Obviously this additional facility is to be preferred and for an OB of any length and where a number of broadcasts are made from the same site, it becomes essential. The same applies if radio links are used — is there to be a bi-directional control channel in addition to the programme circuit from OB to base? If all else fails however, it is a wise precaution to know the whereabouts of the nearest accessible telephone whether it is in a private house or office, or a public call box. Many a programme has been saved by having the right coins available!

People

By this stage it should be clear as to how many people will be involved at the OB site. Anything more than a simple one-man job may require a number of skills — producer, engineer, commentator, technical operator, secretary, driver, caterer etc.

A large event with the public present, such as an exhibition, may require the services of a security man, or publicity specialist. The list grows with the complexity of the programme, as does the cost.

The exact number of people is an important piece of anticipation — getting it right depends on being able to visualise whether for example there is a script writing and typing requirement on-site. It will also depend on whether the working day is to be so long as to warrant the employment of duplicate staff working in shifts.

Equipment

This is best organised on a category basis by the individuals most closely involved:

1. *Engineering:* microphones, cables, sound mixers, turntables, tape recorders, amplifiers, loudspeakers, headphones, power cables and distribution boards, spare fuses, sticky tape, editing materials, recording tape, spare spools, tool kit, radio, spare batteries.
2. *Programme:* records, tapes, carts, scripts.
3. *Administrative*: tables, chairs, paper, typewriters, pencils, torches, clipboards, money, stop-watches, string, publicity material.
4. *Personal*: food and drink, special clothing, first aid kit.
5. *Transport*: vehicles.

There are always things which get forgotten, but if they are really important, this only happens once.

Accommodation

In further discussion with the event organiser there has to be agreement on the exact location of the broadcasting personnel and equipment. There may be special regulations governing car parking or access to the site, in which case the appropriate passes need to be obtained.

In order to rig equipment it will be necessary to gain access well before the event — are any keys required? Who will be there? and what security exists to safeguard equipment once it is rigged? At this stage the producer must also satisfy himself as to the whereabouts of lavatories, fire exits, catering facilities, lifts and any special features of the site.

Programme research

Further discussion with the event organiser will establish the detailed timetable and list of participants. With an open-air event such as a parade or sports meeting, it is important to discover any alternative arrangements in case of rain. As much information as possible about who is taking part, the history of the event, how many people have attended on previous occasions, and so on, is useful preparatory material for the broadcast itself. Additional research may be necessary at this stage for the commentators — see under 'Commentary'.

The producer is then in a position to draw up a running order and to tell everyone his or her precise role both on and off the air. The running order should give as much relevant information as possible including 'who is doing what', 'when', and details of cues and timings, where these are known.

Liaison with the base studio

Particularly in the case of a 'live' OB, staff at the base studio need to be kept informed. They should have copies of the running order and be involved in a discussion of any special fill-up material or other instructions in case of a technical failure. Arrangements should be made for a 'live' OB to be recorded at the base studio so that a possible feature can be made for a highlight or follow-up programme.

Publicity

The producer should ensure he has done everything he can to provide the appropriate advance publicity. This may be in the form of programme billings, printed posters, a press release, or simply on-air trails and announcements. It is a matter of common experience that broadcasters go to immense pains to cover an important public event, but overlook the necessity of telling people about it in advance. It is true that some promoters claim that broadcast coverage keeps people away from attending the event itself, but on the other hand it is frequently the case that advance publicity, particularly on radio as opposed to television, will stimulate public interest and swell the crowds, many of whom will have transistor sets pressed to their ears.

Safety

In a situation where crowds of people are present and their attention is inevitably drawn to the spectacle they have come to see, the broadcaster has a special responsibility to ensure that his own operation does not present any hazards. The broadcaster is of course affected by, and must observe, any local bye-laws or other regulations which apply to the OB site. His equipment must not obstruct gangways or obscure fire exit notices, or the fire equipment itself.

Cables across pavements or passage-ways must either be covered by a ramp, or should be lifted clear of any possibility of causing an obstruction.

Microphones suspended over an audience must be securely fixed, not just with sticky tape which can become loosened with a temperature change, but secured in such a way as to prevent any possibility of their being untied by inquisitive or malicious fingers.

Cable Runs

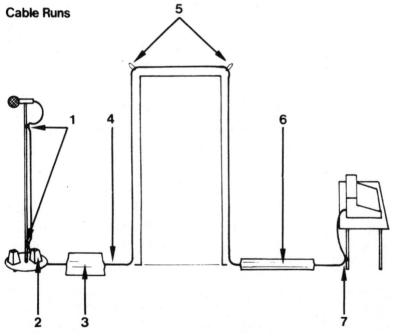

Microphones and cables must be safely rigged. 1. Cable taped to mic stand. 2. Stand weighted. 3. Mat covers cable at walkway. 4. Cable laid without loops or knots. 5. Cable slung over doorways. 6. Cable taped to floor. 7. Cable made fast at mixer end.

195

Members of the public are generally curious of the broadcasting operation and all equipment must be completely stable, for instance microphone stands or loudspeakers should not be able to fall over. Nor of course must straying hands be able to touch mains electricity connections. A little discreet fencing off may be desirable.

This will almost certainly be necessary where a ground level public address system is in use. For a DJ show where the broadcaster is providing an on-site loudspeaker output, the sound intensity close to the speakers is often sufficient to cause temporary, and in some cases permanent damage to ears. To prevent this some form of barrier three feet or so from the speaker is generally needed, but a better alternative is to raise the speakers, fixing them securely well above head height.

Tidiness

The broadcaster is working in a public place and both his appearance and his general behaviour will contribute to the station's image. This is recognised by the more senior staff but may not always be appreciated by freelance contributors. A small but important aspect of public relations is the matter of leaving the OB site in a sensibly tidy state. It is clearly undesirable to leave any equipment behind but this should also apply to the accumulated rubbish of a working visit — scripts, notes, food tins, plastic bags, empty boxes etc. To be practical, a good OB site will be required again and it is not in the broadcaster's interests to be remembered for the wrong reasons.

Gratuities

It is common sense to recognise that the broadcaster's presence at an OB site is likely to cause extra effort for those who normally work there. It will not be necessary to consider this point in every case, and it may even be felt that where there is some special distinction attached to broadcasting it is possible to live off that good name. This temptation should be resisted, for every time that status is used in this way, it is likely to be diminished. A facility fee should be paid where local assistance was provided beyond the requirements of their normal job, and to any outsiders who were asked for some special service, for example, use of a telephone, electricity or water supply, parking of vehicles. The amounts should obviously be related to the service provided – too much and one is open to charges of profligate wastage, too little and one quickly does more harm than good.

16

COMMENTARY

RADIO has a marvellous facility for creating pictures in the listener's mind. It is more flexible than television in that it is possible to isolate a tiny detail without waiting for the camera to 'zoom in' and it can create a breadth of vision much larger than the dimensions of a glass screen. The listener does more than simply eavesdrop on an event; radio, more easily than television or film, can convey the impression of actual participation. The aim of the radio commentator is therefore to recreate in the listener's mind not simply a picture but a total impression of the occasion. This is done in three distinct ways:

1. The words used will be visually descriptive of the scene.
2. The speed and style of their delivery will underline the emotional mood of the event.
3. Additional 'effects' microphones will reinforce the action, or the public reaction to it.

Attitude to the listener

In describing a scene it has been said that the commentator should have in mind 'a blind friend who couldn't be there'. It is important to remember the obvious fact that the listener cannot see. Without this it is easy to slip into the situation of simply chatting about the event to 'someone beside you'. The listener should be regarded as a friend because this implies a real concern to communicate accurately and fully. The commentator must use more than his eyes and convey information through all the senses, so as to heighten the feeling of participation by the listener. Thus for example temperature, the proximity of people and things, or the sense of smell are important factors in the overall impression. Smell is particularly evocative – the scent of newly mown grass, the aroma inside a fruit market or the timeless mustiness of an old building. Combine this with the appropriate style of delivery, and the sounds of the place itself, and you are on the way to creating a powerful set of pictures.

Preparation

Some of the essential stages are described under 'Outside Broadcasts' but the value of a pre-transmission site visit cannot be over-emphasised. Not only must the commentator satisfy himself as to his field of vision and whether the sun is in his eyes, but he must use the time to obtain essential facts about the event itself. For example in preparing for a ceremonial occasion he will need to discover:

1. The official programme of events with details of timing etc.
2. The names of the flowers used for decoration, or the trees in the area.
3. The history of the buildings and streets, and their architectural detail.
4. The background of the people taking part – unseen as well as seen, for example organisers, caretakers.
5. The titles of music to be played, and any special association it may have with the people and the place.

It adds immeasurably to the description of a scene to be able to mention the type of stonework used in a building, or that 'around the platform are fuchsias and hydrangeas'. The point of such detail is to use it as contrast with the really significant elements of the event so letting them gain in importance. Contrast makes for variety and for more interesting listening and mention of matters both great and small is essential, particularly for an extended piece. An eye for detail can also be the saving of a broadcast when there are unexpected moments to fill. There is no substitute for a commentator doing his homework.

In addition to personal observation and enquiry, useful sources of information will be the reference section of libraries or museums, newspaper cuttings, back copies of the event programme, previous participants, specialist magazines, and commercial or government press offices.

Having obtained all the factual information in advance, the commentator must assemble it in a form which he can use in the conditions prevailing at the OB. If he is perched precariously on top of the radio car in the rain, clutching a guardrail to steady himself and holding a microphone, stopwatch, and an umbrella, the last thing he wants is a bundle of easily windblown papers! Notes should be laid out on as few sheets as possible and held firmly on a clipboard. Cards may be useful since they are silent to handle. The important thing is their order and logic. The information will often be chronological in nature listing the background of the people taking part. This is particularly so where the participants appear in a predetermined sequence — a procession or parade, variety show, race meeting, athletics event, church service, or civic ceremony. Further information on the event or the environment can be on separate pages so long as they can be referred to easily. If the event is non-sequential, for instance a football match or public meeting, the personal information may be more useful in alphabetical form, or better still memorised.

Working with the base studio

The commentator will need to know the precise handover details. This applies both from the studio to himself, and from his own end cue for the return to the studio. These details are best written down for they easily slip the memory under such conditions. He should also be fully aware of the procedures to be followed in the event of any kind of circuit failure — the back-up music to be played, and who makes the decision to restore the programme. It may be necessary to devise some system of hand signals or other means of communication with technical staff, and he will want to know whether he will be able to hear 'talk-back' in his headphones etc. These matters are the 'safety nets' which enable the commentator to fulfil his role with a proper degree of confidence.

As with all outside broadcasts, the base studio should ensure that the commentary output is recorded. Not only will the commentator be professionally curious as to how it came over, but the material may be required for archive purposes. Even more important is that an event worthy of a 'live' OB will almost certainly merit a broadcast of edited highlights later in the day. Thus two recordings may be needed, a complete original and one which can be cut for subsequent rebroadcast.

Sport

First and foremost the sports commentator must know his sport and have detailed knowledge of the particular event. He should know the sequence which led up to it, its siginficance in any overall contest, the participants and something of their history. The possession of this background information is elementary, but what is not so obvious is how to use it. The tendency is to give it all out at the beginning in the form of an encyclopaedic but fairly indigestible introduction. Certainly the basic facts must be provided at the outset, but a much better way of using background detail is as the game itself proceeds, at an appropriate moment or during a pause in the action. This way the commentator sounds as though he is part of what is going on instead of being a rather superior observer.

Traditionally, for technical reasons, the commentator has often had to operate from inside a soundproof commentary position, isolated from his immediate surroundings. He can easily lose something of the atmosphere by creating his own environment and there is a strong argument in favour of the ringside seat approach, provided that he uses a noise-cancelling microphone and his communication facilities, such as headphone . talkback, are secure.

Sports stadia seem to undergo more frequent changes to their layout than other buildings and unless a particular site is in almost weekly use for radio work, a special reconnaissance visit is strongly advised. It is easy to forego the site reconnaissance assuming that the place will be the same as it was six months ago. However unless there are strong reasons to the contrary, a visit and technical test should always be made.

Where the action is spread out over a large area as with motor racing, a full scale athletics competition or rowing event, more than one commentator is likely to be in action. Cueing, hand-overs, timing, liaison with official results — all these must be precisely arranged. The more complex an occasion, the more necessary is observance of the three golden rules for all broadcasts of this type:

1. Meticulous production planning so that everyone knows what is *likely* to be asked of him.
2. First class communications for control.
3. Only one person in charge.

Communicating mood

The key question is 'what is the overall impression here?' Is it one of joyful festivity or is there a more intense excitement? Is there an urgency to the occasion or is it relaxed? At the other end of the emotional scale there may be a sense of awe, a tragedy or a sadness which needs to be reflected in a sombre dignity. Whatever is happening, the commentator's sensitivity to its mood, and to that of the spectators, will control his style, use of words and speed of delivery. More than anything else this will carry the impressions of the event in the opening moments of the broadcast. The mood of the crowd should be closely observed — anticipatory, excited, happy, generous, relaxed, impressed, restive, sullen, tense, angry, solemn, sad. Such feelings should be conveyed in the voice of the commentator and their accurate assessment will help him to know when to stop and let the sounds of the event speak for themselves.

Co-ordinating the images

It is all too easy to fall short of an overall picture but to end up instead with some accurately described but separate pieces of jig-saw. The great art, and challenge, of commentary is to fit them together, presenting them in a logically co-ordinated way which allows your 'blind friend' to place the information accurately in his mind's eye. The commentator must include not only the information relating to the scene, but also something about how this information should be used to build the appropriate framework of scale. Having provided this contextual information, other items may then be related to it. Early on, it should be mentioned where the commentator's own position is relative to the scene; also giving details of distance, size, foreground, left and right etc. Movement within a scene needs a smooth, logical transition if the listener is not to become hopelessly disorientated.

Content and style

The commentator begins with a 'scene-set'. He says first of all where he is and why — this is best not given in advance by the continuity handover and duplication of this information must be avoided. The listener should be helped to identify with

203

the location, particularly if it is likely to be familiar to him. The description continues from the general to the particular noting, as appropriate, the weather, the overall impression of lighting, the mood of the crowd, the colour content of the scene and what is about to happen. Perhaps two minutes or more should be allowed for this 'scene setting', depending on the complexity of the event, during which time nothing much may be happening. By the time the action begins the listener should have a clear visual and emotional picture of the setting, its sense of scale and overall 'feel'. Even so, the commentator must continually refer to the generalities of the scene as well as to the detail of the action. The two should be woven together.

Time taken for scene-setting does not of course apply in the case of news commentary where one is concerned first and foremost with what is happening. Arriving at the scene of a fire of demonstration, one deals first with the event and widens later to include the general environment. Even so, it is important to provide the detail with its context.

Many commentaries are greatly improved by the use of colour. Colour whether gaudy or sombre is easily recreated in the mind's eye and mention of purple robes, brilliant green plumage, dark grey leaden skies, the blue and gold of ceremonial, the flashes of red or the sparkling white surf — such specific references conjure up the reality much better than the short cut of describing a scene simply as multi-coloured.

In describing the action itself, the commentator must proceed at the same pace as the event, combining prepared fact with spontaneous vision. In the case of a planned sequence as a particular person appears, or slightly in anticipation, reference is made to the appropriate background information, title, relevant history and so on. This is more easily said than done and requires a lot of practice — perhaps using a tape recorder to help perfect the technique.

Sports action

The description of sport, even more than that of the ceremonial occasion, needs a firm frame of reference. Most listeners will be very familiar with the layout of the event and can orient themselves to the action so long as it is presented to them the right way round. They need to know which team is playing from left to right; in cricket which end of the pitch the bowling

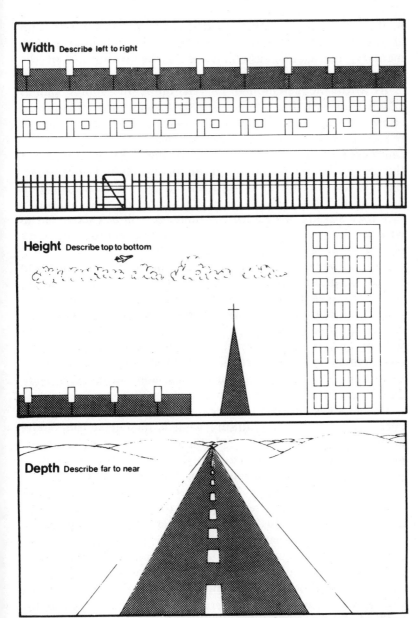

The dimensions of commentary. The listener needs 3-dimensional information in which to place the action. Such orientation should not be confined to the scene-set but should be maintained throughout the commentary.

is coming from; in tennis, who is serving from which court; in horse racing or athletics, the commentator's position relative to the finishing line. It is not sufficient to give this information at the beginning only, it has to be used throughout a commentary, consciously associated with the description of the action.

As with the ceremonial commentator, the sports man is keeping up with the action but also noticing what is going on elsewhere, for instance the injured player, or a likely change in the weather. Furthermore, the experienced sports commentator can increase interest for the listener by highlighting an aspect of the event which is not at the front of the action. For example, the real siginificance of a motor race may be the duel going on between the 4th and 5th place; the winner of a 10,000 metre race may already be decided but there can still be excitement in whether the man in second place will set a new European record or a personal best.

With slower games, such as cricket, the art is to use pauses in the action interestingly, not as gaps to fill but opportunities to add to the general picture or give further information. This is where another commentator or researcher can be useful in supplying appropriate information from the record books or with an analysis of the performance to date. Long stretches of commentary in any case require a change of voice, as much for the listener as for the commentators, and changeovers every 20 - 30 minutes are about the norm.

If for some reason the commentator cannot quite see a particular incident or is unsure what is happening, he should avoid committing himself – "I think that . . ." A better, more positive way is – "It looks as though . . ." Similarly it is unwise for a commentator to speculate on what a referee is saying to a player in a disciplinary situation. Only what can be seen or known should be described. It is easy to make a serious mistake affecting an individual's reputation through the incorrect interpretation of what may appear obvious. And it must be regarded as quite exceptional to voice a positive disagreement with a referee's decision. After all he is closer to the action and may have seen something which the commentator, with his general view, missed. The reverse can also be true but in the heat of the moment it is sensible policy to give referees and umpires the benefit of any doubt.

Scores and results should be given frequently for the benefit of listeners who have just switched on but in a variety of styles in order to avoid irritating those who have listened throughout. Commentators should remember that the absence of goals or points can be just as important as a positive score-line.

Actuality and silence

It may be that during the event there are sounds to which the commentary should refer. The difficulty here is that the noisier the environment, the closer on-microphone will be the commentator so that the background will be relatively reduced. It is essential to check that these other sounds can be heard through separate microphones otherwise references to 'the roar of the helicopters overhead', 'the colossal explosions going on around me' or 'the shouts of the crowd' will be quite lost on the listener. It is important in the circumstances for the commentator to stop talking and to let the event speak for itself.

There may be times when it is virtually obligatory for the commentator to be silent – during the playing of a national anthem, the blessing at the end of a church service, or important words spoken during a ceremonial. Acute embarrassment on the part of the over talkative commentator and considerable annoyance for the listener will result from his being caught unawares in this way. A broadcaster unfamiliar with such things as military parades or church services must be certain to avoid such pitfalls by a thorough briefing beforehand.

The ending

Running to time is helped by having a stop-watch synchro-nised with the studio clock. This will provide for an accurately timed handback, but if open-ended, the cue back to the studio is simply given at the conclusion of the event.

It is all too easy after the excitement of what has been happening to create a sense of anti-climax. Even though the event is over and the crowds are filtering away, the commentary should maintain the spirit of the event itself perhaps with a brief summary, or with a mention of the next similar occasion. Another technique is radio's equivalent of the television wide-angle shot. The commentator 'pulls back' from the detail of the scene, concluding as he began with a general impression of the whole picture before ending with a positive and previously agreed form of words which indicates a return to the studio.

Many broadcasters prefer openings and closings to be scripted. Certainly if you have hit upon the neat well turned phrase, its inclusion in any final paragraph will contribute appropriately to the commentator's endeavour to sum up both the spirit and the action of the hour.

An example

One of the most notable commentators was the late Richard Dimbleby of the BBC. Of many, perhaps his most memorable piece of work was his description of the lying-in-state of King George VI at Westminster Hall in February 1952. The printed page can hardly do it justice, it is radio and should be heard to be fully appreciated. Nevertheless it is possible to see here the application of the commentator's 'rules'. A style of language, and delivery, that is appropriate to the occasion. A 'scene-set' which quickly establishes the listener both in terms of the place and the mood. 'Signposts' which indicate the part of the pictures being described. Smooth transitions of movement that takes you from one part of the picture to another. Researched information, short sentences or phrases. direct speech, colour and attention to detail, all used with masterly skill to place the listener at the scene.

"It is dark in New Palace Yard at Westminster tonight. As I look down from this old, leaded window I can see the ancient courtyard dappled with little pools of light where the lamps of London try to pierce the biting, wintry gloom and fail. And moving through the darkness of the night is an even darker stream of human beings, coming, almost noiselessly, from under a long, white canopy that crosses the pavement and ends at the great doors of Westminster Hall. They speak very little, these people, but their footsteps sound faintly as they cross the yard and go out through the gates, back into the night from which they came.

They are passing, in their thousands, through the hall of history while history is being made. No one knows from where they come or where they go, but they are the people, and to watch them pass is to see the nation pass.

It is very simple, this lying-in-state of a dead king, and of incomparable beauty. High above all light and shadow and rich in carving is the massive roof of chestnut that Richard II put

208

over the great hall. From that roof the light slants down in clear, straight beams, unclouded by any dust, and gathers in a pool at one place. There lies the coffin of the King.

The oak of Sandringham, hidden beneath the rich golden folds of the Standard; the slow flicker of the candles touches gently the gems of the Imperial Crown, even that ruby that King Henry wore at Agincourt. It touches the deep purple of the velvet cushion and the cool, white flowers of the only wreath that lies upon the flag. How moving can such simplicity be. How real the tears of those who pass and see it, and come out again, as they do at this moment in unbroken stream, to the cold, dark night and a little privacy for their thoughts."

17

MUSIC RECORDING

THERE are three questions which a producer must ask himself before becoming involved in the production of any music.

Firstly, is the material offered relevant to programme needs? The technically minded producer, audiophile or engineer can easily create reasons for recording a particular music occasion other than for its value as good programming. It may represent an attractive technical challenge, or be the sort of concert which at the time seems a good idea to have 'in the can'. Alternatively the desire to record a particular group of performers may outweigh considerations of the suitability of what they are playing. Sometimes musicians are visually persuasive but aurally colourless, or as with many club performers dependent on an atmosphere difficult to reproduce on radio. To embark on music with little prospect of broadcasting it is a speculative business and the radio producer should not normally commit resources unless he knows perhaps only in outline how he intends to use the material.

The second question asks whether the standard of performance is good enough for broadcasting? There cannot be a single set of objective criteria for standards since much depends on the programme's purpose and context. A national broadcaster will undoubtedly demand the highest possible standards; regionally and locally there is an obligation to broadcast the music-making of the area which will almost certainly be of less than international excellence. The city orchestra, college swing band, amateur pop group, all have a place in the schedules but for broadcasting to a general audience, as opposed to a school concert which is directed only to the parents of performers, there is a lower limit below which the standard must not fall. In identifying this minimum level, the producer has to decide whether he is primarily broadcasting the music, the musician, or the occasion. Certainly he should not go ahead without a clear indication of the likely outcome – new groups should be auditioned first, preferably 'live' rather than from a submitted tape. If the technical limits of performance are apparent, musicians should be persuaded to play items that lie within their abilities. Simple music well played is infinitely preferable to the firework display that does not come off.

And finally, is the recording or broadcast within the technical capability of the station? Even at national level there are limits to what can be expended on a single programme. Numbers and types of microphones, the best specification for stereo lines, special circuits, engineering facilities at a remote OB site,

Choir - 34 performers ▪ 1 Mic

Pop Group - 4 performers ▪ 12 Mics

The technical complexity of broadcasting live music is not related to how many performers there are. The producer must decide whether adequate programme standards can be achieved within his available resources.

the availability of more than one echo source and so on — these are considerations which affect what the listener will hear and will therefore contribute to his appreciation of the performer. The broadcaster has an obvious obligation to the artist to present him in the most appropriate manner without the intervention of technical limits. This presupposes that the producer knows exactly what is involved in any given situation, that for example he understands the implications of a 'live' concert where the members of a 'pop' group sing as they play, where public address relay is present, or hyper-cardioid, variable pattern or 'lanyard' microphones are required to do justice to a particular sound balance. The smaller programme-making units should avoid taking on more than they can adequately handle, and instead should stay within the limits of their equipment and expertise. Much better for a local station to refuse the occasional music OB as beyond its technical scope than it should broadcast a programme which it knows could have been improved upon given the appropriate equipment.

The remainder of this chapter is directed to help producers in their understanding of the technical factors of music recording.

The philosophy of music balance is divided into two main groups — firstly, the reproduction of a sound which is already in existence, and secondly, the creation of a synthetic overall balance which exists only in the composer's or arranger's head and subsequently in the listener's loudspeaker.

Reproduction of internal balance

Where the music produced results from a carefully controlled and self-regulating relationship between the performers, it would be wrong for the broadcaster to alter what the musicians are trying to achieve. For example the members of a string quartet are sensitive to each other and adjust their individual volume as the music proceeds. They produce a varying blend of sound which is as much part of the performance as the notes they play or the tempo they adopt. The finished product of the sound already exists and the art of the broadcaster is to find the place where his microphone(s) can most faithfully reproduce it. Other examples of internally balanced music are symphony orchestras, concert recitalists, choirs and brass bands. The dynamic relationship between the instruments and sections of a good orchestra is under the control of its conductor; the broadcaster's task is to reproduce this interpretation of the music. He should not create a new sound by boosting the woodwind or unduly accentuating the trumpet solo. Since the conductor controls the internal balance by what he hears, it is in this area that one searches initially for the 'right' sound. Using a 'one-mic balance' or stereo pair, the rule of thumb is to place it with respect to the conductor's head — 'three metres (10 feet) up and three metres (10 feet) back'.

Similarly the conductor of a good choir will on his own

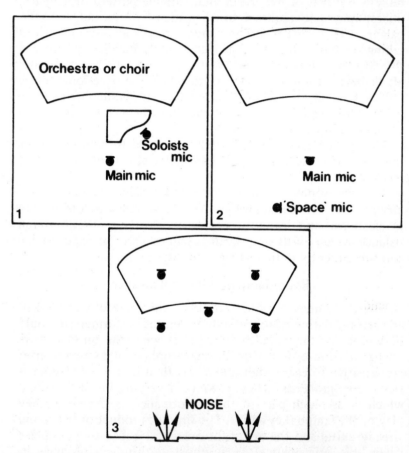

Basic considerations for mic placing with an internally balanced group. 1. Mic balance suitable under low noise conditions in a good acoustic. A soloist's mic or occasional 'filler' mic may be added. 2. In too 'dry' an acoustic a space mic is added to increase the pick-up of reflected sound. 3. Under conditions of unacceptable ambient noise the microphones are moved closer to the source and increased in number to preserve the overall coverage. It may be necessary to add artificial reverberation.

assessment regulate the balance between the soprano, contralto, tenor and bass parts. If the choir is short of tenors and this section needs reinforcing, this adjustment can of course be made in the microphone balance. But this is at once to create a sound not made simply by the musicians and raises interesting questions about the lengths to which broadcasters may go in repairing the deficiencies of performers.

It is possible to 'improve' a musician's tone quality, to clarify the diction of a choir or to correct an unevenly balanced group. The ultimate in such cosmetic treatment is to use the techniques of the recording studio so to enhance a performer's work that it becomes impossible for him ever to appear 'live' in front of an audience, a not unknown situation. But while it is entirely reasonable to make every possible adjustment in order to obtain the best sound from a school orchestra, it would be unthinkable to tamper with the performance of an artist who had a personal reputation. It is in the middle ground, including the best amateur musicians, where the producer is required to exercise his judgement — to do justice to the artist but without making it difficult for the performer in other circumstances.

The foregoing assumes that the music is performed in a hall that has favourable acoustics. Where this is not the case, steps have to be taken to correct the particular fault. For example in too 'dry' an acoustic, some artificial reverberation will need to be added, preferably on-site at the time of recording, although it is possible for it to be added later. Alternatively a 'space' microphone can be used to increase the pick-up of reflected sound. If the hall is too reverberant or the ambient noise level, from air-conditioning plant or outside traffic, is unacceptably high, the microphone should be moved closer to the sound source. If this tends to favour one part at the expense of another, further microphones are added to restore full coverage. The best sound quality from most instruments and ensembles is to be found not simply in front of them, but above them. A good music studio will have a high ceiling and the microphone for an internally balanced group will be kept well above head height. As mentioned previously, the standard starting procedure is to place a main microphone 'three metres (10 feet) up and three metres (10 feet) back' from the conductor's head, with a second microphone perhaps further back and a little higher. The output of the two microphones are then compared. The one giving the better overall blend without losing the detail then remains and the other microphone is moved to another place for a second comparison. An alteration in distance of even a few centimetres can make a significant difference to the sound produced. To avoid the effects of either the reinforcement or the phase cancellation of the reflected sound, microphones are best placed asymetrically within a hall, off the centre line. Similarly one avoids the axis of a concave surface such as a dome.

The process of comparison continues until no further improvement can be obtained. It is essential that such listening is done with reference to the actual sounds produced by the musicians. It is important that producers and sound balance engineers do not confine themselves to the noises produced by their monitoring equipment, good though they may be, but listen in the hall to what the performers are doing.

Having achieved the best placing for the main microphone, soloists', 'filler' or 'space' mics may be added. These additional microphones must not be allowed to take over the balance nor should their use alter the 'perspective' during a concert. For a group that is balanced internally the only additional control is likely to be a compression of the dynamic range as the music proceeds. An intelligent anticipation of variations in the dynamics of the sound is required and although a limiter/compressor will avoid the worst excesses of overload, it can also iron out all artistic subtlety in the performance. There is no substitute for a manual control that takes account of the information from the musical score and is combined with a sensitive appreciation of what comes out of the loudspeaker.

The aim is to broadcast the music together with whatever atmosphere may be appropriate. To secure the confidence of the conductor, bandmaster or leader, it is useful to invite him into the sound mixing and monitoring area to listen to the balance achieved during rehearsal. It should be remembered that since he normally stands close to the musicians, he is used to a fairly high sound level and the playback of rehearsal recordings should take this into account. Recordings should never be played back into the room in which they were made since this can lead to an undue emphasis of any acoustic peculiarity. A balance should also however be monitored at low level, at what more closely resembles domestic listening conditions. This is particularly important with vocal work

216

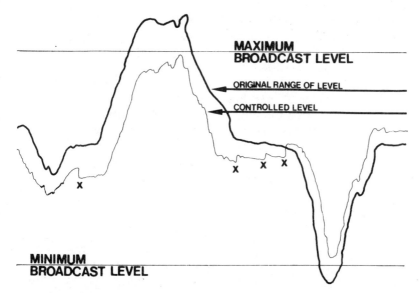

MAXIMUM
BROADCAST LEVEL

ORIGINAL RANGE OF LEVEL

CONTROLLED LEVEL

X   X   X

X

MINIMUM
BROADCAST LEVEL

Dynamic compression. The range of loudness in the studio can easily rise above the maximum and fall below the minimum levels acceptable to the broadcast system. By anticipating a loud passage the main fader is used to reduce the level before it occurs. Similarly the level prior to a quiet part is increased. Faders generally work in small steps, each one introducing a barely perceptible change (X).

when the clarity of diction may suffer if the final balance is only judged at high level.

Creation of a synthetic balance

Whereas the reproduction of an existing sound calls for the integration of performance and acoustic using predominantly one microphone, the creation of a synthetic balance, which in reality exists nowhere, requires the use of many microphones to separate the musical elements in order to 'treat' and reassemble them in a new way. For example, a concert band arrangement calling for a flute solo against a backing from a full brass section would be impossible unless for the duration of the solo the flute can be specially favoured at the expenses of the brass. Achieving this relies on the ability to separate the flute from everything else in such a way that it can be individually emphasised at will without affecting the sound from other instruments. The factors involved in achieving this separation are: studio layout, microphone types, source treatment, mixing technique, and recording technique.

217

Studio layout

The physical arrangement of a music group has to satisfy several criteria, some of which may conflict. These criteria can be listed as:

1. To achieve 'separation', quiet instruments and singers should not be too close to loud instruments.
2. The spatial arrangement must not inhibit any stereo effect required in the final balance.
3. The conductor or leader must be able to see everyone.
4. The musicians must be able to hear themselves and each other.
5. Certain musicians will need to see other musicians.

The producer should not force players to adopt an unusual layout against their will since the standard of performance is likely to suffer. He must resolve any difficulty by suggesting alternative means of meeting the musical requirements. For example a rhythm section of piano, bass, drums and guitar,

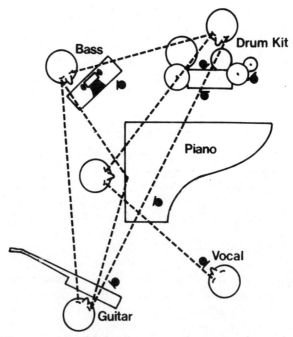

Studio layout. The musicians need to see each other and the microphones placed so as to avoid undue pick-up of other instruments.

needs to be tightly grouped together so that they can all see and hear each other. If there is a tendency for them to be picked up on the microphones of adjacent instruments they may need to be screened off. If this in turn affects their, or other musicians' ability to see or hear, the sight-line can be restored by the use of screens with inset glass panels, and aural communications maintained by means of headphones fed with whatever source is required.

Left to themselves, musicians often adopt the layout usual to them for cabaret or stage work. This may be unsuitable for broadcasting and it is essential that the producer knows the instrumentation detail beforehand in order to make positive suggestions for the studio arrangements. He must know whether bass and guitar players have an electric or acoustic instrument. Also how much 'doubling' is anticipated, that is, one musician playing more than one instrument, sometimes within the same musical piece, and whether the players are also to sing. This information is also useful in knowing how many music stands to provide.

It is preferable to avoid undue movement in the studio during recording or transmission but it may be necessary to ask a particular musician to move to another microphone, for example for a solo. It is also usual to ask brass players to move into the microphone slightly when using a mute. This avoids opening the fader to such an extent that the separation might be affected.

Microphone types

As an aid in achieving separation, the sound recordist's best friend is the directional microphone. The physical layout in the studio is obviously arrived at in the light of what microphones are available. A ribbon microphone with its figure of eight directivity pattern is most useful for its lack of pick-up on the two sides. Used horizontally just above a flute or piano, it is effectively dead to other instruments in the same plane. A cardioid microphone gives an adequate response over its front 180° and will reject sounds arriving at the back – good for covering a string section. A hyper-cardioid microphone will narrow the angle of acceptance giving an even more useful area of rejection. Condenser or electrostatic types of microphone with variable directivity patterns are valuable for the flexibility

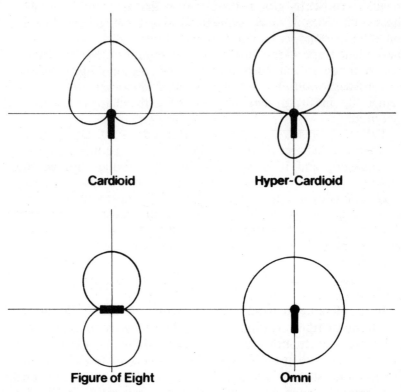

Cardioid **Hyper-Cardioid**

Figure of Eight **Omni**

Microphone polar diagrams or directivity patterns. A microphone is sensitive to sounds within its area of pick-up but in selecting one for a particular purpose consideration must also be given to how well it will reject unwanted sounds from another direction.

they afford in being adjustable to meet particular needs.

The closer a microphone is placed to an instrument the greater the relative balance between it and the sounds from other sources. However while separation is improved, other effects have to be considered:

1. The pick-up of sound very close to an instrument may be of inferior musical quality. It can be uneven across the frequency range or sound 'rough' due to the reproduction of harmonics not normally heard. There may be an undue emphasis of finger noise or the instrument's mechanical action.
2. The volume of sound may produce overload distortion in the microphone, or subsequently.

3. Movement of the player relative to the microphone becomes very critical, causing significant variations in both the quantity and quality of the sound.
4. Close microphone techniques require more microphones and more mixing channels thus increasing the complexity of the operation and the possibility of error.

The choice and placing of microphones around individual instruments is a matter of skill and judgement by the recording engineer. But no matter how complex the technical operation, the producer must also be aware of other considerations. He must not allow the changing of microphones, alterations to the layout, the running of cables or audio feeds to interfere unduly with the music-making or human relations aspects. It is possible

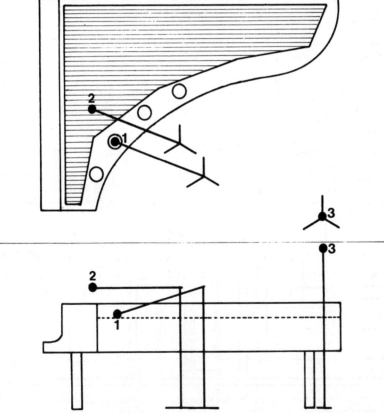

Piano balance. Typical microphones for different styles of music. 1. Emphasises percussive quality for pop music and jazz. 2. Broader intermediate position for light music. 3. Full piano sound for recitals and other serious or classical music.

to be technically so pedantic as to inhibit the performance. If major changes in the studio arrangements are required, it is much better to do them while the musicians are given a break. Under these circumstances the broadcaster has an obvious additional responsibility to safeguard instruments left in the studio.

The ultimate in separation is to do away with the microphone altogether. This is possible with certain electric instruments where their output is available via an appropriately terminated lead, as well as acoustically for the benefit of the player and other musicians. The lead should be connected through a 'direct inject' box to a normal microphone input cable. Detailed in the diagram, a D/I box is essentially a high impedance to 600 ohms matching and isolating transformer, which bridges across the

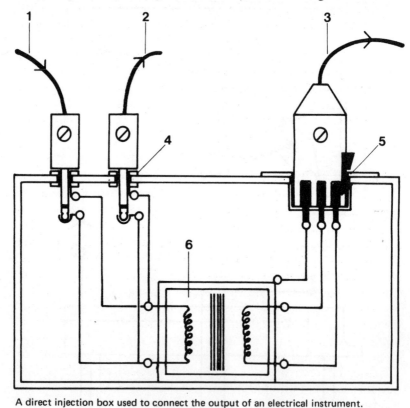

A direct injection box used to connect the output of an electrical instrument.
1. electrical output of instrument; 2. supply to musician's amplifier for his own acoustic reproduction; 3. output, as source for mixer channel via normal microphone connection; 4. 2-pole Jack (unbalanced); 5. 3-pole mic connector (balanced); 6. matching and isolating transformer.

222

input of the instrument's amplifier and correctly terminates the input to the microphone channel. Used particularly in conjunction with electric guitars, the box obviates the hum, rattles and resonances often associated with the alternative method, namely placing a microphone in front of the instrument's loudspeaker.

A further point in the use of any electrically powered instrument is that it should be connected to a studio power socket through a mains isolating transformer. This will protect the power supply in the event of a failure within the instrument and will exclude the possibility of an electrocution accident — so long as the studio equipment and the individual instrument are correctly wired and properly earthed. Faulty wiring or earthing arrangements can cause an accident for example in the event of a performer touching simultaneously two 'earths' ('grounds') — his instrument and a microphone stand — which in fact are at a different potential. While comparatively rare it is a matter which needs attention in the broadcasting of amateur pop groups using their own equipment.

A number of techniques may be applied to individual sound sources, some of which may affect the separation. The main techniques are frequency control, dynamic control and echo.

Frequency control

The tone quality can be altered by the emphasis or suppression of a given portion of the frequency spectrum. A singer's voice is given added 'presence' and clarity of diction is improved by a lift in the frequency response in the octave between 2.8 kHz and 5.6 kHz. A string section can be 'thickened' and made 'warmer' by an increase in the lower and middle frequencies, while brass is given greater 'attack' and a sharper edge by some 'top lift'. It should be noted however that in effectively making the microphone for the brass section more sensitive to the higher frequencies, spill-over from the cymbals is likely to increase and separation in this direction is therefore reduced. Fairly savage frequency control is often aplied to jazz or rhythm piano to increase its percussive quality. It is also useful on a one-microphone balance, particularly on an outside broadcast, to reduce a pronounced resonance or other acoustic effect inherent in the hall.

Dynamic control

This can be applied automatically by inserting a compressor/limiter device in the individual microphone chain. Once set, the level obtained from any given source will remain constant – quiet passages remain audible, loud parts do not overload. It becomes impossible for the flute to be swamped by the brass. Because of the economics of popular music, commercial recording companies have attained a high degree of sophistication in the use of dynamic control. This is unlikely to be reached by broadcasters who are not able to go to such lengths in recording their music. However devices of this type can save studio time and their progressive application is likely. Variations include a 'voice-over' facility which enables one source to take precedence over another. Originally intended for DJs, its obvious use is in relation to singers and other vocalists but it can be applied to any source relative to any other.

Echo

The various means of adding the echo effect more correctly described as reverberation are echo room, mechanical plate or spring, tape echo and digital delay line.

An *echo room* is a bare room with a live acoustic, often in the basement of the studio building. It contains a loudspeaker fed with the appropriate source, and facing away from it a microphone, mono or stereo as required, which will pick up the loudspeaker output after its reflection from the wall surfaces. The output of the microphone is returned to the mixing desk as the echo source. An echo room should also contain several small obstructions – such as disused or broken furniture – to break up the natural standing wave patterns. In the absence of a permanent installation, an echo room may be rigged in a reverberant stair well or lavatory, so long as it is not in use!

The output from the source can be made to vibrate a *mechanical plate or spring*, the vibrations travelling through it to a transducer which converts them back into electrical energy, returning as echo to the mixing desk. Equivalent to a two-dimensional room, the reverberation time is adjustable depending on the mechanical damping applied. Some such devices are in portable form and have useful OB applications.

A crude form of echo, known as *tape echo*, is possible by feeding an output to a studio tape machine which records it;

224

the playback head reproducing it a moment later acting as the echo source. The actual delay will depend on the tape speed and the distance between the record and replay heads. Recording machines designed expressly to produce reverberation effects have several replay heads with variable spacing to avoid the 'flutter' which can occur when all the sound is returned after a single constant delay.

An electronic device, called a *digital delay line*, breaks up the input fed into it, reprocessing the signal to form an

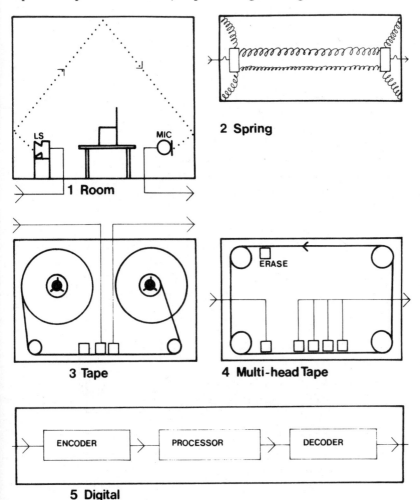

Methods of creating echo. Echo device is fed with a programme signal which it delays. The reverberant output is returned to the mixing desk.

output comprising several components each delayed by a different amount. This output returns to the mixing desk as the echo source. Again, this is a portable device.

A small radio station lacking, or not often needing, specialist facilities, can obtain very acceptable echo at little cost by using the tape delay method in conjunction with an echo spring. The two in series, with the tape first, will produce an extremely effective 'commercial' sound. This method is especially flexible when preceded by a frequency control device that reduces the bass in the system. When echo is added to a singer's voice, it is wise to let him hear the effect since he will almost certainly want to adjust his phrasing to suit the new acoustic.

Mixing technique

Before mixing a multi-microphone balance, each channel should be checked for delivering its correct source, with adequate separation from its neighbours, having the desired amount of 'treatment', and producing a clear distortion-free sound. It is a sensible procedure to label the channel faders with the appropriate source information — solo vocal, piano, trumpets and so on. For a stereo balance a plan has to be drawn up for the placing of each instrument in the stereo picture. Stereo microphones have their 'width' adjusted to spread their output across the required area of the picture, and the mono microphone 'pan pots' set so that their placing coincides with that provided by any stereo microphone also covering the same source. It is possible to create a stereo balance using only

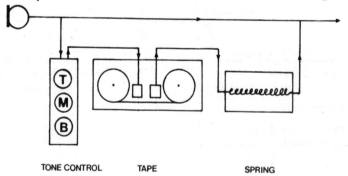

TONE CONTROL   TAPE   SPRING

An echo side-chain. The tone control filters, the tape recorder delays and the spring reverberates. The resultant output is mixed into the main programme circuit to form an original echo effect.

monophonic microphones by 'spotting' them carefully across the stereo picture, but it is an advantage to have at least one genuine stereo channel, even if it is only the echo source.

Microphones should be mixed first in their 'family' groups. The rhythm section, strings or brass, is individually mixed to obtain an internal balance. The sections are then added to each other to obtain an overall mix. Large music desks allow their channels to be grouped together so that sections can be balanced relative to each other by the operation of their 'group' fader without disturbing the individual channel faders. Successful mixing requires a logical progression for if all the faders are opened to begin with, the resulting confusion can be such that it is very difficult to identify problems. It is important to arrive at a trial balance fairly quickly since the ear will rapidly become accustomed to almost anything. The overall control is then

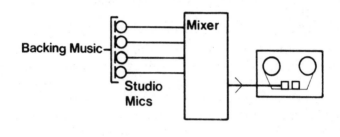

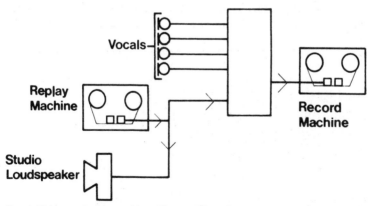

Overdubbing or double tracking. The musicians first record a 'backing track'. This is then replayed so that it is heard on the studio loudspeaker (or headphones) while at the same time mixed with the output of the studio microphones. In this example the final recording consists of 8 performances although of course the process can be repeated further.

adjusted so that the maximum level does not exceed the permitted limit.

The prime requirement for a satisfying music balance is that there should be a proper relationship between melody, harmony and rhythm. Since the group is not internally balanced, listening on the studio floor will not indicate the required result. Only the person with his hands on the faders and listening to the loudspeaker is in a position to arrive at a final result. The melody will almost certainly be passed around the group, and this will need very precise manipulation of the faders. If the strings take the tune from an up-beat, their faders must be opened further *from that point* – no earlier otherwise the perspective will alter. At the end of that section the faders must be returned to their normal position to avoid loss of separation. It is probable that alterations to a source making use of echo will need a corresponding and simultaneous variation in the echo return channel. It is a considerable help therefore to have an elementary music score or 'lead sheet' which indicates which instrument has the melody at any one time. If this is not provided by the musical director, the producer should ensure that notes are taken at the rehearsal – for example how many choruses there are of a song, at what point the trumpets put their mutes in, and perhaps more importantly, when they take them out again, when the singer's microphone has to be 'live' and so on. A professional music balance operator quickly develops a flair for reacting to the unexpected but as with most aspects of broadcasting, some basic preparation is only sensible.

It is important that faders that are opened to accentuate a particular instrument must afterwards be closed to their normal setting. Unless this is done it will be found that all the faders are gradually becoming further and further open with a compensating reduction of the overall control. This is clearly counter-productive and leads to a restriction in flexibility as the channels run out of 'headroom'.

As with all music balance work, the mixing must not take place only under conditions of high level monitoring. The purpose of having the loudspeaker turned well up is so that even small blemishes can be detected and corrected. But from time to time the listening level must be reduced to domestic proportions to check particularly the balance of vocals against the backing, and the acceptable level of applause. The ear has a logarithmic response to volume and is far from being equally sensitive to all the frequencies of the musical spectrum. This means that the perceived relationship between the loudness of different frequencies heard at high level is not the same as when heard at a lower level. Unless the loudspeaker is used with domestic listening in mind as well as for professional monitoring there will be a tendency as far as the listener at home is concerned to underbalance the echo, the bass, and the extreme top frequencies.

Recording technique

The successful handling of a music session requires the co-operation of everyone involved. There are several ways of actually getting the material recorded and the procedure to be adopted should be agreed at the outset.

The first method is obviously to treat a recording in the same way as a live transmission. One starts when the red light goes on and continues until it goes out. This will be the procedure at a public concert when, for example, no retakes are possible.

Secondly, a studio session with an audience present. Minor faults in the performance or mixing will be allowed to pass but the producer must decide when something has occurred that necessitates a retake. The audience may be totally unaware of the problem but he will have lightly and briefly to explain the existence of 'a gremlin' and detail quickly to the musical director the need to retake from point A to point B.

Thirdly, without an audience the musicians can agree to use the time as thought best. This may be to rehearse all the material and then to record it, or to rehearse and record each individual item. In either case breaks can be taken as and when decided by the producer in consultation with the musical director.

Fourthly, to record the most material in the shortest time or to accommodate special requirements, the music may be 'multi-tracked'. This means that instead of arriving at a final mix, the individual instruments, or groups of channels, are recorded on to separate tracks on the tape. These are subsequently mixed in a 'reduction' session without the performers present. The facility to multi-track enables musicians to record their contribution without the necessity of having everyone present. It also permits 'doubling', that is, the performing of more than one role in the same piece of music. This double-tracking is

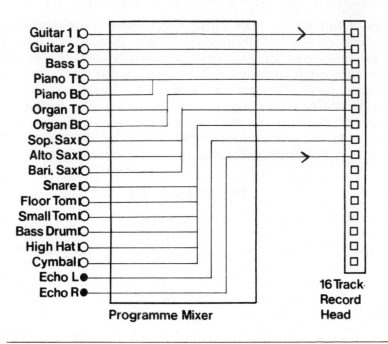

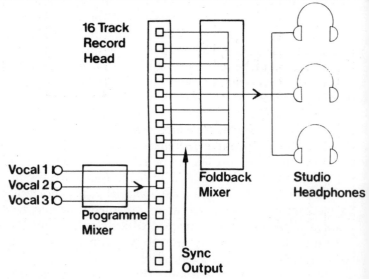

Multi-track recording. In this example the 18 original sources are first recorded as 9 separate tracks. A further 3 vocal tracks are then added, the singers listening to the output of the record heads to maintain synchronisation. The 12 tracks are subsequently mixed together in a reduction session to make the final recording.

most often used for an instrumental group who also sing. The musicians first play the music — either conventionally recorded or multi-tracked, and when this is played back to them on headphones in the form of a 'sync output' actually generated by the record heads, they add the vocal parts. These are recorded on separate tracks or mixed with the music tracks to form a final recording. The process can be repeated to enable singers to sing with themselves as many times as is required to create the

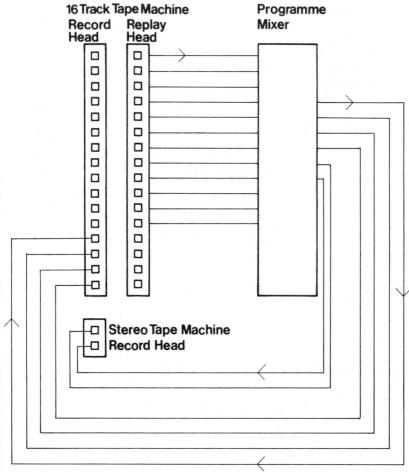

Multi-track reduction. In this example the 12 tracks are mixed to form two separate outputs. The first is in 4 channels for quadraphonic reproduction and is recorded on the remaining 'empty' tape tracks. These recordings are not synchronous with tracks 1-12. The second is a stereo output recorded separately. The advantage of a separate reduction session is that the final mix may be attempted any number of times without keeping the musicians waiting.

desired sound. An added advantage of multi-tracking is that any mistake does not spoil the whole performance — a retake may only be required to correct the individual error.

Since recording at different times represents total separation, multi-tracking techniques can solve other problems. For instance the physical separation or screening of loud instruments such as a drum kit. It is therefore a useful technique to apply to music recording which has to be done in a small non purpose-built studio.

Unless special noise reduction facilities are employed, the re-recording of tape tracks will increase the hiss level on the final recording. It is essential therefore that the best equipment is used and the original recordings are made at the highest tape speed available.

Other production points

Essentially the producer's job is to obtain a satisfactory end product within the time available. He should avoid running into overtime which with professional musicians is expensive. Neither should he be an oppressively hard taskmaster so that the session ends with time to spare, and everyone is relieved to get out. The producer must remember that all artists need encouragement and he has a positive duty to contribute to their giving the best performance possible.

He avoids using the general talkback into the studio to make disparaging comments about individual performers. Instead, he directs all his remarks to the conductor or group leader via a special headphone feed, or better still by going into the studio for a personal talk.

He fosters a professionally friendly atmosphere and sounds relaxed even when under pressure. He anticipates the need for breaks and rest periods.

He avoids displaying a musical knowledge which, while attempting to impress, is based on uncertain foundations. "Can we have a shade more 'arco' on the trombones?" is a guaranteed credibility loser.

He makes careful rehearsal notes for the recording or transmission, and takes details of the final timings and any retakes for subsequent editing.

When an audience is present he decides how they are best

handled and what kind of introduction and warm-up is appropriate.

He resolves the various conflicts which arise — whether the air conditioning is working properly, whether the lights are too bright or whether the banging in another part of the building can be stopped.

When a retake is required, he makes a positive decision and communicates it quickly to the musical director. The producer exercises the broadcaster's normal editorial judgement and is responsible for the quality of the final programme.

He ensures that the musicians are paid — those performers who signed a contract and made the music and, through the appropriate agencies, those who wrote, arranged and published the work still in copyright.

After the session he says thank you — to everyone.

18

DRAMA – SOME PRINCIPLES

THE radio medium has a long and distinguished history of turning thoughts, words and actions into satisfying pictures within the listener's mind by using the techniques of drama. But there is no need for the producer to think only in terms of the Shakespeare play – the principles of radio drama apply to the well made commercial, a programme trail, dramatised reading, five-minute serial or two-minute teaching point in a programme for schools. Since the size and scope of the pictures created are limited only by the minds which devise and interpret them, the medium in its relationship to drama is unique, and any radio service is the poorer for not attempting to work in this area.

As an illustration of the effective simplicity of the use of sound alone, listen now to the well known example by Stan Freberg who gave it as part of his argument for selling advertising time on radio.

MAN: Radio? Why should I advertise on radio? There's nothing to look at . . . no pictures.

GUY: Listen, you can do things on radio you couldn't possibly do on TV.

MAN: That'll be the day.

GUY: Ah huh. All right, watch this. (Clears throat). O.K. people, now when I give you the cue, I want the 700-foot mountain of whipped cream to roll into Lake Michigan which has been drained and filled with hot chocolate. Then the Royal Canadian Air Force will fly overhead towing the 10-ton maraschino cherry which will be dropped into the whipped cream, to the cheering of 25,000 extras. All right . . . cue the mountain . . .

SOUND: GROANING AND CREAKING OF MOUNTAIN INTO BIG SPLASH

GUY: Cue the Air Force!

SOUND: DRONE OF MANY PLANES

GUY: Cue the maraschino cherry . . .

SOUND: WHISTLE OF BOMB INTO BLOOP! OF CHERRY HITTING
         WHIPPED CREAM

GUY: Okay, twenty-five thousand cheering extras . . .

SOUND: ROAR OF MIGHTY CROWD. SOUND BUILDS UP AND CUTS OFF
         SHARP!

GUY: Now . . . you wanta try that on television?
MAN: Well . . .
GUY: You see . . . radio is a very special medium, because it
         stretches the imagination.
MAN: Doesn't television stretch the imagination?
GUY: Up to 21 inches, yes.

Courtesy Freberg Ltd.

The aim with all dramatic writing is for the original ideas to be
re-created in the listener's mind and since the end result occurs
purely within the imagination, there are few limitations of size,
reality, place, mood, time or speed of transition. Unlike the
visual arts where the scenery is provided directly, the listener
to radio supplies his own mental images in response to the
information he is given. If the 'signposts' are too few or of the
wrong kind, the listener becomes disorientated and cannot
follow what is happening. If there are too many the result is
likely to be obvious and 'corny'. Neither will satisfy. The
writer must therefore be especially sensitive to how his audience
is likely to react – and since the individual images may stem
largely from personal experience, of which the writer of course
knows nothing, this is not easy. But it is the ageless art of the
storyteller – saying enough to allow listeners to follow the
thread but not so much that they do not want to know what is
to happen next or cannot make their own contribution.

   The writer must have a thorough understanding of the medium
and the production process, while the producer needs a firm
grasp of the writing requirements. If they are not one and the

236

same person, there must be a strong collaboration. There can be no isolation, but if there is to be a dividing line, let the writer put everything down knowing how it is to sound, while the producer turns this into the reality of a broadcast knowing how it is to be 'seen' in the mind's eye.

The component parts with which both are working are speech, music, sound effects, and silence.

The idea

Before committing anything to paper, it is essential to think through the basic ideas of plot and form – once these are decided, a great deal follows naturally. The first question is to do with the material's suitability for the audience, the second with its technical feasibility.

Assuming that the writer is starting from scratch and not adapting an existing play, he should be clear as to his broad intention – to make people laugh, to comment on or explain a contemporary situation, to convey a message, to tell a story, to entertain. How can he best enable the listener to 'connect' with his intention? Does he want him to identify with one of the characters? Should the basic situation be one with which the listener can easily relate? This does not mean that plays can only be set in the same domestic circumstances as that of the audience, far from it. But it does assume that whether the scene is in the royal household of ancient Egypt, or in a space capsule journeying to a distant planet, the listener will meet people he can recognise – fallible, courageous, argumentative, greedy, compassionate and so on. It follows therefore that characterisation is important and it is often useful before beginning a play to sketch out a 'pen portrait' of each character. This helps to stabilise them as people and it becomes easier to give them convincing dialogue. In radio, a person's character is expressed almost entirely by what he says and how he says it.

The second point at this initial stage is to know whether the play has to be written within certain technical or cost limitations. To do something simple and well is preferable to failing with something complicated. There seems little point in writing a play which calls for six sound effects turntables, echo, a variety of acoustics, distorted voice over, and a crowd chanting specific lines of script, if the studio facilities are not able to meet these demands. Of course with ingenuity even a simple studio can provide most if not all of these devices. But the most crucial factor is often simply a shortage of time. There may be limitations too in the capabilities of the talent available. The writer for example should beware creating a part which is emotionally exceptionally demanding only to hear it inadequately performed. Writing for the amateur or child actor can be very rewarding in the surprises which their creative flowering may bring, but it can also be frustrating if you automatically transfer into the script the demands and standards of the professional stage.

Thus the writer must know at the outset how to tailor his play for the medium, what he is attempting to put over, how he expects his audience to relate to the material, and whether what he wants is technically and financially possible.

Construction

The simplest way of telling a story is to:

1. Explain the situation.
2. Introduce 'conflict'.
3. Develop the action.
4. Resolve the conflict.

Of course there will be complications and sub-plots but the essence of a good story is to want to find out 'what happens in the end'. Who committed the crime? Were the lovers reunited? Did the cavalry arrive in time? The element which tends to interest us most is the resolution of conflict and since this comes at the end there should be no problem of maintaining interest once into the play.

The difficulties lie in the earlier expository stages. In radio scenes can be shorter than in the theatre, and intercutting between different situations is a simple matter of keeping the listener informed about where he is at any one time. This ability to move quickly in terms of location should be used positively to achieve a variety and contrast which itself adds interest. The impact of a scene involving a group of fear-stricken people faced with impending disaster is heightened by its direct juxtaposition with another, but related, group unaware of the danger. If the rate of intercutting becomes progressively faster and the scenes shorter, the pace of the play increases. This sense of acceleration or at least of movement, may be in the plot itself

238

but a writer can inject greater excitement or tension simply in his handling of the scene length and in their relation to one another. Thus the overall shape of the play may be a steady development of its progress, heightening and increasing. Or it may revolve around the stop-go tempo of successive components. Interest through contrast may be obtained by a variety of means, for example:

1. Change of pace: fast/slow action, noisy/quiet locations, long/short scenes.
2. Change of mood: tense/relaxed atmosphere, angry/happy, tragic/dispassionate.
3. Change of place: indoors/open air, crowded/deserted, opulent/poverty stricken.

The radio writer is concerned with images created by sound alone; if he wants colour and mood he must paint them with the words he uses and choose locations that are aurally evocative.

On a personal note to illustrate the impact of contrast within a play, I recall a moment from a drama on the life of Christ. The violence and anger of the crowd demanding his execution is progressively increased, the shouting grows more vehement. Then we hear the Roman soldiers, the hammering of nails and the agony of the crucifixion. Human clamour gives way to a deeper, darker sense of tragedy and doom. Christ's last words are uttered, a crash of thunder through to a climax of discordant music gradually subsiding, quietening to silence. A pause. Then slowly – bird song.

How wrong it would have been to spoil that contrast by using the narrator, as elsewhere in the play.

Dialogue

"Look out, he's got a gun". Lines like this, unnecessary in film, television or theatre where the audience can see that he has a gun, are essential in radio as a means of conveying information. The difficulty is that such 'point' lines can so easily sound contrived and false. All speech must be the natural colloquial talk of the character by whom it is uttered. In reproducing a contemporary situation, a writer can do no better than to take his notebook to the market place or cocktail party and observe what people actually say, and their manner of saying it.

Producers should beware writers who preface a scene with stage directions: the scene is set in a lonely castle in the Scottish Highlands. A fire is roaring in the grate. Outside a storm is brewing. The Laird and his visitor enter.

Such 'picture setting' designed for the reader rather than the listener should be crossed out and the dialogue considered in isolation. If the words themselves create the same scene, the directions are superfluous; if not, the dialogue is faulty.

Laird: (Approaching) Come in, come in. It looks like a storm is on the way.

Visitor: (Approaching) Thank you. I'm afraid you're right. It was starting to rain on the last few miles of my journey.

Laird: Well come and warm yourself by the fire; we don't get many visitors.

Visitor: You are a bit off the beaten track, but since I was in the Highlands and've always been fascinated by castles I thought I would call in – I hope you don't mind.

Laird: Not at all, I get a bit lonely by myself.

Visitor: (Rubbing hands) Ah, that's better. This is a lovely room – is this oak panelling as old as it looks?

etc. etc.

The producer is able to add considerably to such a scene in its casting, in the voices used – for example in the age and accents of the two characters, and whether the mood is jovial or sinister.

In addition to visual information, character and plot, the dialogue must remind us from time to time of who is speaking to whom. Anyone 'present' must either be given a line or be referred to, so that they can be included in the listener's mental picture.

Andrew: Look John, I know I said I wouldn't mention it but . . . well something's happened I think you should know about.

John: What is it Andrew? What's happened?

The use of names within the dialogue is particularly important at the beginning of the scene.

Characters should also refer to the situation not within the immediate picture so that the listener's imagination is equipped with all the relevant information.

Robins: . . . And how precisely do you propose to escape? There are guards right outside the door, and more at the entrance of the block. Even if we got outside, there's a barbed wire fence two storeys high – and it's all patrolled by dogs, I've heard them. I tell you there isn't a chance.

Jones: But aren't you forgetting something – something rather obvious?

An obvious point which the writer does not forget is that radio is not only blind, but unless the drama is in stereo, it is half deaf as well. Movement and distance have to be indicated, either in the acoustic or other production technique, or in the dialogue. Here are three examples:

- (off mic) I think I've found it, come over here.
- Look there they are – down there on the beach. They must be half a mile away by now.
- (softly) I've often thought of it like this – really close to you.

We shall return later to the question of creating the effects of perspective in the studio.

To achieve a flow to the play, consecutive scenes can be made to link one into the other. The dialogue at the end of one scene pointing forward to the next.

Voice 1: Well, I'll see you on Friday – and remember to bring the stuff with you.

Voice 2: Don't worry, I'll be there.

Voice 1: Down by the river then, at 8 o'clock – and mind you're not late.

If this is then followed by the sound of water, we can assume that the action has moved forward to the Friday and that we are down by the river. The actual junction is most often through a fade out of the last line – a line incidentally, like the second half of the one in this last example, words we can afford to miss. There is a moment's pause, and a fade up on the first line of the new scene. Other methods are by direct cutting without fades, or possibly through a music link. The use of a narrator will almost always overcome difficulties of transition so long as the script avoids clichés of the 'meanwhile, back at the ranch' type.

Narrator: Shortly afterwards, Betty died and John, now destitute and friendless, was forced to beg on the streets in order to keep himself from starvation. Then one afternoon, ragged and nearing desparation, he was recognised by an old friend.

A narrator is particularly useful in explaining a large amount of background information which might be unduly tedious in conversational form or where considerable compressions have to be made, for example in adapting a book as a radio play. In these circumstances the narrator can be used to help preserve the style and flavour of the original, especially in those parts which have a good deal of exposition and description but little action.

When in doubt, the experienced writer will almost certainly follow the simplest course remembering that the listener will appreciate most what he can readily understand.

Script layout

Following the normal standard of scripts intended for broadcast use, the page should be typed on one side only to minimise handling noise, the paper being of a firm 'non-rustle' type. The lines should be triple spaced to allow room for alterations and actors' notes, and each speech numbered for easy reference. Directions, or details of sound effects and music should be bracketed, underlined, or in capitals so that they stand out clearly from the dialogue. The reproduction of scripts should be absolutely clear and there should be plenty of copies so that spares are available.

The following is an example of page layout:

1. BRADY: Why isn't Harris here yet? — you people at the Foreign Office seem to think everyone has got time to waste.

2. SALMON: I don't know Colonel, it's not like him to be late.

1. BRADY: Well it's damned inconsiderate, I've a good

mind to . . . (KNOCK AT DOOR)

2. SALMON: (RELIEVED) That's probably him.
(GOING OFF)
I'll let him in (DOOR OPENS OFF)

3. HARRIS (OFF) Hallo John.

4. SALMON: (OFF) thank goodness you've arrived. We've

been waiting some time. (APPROACH)

Colonel Brady I don't think you've met

Nigel Harris. He's our representative . . .

5. BRADY: (INTERRUPTING) I know perfectly well

who he is, what I want to know is where

he's been.

6. HARRIS: Well, I've been trying to get us out of

trouble. It's bad news I'm afraid. The money

we had ready for the deal has gone, and

Holden has disappeared.

7. BRADY: This is preposterous! Are you suggesting

he's taken it?

243

1. HARRIS: I'm not suggesting anything Colonel but we
                know that last night he was at Victoria
                Station, — and bought a ticket for Marseilles.

2. SALMON: Marseilles? By train?

3. HARRIS: By train. At this moment I should think he,
                and the money, are half-way across Europe.

                TRAIN WHISTLE APPROACH AND
                ROAR OF TRAIN PASSING. CROSS-
                FADE TO INTERIOR TRAIN RHYTHM
                CONTINUES UNDERNEATH.

4. STEWARD: (APPROACHING) Take your last sitting for
                lunch please.
                (CLOSER) Last sitting for lunch. Merci
                Madame.

                COMPARTMENT DOOR SLIDES OPEN.

                (CLOSE) Last sitting for lunch Sir. Excusez
                moi Monsieur, — will you be wanting lunch?
                Monsieur?

244

(TO SELF) C'est formidable. Quite a sleeper.
(LOUDER) Excuse me Sir, — Allow me to
remove the newspaper (PAPER RUSTLE).
Will you be . . . (GASP) Oh . . . Terrible . . .
Terrible.

TRAIN NOISE PASSING AND FADES
INTO DISTANCE.
PHONE RINGS. RECEIVER PICKED UP.
RINGING STOPS.

1. BRADY: Hello.

2. VOICE: (DISTORT) Is that Colonel Brady?

3. BRADY: Yes. Who's that?

4. VOICE: (DISTORT) It doesn't matter but I thought
              you ought to know he's dead.

5. BRADY: Who's dead? Who is this?

6. VOICE: (DISTORT) Oh you know who's dead
              all right, — and I've got the money.

1. BRADY: You've got what money? Who are you?

2. VOICE: You'll know soon enough. I'll be in touch . . .

      TELEPHONE CLICK. DIALLING TONE.

3. BRADY: Hello, Hello . . . oh blast it.

      RECEIVER SLAMMED DOWN.

      OFFICE INTERCOM BUZZER.

4. SECRETARY: (DISTORT) Yes Sir?

5. BRADY: Joan, I want you to get hold of Salmon and

      Harris — can you do that?

6. SECRETARY: (DISTORT) Yes Sir — they went back to

      the Foreign Office.

7. BRADY: Well I want them — at once. And get me on

      tonight's plane, — to Marseilles.

      MUSIC TO END.

The actors

Casting a radio drama, whether it is a one hour play or a short illustration will nearly always end by being a compromise between who is suitable and who is available. Naturally, the producer will want the best performers but this is not always possible within the constraints of money. It is also difficult to assemble an ideal cast at one place and possibly at several times for rehearsal and recording, and this to coincide with the availability of studio space. Again, it may be that two excellent players are available, but their voices are too similar to be used in the same play. So there are several factors which will determine the final cast.

Actors new to radio have to recognise the limitations of the typewriter, a machine designed to place words in clearly readable lines on the page. It cannot overlay words in the same way that voices can, and do.

Voice one: The cost of this project is going to be 3 or 4 million – and that's big money by anyone's reckoning.

Voice two: But that's rubbish, why I could do the job for . . .

Voice one: (Interrupting) Don't tell me it's rubbish, anyway that's the figure and it's going ahead.

Although this is what might appear on the page, voice two is clearly going to react to the cost of the project immediately on hearing the figures – half way through voice one's first line. The script writer may insert at that point (react) or (intake of breath) but generally it is best left to the imagination of the actor. Actors sometimes need to be persuaded to act, and not to become too script bound. Then voice one interrupts. This does not mean that he waits until voice two has finished his previous line before starting with the "Don't tell me . . ." He starts well before voice two breaks off, say on the word 'could'. The two voices will overlay each other for a few words thereby sounding more natural. Real conversation does this all the time.

On the matter of voice projection, the normal speaking range over a conversational distance will suffice – intimate and confidential, to angry and hysterical. As the apparent distance is increased, so the projection also increases. In the following example, the actor goes over to the door and ends the line with more projection than he was using at the start. The voice gradually rises in pitch throughout the speech.

Voice: Well I must go. (DEPARTS) I shan't be long but there are several things I must do. (DOOR OPENS, OFF) I'll be back as soon as I can. Goodbye. (DOOR SHUTS).

In moving to the 'dead' side of the microphone the actor's actual movement may have been no more than a metre (3 feet). The aural impression given may be a retreat of at least five metres (16 feet). It is important that such 'moves' are made only during spoken dialogue otherwise the actor will appear to have 'jumped' from a near to a distant position. Of course moving off-mic, which increases the ratio of reflected to direct sound, can only serve to give an impression of distance in an interior scene.

When the setting is in the open air, there is no reflected sound and distance has to be achieved by a combination of the actor's higher voice projection and the small volume derived from a low setting of the microphone channel fader. By this means it is possible to have a character shouting to us from 'over there', having a conversation with another person 'in the foreground' who is shouting back. Such a scene requires considerable manipulation of the microphone fader with no overlay of the voices. A preferred alternative is to have both actors in separate rooms, each with his own microphone and with a headphone feed of the mixed output.

The acoustic

In any discussion of monophonic perspective, distance is a function which separates characters in the sense of being near or

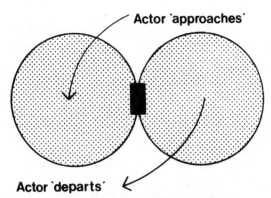

The shaded circles are the normal areas of pick-up on both sides of a bi-dimensional microphone. An Actor 'approaching' says his lines as he moves from the dead side to the live side, reducing his voice projection as he dces so. Effective for indoor scenes.

far. The producer must always know where the listener is placed relative to the overall picture. Generally, but not necessarily, 'with' the microphone, the listener placed in a busily dynamic scene will need some information which distinguishes his following the action by moving through the scene, from his simply watching it from a static position.

Part of this distinction may be in the use of an acoustic which itself changes. Accompanied by the appropriate sound effects a move out of a reverberant courtroom into a small ante-room, or from the street into a telephone box, can be highly effective. There are four basic acoustics comprising the combinations of the quantity, and duration of the reflected sound:

1. No reverberation   outdoor   created by fully absorbent 'dead' studio.

2. Little reverberation but long reverberation time   library or large well-furnished room   bright acoustic or a little reverberation added to normal studio.

3. Much reverberation but short reverberation time   telephone box, bathroom   small enclosed space of reflective surfaces — 'boxy' acoustic.

4. Much reverberation and long reverberation time.   cave, 'Royal Palace', concert hall   artificial echo added to normal studio output.

Frequency discrimination applied to the output of the echo device will add the distinctive colouration of a particular acoustic. The characteristic of a normal drama studio with a 'neutral' acoustic would limit the reverberation time to about 0.2 seconds. Associated with this would be a 'bright' area with a reverberation time of, say 0.6 seconds, and a separate cubicle for a narrator. The key factor is flexibility so that by using screens, curtains and carpet, a variety of acoustic environments may be produced.

Sound effects

When the curtain rises on a theatre stage the scenery is

immediately obvious and the audience is given all the contextual information it requires for the play to start. So it is with radio, except that to achieve an unambiguous impact the sounds must be refined and simplified to those few which really carry the message. The equivalent of the theatre's 'backdrop' are those sounds which run throughout a scene — for example rain, conversation at a party, traffic noise or the sounds of battle. These are most likely to be pre-recorded and reproduced from records or tape. The 'incidental furniture' and 'props' are those effects which are specially placed to suit the action — for instance dialling a telephone, pouring a drink, closing a door or firing a gun. Such sounds are best made in the studio at the time of the appropriate dialogue, if possible by the actors themselves — for example lighting a cigarette or taking a drink, but by someone else if hands are not free due to their holding a script.

The temptation for a producer new to drama is to use too many effects. While it is true that in the real world the sounds we hear are many and complex, radio drama in this respect purveys not what is real but what is understandable. It is possible to record genuine sounds which divorced from their visual reality convey nothing at all. The sound of a modern car drawing up has very little impact, yet it may be required to carry the dramatic turning point of the play! In the search for clear associations between situation and sound, radio over the years has developed conventions with generally understood meanings. The urgently stopping car virtually demands a screech of tyres, slamming doors and running footsteps. It becomes a little larger than life. Overdone, and it becomes comical.

Some other sounds which have become immediately understood are:

1. Passage of time — clock ticking
2. Night time — owl hooting.
3. On the coast — seagulls and seawash.
4. On board sailing ship — creaking of ropes.
5. Early morning — cock crowing.
6. Out of doors, rural — birdsong.

The convention for normal movement is to do without footsteps. These are only used to underline a specific dramatic point.

Background sounds may or may not be audible to the actors in the studio, depending on the technical facilities available. It is important however for actors to know what they are up against, and any background sounds should be played over to them to help them visualise the scene and judge their level of projection. This is particularly important if the sounds are noisy — the cockpit of a light aircraft, a fairground or battle. If an actor has to react to a sound reproduced from a record or tape he will require a feed of the output either to his headphones or through a loudspeaker. Such a speaker remains on even though the studio microphones are 'live' and is therefore different from the normal arrangement. This facility is called

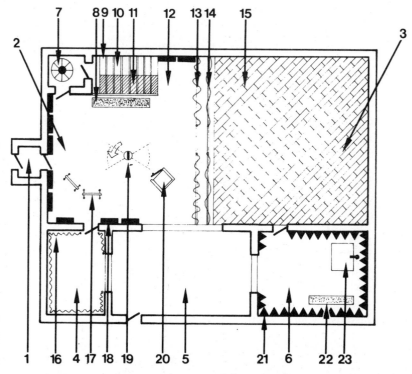

Features of a drama studio. 1. Entrance through sound lobby. 2. Studio 'dead' end. 3. Studio 'live' end. 4. Narrator's studio. 5. Control cubicle with windows to all other areas. 6. Dead room — outdoor acoustics. 7. Spiral staircase — iron. 8. Gravel trough. 9. Sound effects staircase. 10. Cement tread stairs. 11. Wooden tread stairs. 12. Carpet floor. 13. Soft curtain drapes. 14. 'Hard' curtain — canvas or plastic. 15. Wood block floor. 16. Curtains. 17. Moveable acoustic screen. 18. Acoustic absorber — wall box. 19. Bi-directional microphone. 20. Sound effects door. 21. Acoustic wedges — highly absorbent surface. 22. Sand or gravel trough. 23. Water tank.

foldback, and has the advantage not only that the cast can hear the effects, but that any sounds reproduced in this way and picked up on the studio microphone will share the same acoustic as the actors' voices. Producers working in drama will soon establish their own methods of manufacturing studio sounds. The following are some which have saved endless time and trouble:

1. Walking through undergrowth or jungle – a bundle of recording tape rustled in the hands.
2. Walking through snow – a roll of cotton wool squeezed and twisted in the hands, or two blocks of salt rubbed together.
3. Horses' hooves – halved coconut shells are still the best from pawing the ground to a full gallop. They take practice though. A bunch of keys will produce the jingle of harness.
4. Pouring a drink – put a little water into the glass already so that the sound starts immediately the pouring begins.
5. Opening champagne – any good sound man ought to be able to make a convincing 'pop' with his mouth, otherwise blow a cork from a sawn-off bicycle pump. A little water poured on to Alka-Seltzer tablets or fruit salts close on-mic should do the rest.
6. A building on fire – cellophane from a cigarette packet rustled on-mic plus the breaking of small sticks.
7. Marching troops – a marching box is simply a cardboard box approximately 20 x 10 x 5 cm, containing some small gravel. Held between the hands and shaken with precision it can execute drill movements to order.
8. Creaks – rusty bolts, chains or other hardware are worth saving for the appropriate aural occasion. A little resin put on a cloth and pulled tightly along a piece of string fastened to a resonator is worth trying.

The essential characteristic for all sound-making devices is that they should be simple, reliable and consistent. And if the precise effect cannot be achieved, it is worth remembering that by recording a sound and playing it back at a different speed, it can be altered in 'size' or made unrelatable to the known world. Hence the fantasy sounds varying from dinosaurs to outer space.

In making a plea for authenticity and accuracy, it is worth noting that such attention to detail saves a producer considerable letter writing to those among his audience who are only too ready to display their knowledge. Someone will know that the firing of the type of shot used in the American War of Independence had an altogether characteristic sound, of course certain planes used in the Australian Flying Doctor service had three engines not four, and whoever heard of an English cuckoo in February?! The producer must either avoid being too explicit, or he must be right.

Music

An ally to the resourceful producer, music can add greatly to the radio play. However if it is over-used or badly chosen, it becomes only an irritating distraction. The producer must decide in which of its various roles music is to be used:

1. As a 'leitmotif' to create an *overall style*. Opening and closing music plus its use within the play as links between some of the scenes will provide thematic continuity. The extracts are likely to be the same piece of music, or different passages from the same work, throughout.
2. Music chosen simply to *create mood* and establish the atmosphere of a scene. Whether it is 'haunted house' music or 'a day at the races', music should be chosen that is not so familiar that it arouses in the listener his own preconceived ideas and associations. In this respect it pays the producer to cultivate an awareness of the lesser known works in his record library.
3. Reiterative or relentless music can be used to mark the *passage of time*, thus heightening the sense of passing hours, or seconds. Weariness or monotony is economically reinforced.

In using music to be deliberately evocative of a particular time and place, the producer must be sure of his research. Songs of the first world war, or ballads of Elizabethan England — there is sure to be at least one expert listening ready to point out errors of instrumentation, words or date. To use a piano to set the mood of a time when there was only the harpsichord and virginals is to invite criticism.

The drama producer must not search automatically on the shelves of his library but should consider the use of specially written material. This need not be unduly ambitious or costly,

253

a simple recurring folk song, or theme played on a guitar or harmonica can be highly effective. There are considerable advantages in designing the musical style to suit the play, and having the music durations to fit the various introductions and voice-overs.

Production technique

Producers will devise their own methods and different plays may demand an individual approach, as will working with children or amateurs as opposed to professional actors. However the following is a practical outline of general procedure:

1. The producer works with the writer, or on the script alone re-writing for the medium, and making alterations to suit the transmission time available.
2. He casts the play, issues contracts, distributes copies of the script, arranges rehearsal or recording times.
3. He, or his team, assembles the sound effects, books the studio, arranges for any special technical facilities or acoustic requirements, and chooses the music.
4. The cast meets, not necessarily in the studio, for a read through. Awkward wordings may be altered to suit individual actors. The producer gives points of direction on the overall structure and shape of the play and the range of emotion required. This is to give everyone a general impression of the piece. Scripts are marked with additional information such as the use of cue lights.
5. In the studio, scenes are rehearsed on-mic, with detailed production points concerning inflection, pauses, pace, movement etc. The producer should be careful not to cause resentment by 'over-direction', particularly of professional actors. Sound effects from 'grams', tape or in the studio are added. The producer's main task is to encourage the actors and to listen carefully for any additional help they may need or for any blemish that should be eradicated.
6. As each scene is polished to its required perfection, a recording 'take' is made. Are the pictures conjured up at the original reading of the script being brought to life? Is the atmosphere, content and technical quality exactly right? Necessary retakes are made and the script marked accordingly.

7. The tape is edited using the best 'takes', removing fluffs and confirming the final duration.
8. The programme is placed in the transmission system and the remaining paperwork completed.

There are many variations on this pattern of working. For example to do away with the studio. If the play is suitable then for example the recording can be made out of doors among the back alleys and railway tracks of the city — a radio verité? Again, there is no need for the producer to think only in terms of the conventional play. A highly effective yet simple format is to use a narrator as the main storyteller with only the important action dialogue spoken by other voices. Few but vivid effects complement this radio equivalent of the strip cartoon — excellent as a children's serial.

A producer finding his way into the drama field is well advised to listen to as many radio plays and serials as possible. He will gather ideas and recognise the value of good words simply spoken.

In realising the printed page into an aural impression, he must not expect that the visual images in his mind at the start will be exactly translated into the end result. The actors are not puppets to be manipulated at will, they too are creative people and will want to make their own individual contribution. The finished play is an amalgam of many skills and talents, it is a 'hand-made', 'one-off' product which hopefully represents a richer experience than was envisaged by any one person at the outset.

19

DOCUMENTARY AND FEATURE PROGRAMMES

THE terms are often used as if they were interchangeable and there is some confusion as to their precise meaning. But here are exciting and creative areas of radio and because of the huge range which they cover, it is important that the listener knows exactly what it is he is being offered. The basic distinctions of type are to do with the initial selection and treatment of the source material. A documentary programme is wholly fact, based on documentary evidence – written records, attributable sources, contemporary interviews and the like. Its purpose is essentially to inform, to present a story or situation with a total regard for honest, balanced reporting. The feature programme on the other hand need not be wholly true in the factual sense, it may include folk song, poetry or fictional drama to help illustrate its theme. The feature is a very free form where the emphasis is often on portraying rather more indefinable human qualities, atmosphere or mood.

The distinctions are not always clear cut and a contribution to the confusion of terms is the existence of hybrids – the feature documentary, the semi-documentary, the drama documentary and so on.

It is often both necessary and desirable to produce programmes which are not simply factual, but are 'based on fact'. There will certainly be times when through lack of sufficient documentary evidence, a scene in a true story will have to be invented – no actual transcript exists of the conversations that took place during Columbus' voyage to the New World. Yet through his diaries and other contemporary records, enough is known to piece together an acceptable account which is valid in terms of reportage. While some compromise between what is established fact and what is reasonable surmise is understandable in dealing with the long perspective of history, it is important that there is no blurring of the edges in portraying contemporary issues. Fact and fiction are dangerous in combination and their boundaries must be clear to the listener. A programme dealing with a murder trial, for example, must keep to the record, to add fictional scenes is to confuse, perhaps to mislead. Nevertheless it is a perfectly admissable programme idea to interweave serious fact, even a court case, with contrasting fictional material, let us say songs and nursery rhymes; but it must be called a feature not a documentary. Ultimately what is important is not the subject or its treatment, but that we all understand what is meant by the terms used. It is essential that the listener knows the purpose of the broadcaster's programme – essentially the difference between what is true and what is not. If the producer sets out to provide a balanced, rounded, truthful account of something or someone – that is a documentary. If he does not feel so bound to the whole truth and his original intent is to give greater reign to the imagination, even though the source material is real – that is a feature.

The documentary

Very often subjects for programmes present themselves as ideas which suddenly become obvious. They are frequently to do with contemporary issues such as race relations, urban development, pollution and the environment, medical research. A programme might explore in detail a single aspect of one of these subjects which broadly attempts to examine how society copes with change. Other types of documentary deal with a single person, activity or event – the discovery of radium, the building of the Concorde aeroplane, the life of a notable figure or the work of a particular factory, theatre group or school.

Essentially these are all to do with people, and while statistical and historical fact is important, the crucial element is the human one – to underline motivation and help the listener understand why certain decisions were made, and what makes people 'tick'.

The main advantage of the documentary approach over that of the straightforward talk is that the subject is made more interesting and brought alive by involving more people, more voices and a greater range of treatment. It should entertain while it informs, and as it illuminates provoke further thought and concern.

Planning

Following on the initial idea is the question of how long the programme should be. It may be that the brief is to produce for a 30 minute or one hour slot, in which case the problem is one of selection, of finding the right amount of material. Given a subject that is too large for the time available, a producer has the choice either of dealing with the whole area fairly superficially, or reducing the topic range and taking a particular aspect in greater depth. It is for example, the difference between a 20 minute programme for schools on the life of Chopin, and the same duration or more devoted to the events leading up to his writing of the 'Revolutionary Study' directed to a serious music audience.

Where no overall duration is specified, simply an intent to cover a given subject, the discipline is to contain the material within a stated aim without letting it become diffuse, spreading into other areas. For this reason it is an excellent practice for the producer to write himself a programme brief in answer to the questions – 'What am I trying to achieve?' 'What do I want to leave with the listener?' Later on, when deciding whether or not a particular item should be included, a decision is easier in the light of the producer's own statement of intent. This is not to say that programmes cannot change their shape as the production proceeds, but a positive aim helps to prevent this happening without the producer's knowledge and consent.

At this stage the producer is probably working on his own, gradually coming to terms with the subject, exploring it at first hand. During this initial research he makes notes, in particular listing those topics within the main subject which must be included. This is followed by decisions on technique – how each topic is to be dealt with. From this emerges the running order in embryo. Very often the title comes much later – perhaps from a significant remark made within the programme. There is no formally recognised way of organising this programme planning, each producer has his own method. By committing thoughts to paper and seeing their relationship one to another – where the emphasis should be and what is redundant – the producer is more likely to finish up with a tightly constructed, balanced programme. Here is an example of the first planning notes for a local radio programme. This radio station serves a coastal region where the trawler fleet has been seriously affected by the loss of fishing rights in international waters.

Working Title:	'The Return of the Trawlermen'.
Aim:	To provide the listener with an understanding of the impact which changes in the deep sea fishing industry over the last ten years have had on the people who work in it.
Duration:	30 minutes
Information:	Annual figures for shipping tonnage, men employed, fish landed, turnover and profit, investment etc.
Content:	Historical account of development in the 10 years,

    — technological change, searching, catching, methods.

    — economic change, larger but fewer ships — implication for owners in the increase in capital cost.

    — social change resulting from fewer jobs, higher paid work, longer voyages, and better conditions on board.

Key Questions: What has happened to the men and the ships that used to work here in large numbers?

What has happened to those areas of the city where previously whole streets were dependent on fishing as a livelihood? Family life, local shopkeepers etc. loss of comradeship?

How significant were the political factors affecting fishing rights in distant waters or was the industry in any case undergoing more fundamental change?

Will the trends continue into the future?

Interview Sources: Trawler Federation.

Docks and Harbour Board?   Shipbuilder?

Trawlermen's Union

Fleet Owner

Skippers — past and present

White Fish Authority

Representative of fish processing industry
    — oils — frozen food

260

```
                        Government – ministry official
                                     members of parliament
                        Wives of seamen etc.
Reference Sources:Newspaper cuttings
                        Library – shipping section
                        Government White Paper
                        Trawler Company reports
                        Magazine – Fishing News International
                        Fred Jones (another producer who did a
                        programme on the docks some time ago)
Actuality:              Bringing in the catch, nets gear running,
                        ships bridge at sea, engine noise, radio com-
                        munications, shoal radar etc.
                        unloading – dockside noises
                        auction
```

By setting out the various factors which have to be included in the programme, it is possible to assess more easily the weight and duration which should be given to each, and whether there are enough ideas to sustain the listener's interest. It probably becomes apparent that there is a lot to get in. It would be possible to do a programme which concentrated solely on the matter of international fishing rights, but in this case the brief was broader and the temptation to dwell on the latest or most contentious issue, such as safety at sea, must be resisted – that's another programme.

There is one final point on planning. A producer's statement of intent should remain fixed, but how he fulfils that aim may change. He plans initially to reach his goals in a certain way, however if in the course of the production he unearths an unforeseen but vital fact, he must alter his plans to include it. The programme material itself will influence decisions on content.

Research

Having written the basic planning notes, the producer must then make the programme within his allocated resources. He must decide whether he will call on a specialist writer or will write his own script. Depending on this will rest the matter of further research – perhaps it is possible to obtain the services of a re-

261

search assistant or reference library. The producer who is working to a well defined brief knows what he wants and in asking the right questions will save both time and money. The principle is always as far as possible to go back to sources, the people involved, eye witnesses, the original documents and so on.

Structure

The main structural decision is whether or not to use a narrator. A linking, explanatory narrative is obviously useful in driving the programme forward in a logical, informative way. This can provide most of the statistical fact and the context of the views expressed, and also the names of various speakers. A narrator can help a programme to cover a lot of ground in a short space of time but this is part of the danger; and may give the overall impression of being too efficient, too 'clipped' or 'cold'. He should *link* and *not interrupt*, and there will amost certainly not be any need to use a narrative voice between every contribution. There are styles of documentary programme which make no use at all of links but each item flows naturally from one to the next, pointing forward in an intelligible juxta-position. This is not easy to do but can often be more atmo-spheric.

Collecting the material

Much of the material will be gathered in the form of location interviews. If it has been decided that there will be no narrator, it is important to ensure that the interviewees introduce them-selves — "speaking as a trawler owner . . ." or "I've been in this business now for thirty years . . ." They may also have to be asked to bring out certain statistical information. This may be deleted in the editing but it is wise to have it in the source material if there is no obvious way of adding it in a linking script.

It must be decided whether the interviewer's voice is to re-main as part of the interviews. It is quite feasible for all the interviewing to be done by one person, who is also possibly the producer, and for the programme to be presented in the form of a personal investigative report. Pursuing this line further, it is possible for the producer to hire a well known personality to make a programme as a personal statement — still a documentary, but seen from a particular viewpoint that is known and understood. Where the same interviewer is used throughout, he becomes the narrator and no other linking voice is needed. Where a straightforward narrator is used, the interviewer's questions are removed and the replies made to serve as statements, the linking script being careful to preserve them in their original context. What can sound untidy and confusing is where in addition to a narrator, the occasional interviewer's voice appears to put a particular question. A programme should be consistent to its own structure. But form and style are infinitely variable and it is important to explore new ways of making programmes — clarity is the key.

Impression and truth

The purpose of using actuality sounds is to help create the appropriate atmosphere. More than this, for those listeners who are familiar with the subject, recognition of authentic backgrounds and specific noises increases the programme's authority. It may be possible to add atmosphere by using material from sound effects discs. These should be used with great care since a sound only has to be identified as 'not the genuine article' for the programme's whole credibility to suffer. The professional broadcaster knows that many simulated sounds or specially recorded effects create a more accurate impression than the real thing. The producer concerned not simply with truth but with credibility, may use non-authentic sounds only if they give an authentic impression.

The same principle applies to the rather more difficult question of fabrication. To what extent may the producer create a 'happening' for the purpose of his programme? Of course he has to 'stage manage' some of the action. If he wants the sound of ships' sirens, the buzzing of a swarm of angry bees, or children in a classroom reciting poetry, these things may have to be made to happen while his recorder is running. Insofar as these sounds are typical of the actual sounds, they are real. But to fabricate the noise of an acutal event, for example a violent demonstration with stones thrown, glass breaking, perhaps even shots being fired; this could too easily mislead the listener unless it is clearly referred to as a simulation. Following the work of broadcasters in war time it is probably true that unless there are clear indications to the contrary, the listener has a right to expect that what he hears in a documentary programme is genuine material to be taken at face value. It is not the documentary producer's job to deceive, or to confuse, for the sake of effect.

Even the reconstructions of a conversation that actually happened, using the same individuals, can give a false impression of the original event. Like the 'rehearsed interview', it simply does not feel right. Similarly it is possible to alter a completely real conversation by the switching on of a tape machine — a house builder giving a quotation for a prospective purchaser is unlikely to be totally natural with a 'live' microphone present!

Faced with the possibility that reality will elude him, both in an original recording or by a later reconstruction, the documentary producer may be tempted to employ secretive methods to obtain his material.

An example would be to use a concealed tape machine to record a conversation with an 'underground' bookdealer for a programme on pornography, This is a difficult area which brings the broadcaster into conflict with the quite reasonable right of every indidvidual to know when he is making a statement for broadcasting. Certainly the BBC is opposed to the use of surreptitious production techniques as being an undue invasion of personal liberty. If such a method is ever used, it is as a result of a decision taken at a very senior level.

The implications for an organisation which broadcasts material which depended in the subliminal or secret, are such that this is a question which the producer, staff or freelance, should not take upon himself. He must obtain clearance from his programme boss.

Of course if the subject is historical, it is an understood convention that scenes are reconstructed and actors used. Practice in other countries differs but in Britain a documentary on even a recent criminal trial must of necessity reconstruct the court proceedings since the event itself cannot be recorded. No explanation is necessary other than a qualification of the authenticity of the dialogue and action. What is crucial is that the listener's understanding of what he hears is not influenced by an undisclosed motive on the part of the broadcaster.

Music

The current practice is to make little use of music in documentary programmes, perhaps through a concern that it can too easily generate an atmosphere, which should more properly be created by real life voices and situations. However, producers will quickly recognise those subjects which lend themselves to special treatment. Not simply programmes which deal with orchestras or pop groups, but where specific music can enhance the accuracy of the impression – as background to youth club material, or to accompany reminiscence of the depressed '30s. A line from a popular song will sometimes provide a suitably perceptive comment, and appropriate music can certainly assist the creation of the correct historical perspective.

Compilation

Having planned, researched, and structured the programme, written the basic script and collected his material the producer must assemble it so as to meet his original brief within the time allotted. First, a good opening. Two suggestions which could apply to the earlier example of the programme on the fishing industry are illustrated by the following script of page one.

Example one:

1. Sound effects	Rattle of anchor chain.
	Splash as anchor enters water.
2. Narrator:	The motor vessel 'Polar Star' drops anchor for the last time. A deep sea trawler for the last twenty four years she now faces an uncertain future.
	Outclassed by a new generation of freezer ships and unable to adapt to the vastly different conditions, she and scores of vessels like her are now tied up – awaiting either conversion, or the scrap yard.
	In this programme we look at the causes of change in the industry and talk to some of the men who make their living from the sea. Or, who like their ships, feel that they too have come to the end of their working life, etc.

Example two:

1. Skipper Matthews:	I've been a trawler skipper for eighteen years — been at sea in one way or another since I was a lad. Never thought I'd see this Rows of vessels tied up like this, just rusting away — nothing to do. We used to be so busy here. I never thought I'd see it.
2. Narrator:	The skipper of the Grimsby 'Polar Star'. Why is it that in the last few years the fishing fleet has been so drastically reduced? How have men like skipper Matthews adapted to the new lives forced on them? And what does the future look like for those who are left? In this programme we try to find some of the answers . . . etc.

The start of the programme can gain attention by a strong piece of sound actuality, or by a controversial or personal statement carefully selected from material that is to be heard within the programme. It opens 'cold' without music or formal introduction preceded only by a time check and station identification. An opening narration can outline a situation in broad factual terms, or it can ask questions to which the listener will want the answers. The object is to create interest, even suspense, and involve the listener in the programme at the earliest possible time.

The remainder of the material may consist of interviews, narrators' links, actuality, vox pop, discussion and music. Additional voices may be used to read official documents, newspaper cuttings or personal letters. It is better if possible to arrive at a fairly homogeneous use of a particular technique, not to have all the interviews together, and to break up a long voice piece or statement for use in separate parts. The most easily understood progression is often the chronological one, but it may be desirable to stop at a particular point in order to counter-balance one view with its opposite. And during all this time the final script is being written around the material as it comes in — cutting a wordy interview to make the point more economically in the narration, leaving just enough unsaid to give the actuality material the maximum impact, dropping an idea altogether in favour of a better one. Always keeping one eye on the original brief.

Programme sequence

There are few rules when it comes to deciding the programme sequence. What matters is that the end result makes sense — not simply to the producer, who is thoroughly immersed in his subject and knows every nuance of what he left out as well as what he put in, but to the listener who is hearing it all for the first time. The most consistent fault with documentaries is not with their content but in their structure. Examples of such problems are insufficient 'signposting', the re-use of a voice heard sometime earlier without repeating the identification, or a change in the convention regarding the narrator or interviewer. For the producer who is close to his material it is easy to overlook a simple matter which may present a severe obstacle to the listener. The programme-maker must always be able to stand back and take an objectively detached view of his work as its shape emerges.

The ending

To end, there are limitless alternatives. Here are some suggestions:

1. To allow the narrator to sum up — useful in some types of schools programme or where the material is so complex or the argument so interwoven that some form of clarifying resumé is desirable.
2. To repeat some of the key statements using the voices of the people who made them.
3. To repeat a single phrase which appears to encapsulate the situation.
4. To speculate on the future with further questions.
5. To end with the same voice and actuality sounds as those used at the opening.
6. To do nothing, leaving it to the listener to form his own assessment of the subject. This is often a wise course to adopt if moral judgements are involved.

Contributors

The producer has a responsibility to those whom he has asked to take part. It is first to tell them as much as possible of what the programme is about. He provides them with the overall context in which their contribution is to be used. Secondly he tells them, prior to transmission, if their contribution has had to be severely edited, or omitted altogether. Thirdly, whenever possible he lets his contributors know in advance the day and time of transmission. These are simple courtesies and the reason for them is obvious enough. Whether they receive a fee or not, contributors to documentary programmes generally take the process extremely seriously often researching additional material to make sure their facts are right. They frequently put their professional or personal reputation at risk in expressing a view or making a prediction. The producer must keep faith with them in keeping them up-to-date as to how they will appear in the final result.

What the producer cannot do is to make the programme conditional upon their satisfaction with the end product. He cannot allow them access to the edited tapes in order to have them approved for transmission. Not only would he seldom have a programme because contributors would not agree, but he would be denying his editorial responsibility. The programme goes out under his name and that of the broadcasting organisation. That, the listener understands, is where praise and blame attaches and editorial responsibility is not to be passed off or avoided through undisclosed pressures or agreements with anybody else.

The feature

Whereas the documentary must distinguish carefully between fact and fiction and have a structure which separates fact from opinion, the feature programme does not have the same formal constraints. Here all possible radio forms meet, poetry, music, voices, sounds — the weird and the wonderful. They combine in an attempt to inform, to move, to entertain or to inspire the listener. The ingredients may be interview or vox-pop, drama or discussion and the sum total can be fact or fantasy. A former Head of BBC Features Department, Laurence Gilliam described the feature programme as "a combination of the authenticity of the talk with the dramatic force of a play, but unlike the play, whose business is to create dramatic illusion for its own sake, the business of the feature is to convince the listener of the truth of what it is saying, even though it is saying it in dramatic form".

It is in this very free and highly creative form that some of the most memorable radio has been made. The possible subject material ranges even more widely than the documentary since it embraces even the abstract. A programme on the development of language, a celebration of St. Valentine's day, the characters of Dickens. Even when all the source material is authentic and factually correct, the strength of the feature lies more in its impact on the imagination than in its intellectual truth. Inter-cut interviews with people who served in the Colonial Service in India mixed with the appropriate sounds can paint a vivid picture of life as it was under the British Raj – not the whole truth, not a carefully rounded and balanced documentary report, it is too wide and complicated a matter to do that in so short a time, but a version of the truth, an impression. The same is true of a programme dealing with a modern hospital, the countryside in summer, the life of Byron, or the wartime exploits of a bomber squadron. The feature deals not so much with issues but with events, and at its centre is the ancient art of telling a story.

The production techniques and sequence are the same as for a documentary – statement of intent, planning, research, script, collection of material, assembly, final editing. In a documentary the emphasis is on the collection of the factual material. Here, the work centres on the writing of the script – a strong story line, clear visual images, the unfolding of a sequence of events with the skill of the dramatist, the handling of known facts but still with a feeling of suspense. Some of the best programmes have come from the producer/writer who can hear the end result begin to come together even as he does his research. It is only through his immersion in the subject that he is qualified to present it to the rest of us. Once again, because of the multiplicity of treatment possible and the indistinct definitions we use to describe them, an explanatory sub-title is often desirable.

'A personal account of . . . . . . '
'An examination of . . . . . . '
'The story of . . . . . . '
'Some aspects of . . . . . . '
'A composition for radio on . . . . . . '

Thus the purpose of the finished work is less likely to be misconstrued.

For the final word on the documentary and feature area of programming, Laurence Gilliam again.

"It can take the enquiring mind, the alert ear, the selective eye, and the broadcasting microphone into every corner of the contemporary world, or into the deepest recess of experience. Its task, and its destiny is to mirror the true inwardness of its subject, to explore the boundaries of radio and television, and to perfect techniques for the use of the creative artist in broadcasting."

20

THE WORK OF THE PRODUCER

SO what does the producer actually do?

First and foremost he, or she, has ideas — ideas for programmes, or items, pieces of music or subjects for discussion — new ways of treating old ideas, or creating a fresh approach to the use of radio. New ideas are not simply for the sake of being different, they stimulate interest and fresh thought, so long as they are relevant. But ideas are not the product of routine, they need fresh inputs to the mind. The producer therefore must not stay simply within the confines of his world of broadcasting, but must involve himself physically and mentally in the community he is attempting to serve. It is all too easy for 'media men' to stay in their ivory tower and to form an elite not quite in touch with the world of the listener. Such an attitude is one of a broadcasting service in decline. Ideas for programmes must be rooted firmly in the needs and language of the audience they serve, the producer's job is to assess, reflect and to anticipate those needs through a close contact with his potential listeners. He probably carries a small notebook to jot down the fleeting thought or snatch of conversation overheard. And if he cannot think of new ideas himself, he must act as a catalyst for others and at least recognise an idea when he sees one. Only then may he retreat to the quiet of his office so that he can think.

There is however a great deal of difference between a new idea and a good idea and any programme suggestion has to be thought through on a number of criteria. An idea needs distilling in order to arrive at a workable form. It has to have a clarity of aim so that all those involved know what they are trying to do. It has to be seen as relevant to its target audience, and it must be practicable in terms of resources. Is there the talent available to support the idea? Is it going to be too expensive in people's time? Does it need additional equipment? What will it cost? Is there sufficient time to plan it properly? Any new programme idea has to be thought through in relation to the four basic resources — people, money, technical equipment and time. It may be depressing to have to modify a really good idea in order to make it work with the resources available, but one of the producer's most important tasks is to reconcile the desirable with the possible.

Given the initial programme idea in a practical format, the producer may have to persuade his boss, the programme controller or station manager, that the proposal is the best thing that could happen to the broadcast output. Further, not only will the programme not fail, but it will enhance the manager's reputation, as well as provide a memorable programme. The first question the manager is likely to ask is "What will it do for the audience?" There are two possible answers — 'satisfy it' or 'increase it'. A good programme may do both. In allocating a transmission slot, the time of day selected can be crucial to the success of the programme. It is no good putting out a programme for children at a time when children are not available, nor is it helpful to broadcast an in-depth programme at a time when the home environment is busy and the necessary level of concentration is unlikely to be sustained. This is where a knowledge of the target audience is useful. Farmers, industrial workers, housewives, teenagers, doctors will all have preferred listening times which will vary according to local circumstances.

The fairly superficial news/information and 'current affairs plus music' type of continuous programme, where all the items are kept short, may be suitable for the general audience at times when other things are happening — such as meal times or at work. But the timing of the more demanding documentary, drama or discussion programme can be critical and will depend on individual circumstances. Factors to be considered when assessing the audience availability may include weekday/weekend work and leisure patterns, the potential car listenership which can represent a significant 'captive' audience, television viewing habits, and so on. The producer is involved in marketing his product and normal consumer principles apply whether or not his radio service is commercially financed.

Having agreed upon a time slot for the broadcast, the producer must ensure there is reasonable time available for its preparation. Is it to be next week or in six month's time? No producer will say that he has sufficient time for production work but there is much to commend his working within definite deadlines for such pressure can lend creative impetus to the programme.

The programme idea is now accepted and a transmission date and time allocated. It will also be at this stage that the producer obtains authorisation for any additional resources which he may need – money for research effort, a special contributor or music group. He will check the availability of appropriate studio facilities and make arrangements for any necessary engineering or other staff support. He must also obtain the clearance of any copyright work which he wishes to use. Conditions for the broadcasting of material in which usage rights are owned by someone outside the broadcasting service vary widely. In the case of literary copyright, books, poems, articles etc., the publisher will normally be the point of reference but if the work is not published, the original author (or if dead his estate) should be consulted. However such rights of ownership exist only for a period of 50 years from the date of publication or from the death of the author, whichever is the later. The rules vary according to the law of the country in which the broadcast is to be made and in cases of doubt it is well worth taking specialist legal advice – discussing copyright fees after the broadcast is, to say the least, a weak negotiating position.

Programme requirements may be very simple and the producer able to fulfil them on his own – some interview material, music selected from the library, and his own crisply written and well presented links may be all that is required. Good ideas are often simple in their translation into radio and can be easily ruined by 'over-production'. On the other hand it may be necessary to involve a lot more people, such as a writer, 'voices', actors, specialist interviewer or commentator. The interpretation of the original idea may call for specially written music or the compilation of sound effects, electronic or actuality. Again, it is easy to get carried away by an enthusiasm for technique, which is why the original brief is such an important part of the process. It should serve as a reference point throughout the production stages.

After selecting his contributors, agreeing fees and persuading them to share his objectives, the producer's task is basically to stay in close touch with them. Remember also, that the producer must always be on the look out for new voices and fresh talent. He then revises draft scripts and clarifies the individual aims and concepts so that when everybody comes together in the studio they all know what they are doing and can work together to a common goal. He must apply himself to this with a great sense of timing so that everything integrates at the same moment — the broadcasting or recording. Above all the producer must give encouragement. The making of programmes has to be both creative and businesslike. There is a product to be made, restrictions on resources and constraints of time to be observed. But it also calls on people to behave uniquely, to write something they have never written before, to give a new public performance, to play music in a personal way. The producer is asking them to give something of themselves. Contributors, artists and performers of all kinds generally give their best in an atmosphere of encouragement, not uncritical, not complacent, but a recognition that they are involved in the process of creative giving. To an extent it is self revealing, and this leaves the artist with a feeling of vulnerability which needs to be reassured by a sense of succeeding in his attempted communication. The producer's role is to provide this feedback in whatever form it is required. He has therefore to be perceptive of his contributors, whether they are professional or amateur.

During this time while material is being gathered and ordered there may be a number of permissions to seek. Broadcasters have no rights over and above those of any other citizen and to interview someone or to make recordings in a home, hospital, school, factory or other non-public place requires the approval of appropriate individuals. In the great majority of cases it is not withheld, and indeed it is most often only an informal verbal clearance that is required. It does not do however to record without the knowledge or consent of the legitimate owner or custodian of the property. But neither is it acceptable to be given permission subject to certain conditions, for example to undertake to play back the material recorded and not to broadcast any of it without the further permission of the person concerned. In response to his request to record, the producer must accept only a 'yes' or a 'no' and not be tempted to accept conditional answers. The listening public has the right to believe that the programme they hear is what the producer whose name attaches to it wants them to hear, and is not the result of some secret deal imposed on him by an outside party.

Accountability for the programme rests with the producer, it can seldom be shifted elsewhere.

So the programme takes shape until the time comes for it to be broadcast or recorded – the studio session. Here again the producer must combine his talents for shrewd business with his yearning for artistic creativity. He has limited resources, particularly of time, and he has people wanting to give of their best, some of whom may be in unfamiliar surroundings, possibly tense, almost certainly nervous. He must set them at their ease and create the appropriate atmosphere. There is no single 'right' way of doing this since people and programmes are all different – the atmosphere in a news studio needs to be different from that of a drama production. A music recording session will be different again from a talk or group discussion. It may be a case of providing coffee all round or even a *small* quantity of something stronger. Any lavish hospitality of this kind is generally much better left until after the programme. But there are two points which a producer must observe. Firstly to make any necessary introductions so that people know who everyone else is and what they are doing, including any technical staff. The second task is to run over the proposed sequence of events so that individual contributors know their own place in the timescale. These two practices help to reassure and provide some security for the anxious. There is nothing worse for a contributor than his standing around wondering what is going on or even whether he has come to the right place. By this time everyone in the studio should have a script or running order, and know what is required of them. They should know of any breaks in the session and be sufficiently acquainted with the building as to be able to find their own way to the source of coffee or to the lavatory. There should be enough chairs.

Rehearsal, recording or transmission can begin.

Whatever the attitude and approach of the producer, it will find its way into the end product. To get the job done, there has to be a certain studio discipline. "That's not quite right yet, let's take it again from the beginning" – this is the signal for a new and better concerted effort. "Everyone check the running order" – means *everyone*. "Start again in twenty minutes" cannot mean people wandering back in half an hour. The producer needs to control, to drive the process forward, to maintain the highest possible quality with the time and talent at his disposal. It is generally a compromise. Too strict a control can be stifling to individual creativity, anxiety increases, the studio atmosphere becomes formal and inflexible. On the other hand, lack of control can mean a drifting timescale, an uncertainty as to what is going on, and a lowering of morale. The appropriate balance is developed with experience but the following points apply generally to this area of man-mangement:

1. Use general talkback for announcements to studio participants sparingly. Such use should be brief and should be overall praise or straightforward administration. Never use talkback from control cubicle into the studio for individual criticism.
2. Listen to suggestions from contributors for alterations but be positive in making up your mind as to what will be done.
3. Provide plenty of individual feedback to contributors.
4. Keep in the mind the needs of the technical, operational or other broadcasting staff — they also want to feel that they are contributing their skills to the programme.
5. Watch the clock, plan ahead for breaks, recording or transmission deadlines. Avoid a last minute rush.
6. Mark the script as a recording proceeds for any retakes needed or editing required.
7. Be encouraging.

In rehearsing a straight talk, it may be necessary for the producer to sit in the studio opposite the speaker in order to persuade him that he is actually talking to someone. The effect of knowing that he has an intent listener is likely to make his delivery much more natural. Moreover, any verbal pedantry or obscure construction in the script is the signal for the producer to ask for clarification. Since it is given in conversational form, this can then become the basis of the suggested re-write. Almost always, constructive suggestions for simplification, professionally given, are gratefully accepted, often with relief. Producers should remember, however, that their role is not to create in their contributors imitations of themselves. In making suggestions for script changes, or how an actor might tackle a certain line, the producer must be visualising not how he himself would do it but how that particular performer can be most effective.

So much for the producer's responsibility to the other people involved in making the programme but of course his prime responsibility is towards the listener. Is the programme providing a clear picture of what it is intending to portray? Are the facts correct and in the right order? Is it legally all right? Is it of good technical quality? Is it interesting? Most of these questions are self-evident and so long as they are borne in mind will answer themselves as the programme proceeds. Some questions however may require a good deal of searching, for example – is it in good taste?

> *Taste:* The disposition or execution of a work of art, choice of language or conduct seen in the light of the faculty of discerning and enjoying beauty or other excellence.
>
> (Concise Oxford Dictionary)

Beauty and excellence are in the eye of the beholder but where there are common standards of acceptability, the producer must be fully aware of them so that his programmes may be directed within them. He must know the generally accepted social tenor of his time and the cultural flavour of his place if he is to succeed with the general audience and avoid giving unwitting offence. He may decide that his programme is only directed to the bawdy revellers in the marketplace with little thought for those who would be shocked at such goings on. He may design his programme simply for a cultural or intellectual elite whose acceptable standards are 'more advanced' than those of more simple folk. So be it, but either way the radio casting of his programme is by definition broad rather than narrow; others will hear and their reaction too must be calculated as part of the overall response. In questions of content, material will be designed for a specific target audience but the matter of acceptable taste is a much broader issue which the radio producer must sense accurately. In stepping outside it, he takes a considerable social risk. In deciding on a style of language, or the inclusion of a particular joke which raises the question of good or bad taste, there is one simple rule: would I say this to someone I did not know very well in a face to face situation? If so, it is fine for broadcasting. If not, the producer must ask himself whether he is using the microphone as a mask to hide behind. Simply because the studio appears to be isolated from contact with the audience it is sometimes tempting to be daring in one's assumed relationship with the individual listener. The matter of taste in broadcasting so often resolves itself in a recognition of the true nature of the medium.

After the recording and while the contributors are still present, it is often possible to put together some additional material for on-air trailing and promotional use. A specially constructed 30 second piece will later pay dividends in the attention which it can attract.

The producer has a responsibility to his professional colleagues who use the same technical facilities. This finds expression in a number of ways.

1. *Studio cleanliness:* The smaller the radio station the more it operates on a 'leave the place as you would wish to find it' basis. He probably will not be required to do the clearing up in detail but he should leave it in its 'technically normal' and usable state.

2. *Fault reporting system:* Every studio user must contribute to the engineering maintenance by reporting any equipment faults which occur. It is extremely annoying for a producer to be seriously hampered by a studio 'bug' only to find that someone else had the same trouble a few days previously but did nothing about it.

3. *Return of borrowed equipment:* A radio station is a communal activity, its facilities are shared. An additional tape recorder or a special microphone taken from one place to another for a specific programme should be returned afterwards. It may not be the producer who actually does this but it is likely to be his responsibility to ensure that some other user is not deprived.

If the programme was 'live', the contributors have been thanked and the occasion suitably rounded off. This may mean the dispensing of some 'hospitality' or simply a discussion of 'how it went'. It is generally unhelpful to be too analytical at this stage, most people know anyway whether as a programme it was any good.

If the programme was recorded, the process is similar but at the end of it, the producer has a tape, or tapes, which may require editing. He should have a running order or script marked in detail with the edits he knows he wants but there may be additional cuts to be made in the light of the overall timing. A further editing session is booked at which he listens to all the material and makes the final judgement on what is to be included.

The finished tape together with the necessary paperwork is

then deposited within 'the approved system' so that the programme finds its way satisfactorily on to the air. Often a producer while excellent as a creative impresario, artistic director or catalyst in the community may have a total blindspot when it comes to simple programme administration. He may be fortunate enough to have a secretary to look after much of this for him, nevertheless it is his responsibility to see that such things are done. The following is a summary of the likely tasks.

1. The completion of a recording or editing report and other details such as library numbers which will enable the tape to get on the air in accordance with the station system.
2. The writing of introductory on-air announcements, cues and other presentation material detailing the transmission context of the programme.
3. The initiation of payment to contributors, and letters of thanks giving the transmission details if these were not known at the time of the recording.
4. The supply of programme details covering the use of music, commercial records or other copyright material for inclusion in the station log. Depending on local circumstances these items will need to be reported to the various copyright societies so that the original performers and copyright holders can receive their proper payment.
5. The issue of a publicity handout, press release, or programme billing for use by newspapers, or programme journal published by the broadcasting organisation. The placing of on-air 'trails' or 'promos' drawing the listeners' attention to his programme.
6. The answering of correspondence generated by the broadcast. While not necessarily representative of listener reaction as a whole, letters form an important part of a producer's public accountability. Apart from the PR value to the particular radio service such enquiries and expressions of praise or criticism constitute a consumer view which should not be treated lightly.

Having completed the programme, the producer is already working on the next. For some it is a constant daily round to report new facts and discover fresh interests. For others it may be a painstaking progress from one epic to another. Unlike the purely creative artist, the producer cannot remain isolated, generating material simply from within himself. His role is that of the communicator, the interpreter who attempts to bring about a form of contact which explains the world a little more. For the most part it is an ephemeral contact leaving an unsubstantial trace. Radio works very much in the present tense, reputations are difficult to build and even harder to sustain. The producer is rarely regarded as any better than his last programme.

BACK ANNOUNCEMENT

HARRY Vardon, one of the great exponents of golf, was asked why he never wrote a book setting out all that he knew about it. His reason was that when he came to put it down on paper it looked so simple that "anyone who didn't know that much about it should not be playing the game anyway!"

It looks as though it is the same with broadcasting. Is there really any more to it than – 'Have something to say, and say it as interestingly as you can?' Yet there are whole areas of output which have hardly been mentioned – educational programmes, consumer advice, light entertainment and comedy, programmes for young people, specialist minorities or ethnic groups. What about the special problems of short wave broadcasting, or programmes for the listener who is a long way away from the broadcaster? The emphasis here has had to be on the production of programmes whose basis lies within the community to which they are directed. A book, like a programme, cannot tell the whole truth. What the reader, or listener, has a right to expect is that the product is 'sold' to him in an intelligible way and then remains true to his expectations. Broadcasters talk a great deal about objectivity and balance, but even more important, and more fundamental, is the need to be fair in the relationship with the listener. A broadcasting philosophy which describes itself in programme attitudes yet ignores the listener is essentially incomplete.

What then is the purpose of being in broadcasting – the aim of it all? It is not enough to say, "I want to communicate" – communicate what? And why? There are several possible answers to this last question – to earn money, to meet the needs of the organisation, to meet your own needs, to become famous, or to persuade others to think as you do. But the purpose of communication is surely to provide options and a freedom of action for other people. Not to close them by offering a half-truth or by weighting them with a personal, political or commercial bias. The reason for providing information, education and the relaxation of entertainment is to suggest alternative courses of action, to explain the implications of one against another, and having done so to allow for a freedom of thought and action. This assumes that people are capable of responding in a way which itself requires a regard for our fellow man.

Having announced his intentions and made his programme, the producer must put his name to it. Programme credits are not there simply to feed the ego or as a reward for your labours. They are a vital element in the power which broadcasting confers on the communicator — personal responsibility for what is said. Many members of a team may contribute to a programme, but only one person can finally decide on the content. Good programmes cannot be made by committee. Group decisions inevitably contain compromise and a weakening of purpose and structure, but worse, they conceal responsibility. Communication that is not labelled or attributed is of little use to the person who receives it.

Programme makers face a hundred difficulties not mentioned here but by engaging a 'professional overdrive', rather than regarding them as a personal undermining, most problems can be made to take on more the aspect of a challenge than a threat. The practicalities of production are encapsulated by the well known Greenwich time signal whose six pips must serve as their final reminder:

1. *Preparation*: State the aims, plan to meet them.
2. *Punctuality*: Be better than punctual, be early.
3. *Presentation*: Keep the listener in mind.
4. *Politeness*: To contributors, listeners and staff.
5. *Punctilious*: Observance of all agreed systems and procedures, and if there is something you don't like, do not ignore it; change it.
6. *Professional*: The putting of the interests of the listener and the broadcasting organisation before your own. And the constant maintenance of a judgement based on a full awareness and a competent technique.

GLOSSARY

A   ABOVE THE LINE COST. Expenditure under the producer's control in addition to fixed overheads (Below the line).

ACCESS BROADCASTING. Programme in which editorial decisions are made by the contributor, not by professional staff.

ACOUSTIC. Characteristic sound of any enclosed space due to the amount of sound reflected from its wall surfaces and the way in which this amount alters at different frequencies. See also REVERBERATION TIME.

ACOUSTIC SCREEN. Free standing movable screen designed to create special acoustic effects or prevent unwanted sound reaching a particular microphone. One side is soft and absorbent, the other is hard and reflective.

ACTUALITY. 'Live' recording of a real event.

AD. Advertisement or commercial.

AD-LIB. Unscripted announcement, "off-the cuff" remark.

AERIAL. Device for transmitting or receiving radio waves at the point of transition from their electrical electromagnetic form.

AGC. Automatic Gain Control. Amplifier circuit which compensates for variations in signal level, dynamic compression.

AM. AMPLITUDE MODULATION. System of applying the sound signal to the transmitter frequency, associated with Medium Wave broadcasting.

APPLE AND BISCUIT. Microphone resembling a black ball with a circular plate fixed on one side. Omni-directional polar diagram.

ASCAP. American Society of Composers, Authors and Publishers — copyright control organisation protecting musical performance rights.

ATMOSPHERE. Impression of environment created by use of actuality, sound effects or acoustic.

ATTENUATION. Expressed in decibels (dBs), the extent to which a piece of equipment decreases the signal strength. Opposite of amplification.

ATTENUATOR. Device of known attenutation deliberately inserted in a circuit to reduce the signal level.

AUDIENCE FIGURES. Expressed as a percentage of the potential audience, or in absolute terms, the number of listeners to a single programme or sequence, daily or weekly patronage, or total usage of the station.

AUDIENCE MEASUREMENT. Research into numbers and attitudes of listeners. Methods used include: 'Aided-Recall' — person to person interview; 'Diary' — the keeping of a log of programmes heard; 'Panel' — permanent representative group reporting on programmes heard.

AUDIO FREQUENCY. Audible sound wave. Accepted range 20 Hz — 20 kHz.

AUTOMATIC GAIN CONTROL. See AGC.

AZIMUTH. The extent to which the gap in the recording or playback heads of a tape machine is truly vertical, i.e. at right angles to the direction of tape travel.

B BACKING TRACK. Recording of musical accompaniment heard by a soloist while he adds his own performance.

BALANCE. Relative proportion of 'direct' to 'reflected' sound apparent in a microphone output. Also the relative volume of separate components in a total mix, e.g. voices in a discussion, musical instruments in an orchestra.

BASS CUT. Device in microphone or other sound source which electrically removes the lower frequencies.

BAY. Standard 7'6" x 19" frame housing power supplies and other technical equipment used in studios or control areas.

BIAS. High frequency signal applied to the recording head of a tape machine to ensure distortion free recording.

BI-DIRECTIONAL. Microphone sensitive in two directions, front and back, but completely insensitive on either side, e.g. ribbon microphone.

BLACK. A carbon copy, generally of typed news story.

BOARD. American term for studio control desk or panel.

BOOM. Wheeled microphone support having a long arm to facilitate microphone placing over performers, e.g. orchestra.

BOOMY. Room acoustic unduly reverberant in the lower frequencies.

BULK ERASER. Equipment capable of demagnetising or 'cleaning' a spool of tape.

C CANS. Colloquial term for headphones.

CAPACITOR MICROPHONE. Microphone type based on principle of conducting surfaces in proximity holding an electrical charge. Requires a power supply.

CAPSTAN. The drive spindle of a tape recorder.

CARDIOID. Heart-shaped area of pick-up around a microphone.

CARTRIDGE or CART. Enclosed endless loop of tape on a single spindle which having finished is ready to start again. Used especially for signature tunes, jingles and idents.

CASSETTE. Enclosed reel to reel device of ⅛ inch wide tape particularly used in domestic or miniature recording machines.

CHANNEL. The complete circuit from a sound source to the point in the control panel where it is mixed with others.

CHINAGRAPH. Soft pencil used to mark tape cutting points during editing. Generally yellow

CLEAN FEED. A supply of cue programme in which a remote contributor hears all the programme elements other than his own. Essential to prevent howl-round.

CLIP. Brief illustrative extract from programme or film soundtrack.

COLOURATION. Effect obtained in a room when one range of frequencies tends to predominate in its acoustic.

COMPRESSOR. Device for narrowing the dynamic range of a signal passing through it.

CONDENSER MICROPHONE. See CAPACITOR MIC.

CONTROL LINE. A circuit used to communicate engineering or production information between a studio and an outside source. Often also used as cue line.

COPY. Written material offered for broadcast e.g. news copy.

COPYRIGHT. The legal right of ownership in a creative work invested in its author, composer, publisher or designer.

COPYTASTER. The first reader of copy sent to a newsroom who decides whether it should be rejected or retained for possible use.

COUGH KEY. Switch under the speaker's control which cuts his microphone circuit.

CROSSFADE. The fading in of a new source while fading out the old.

CROSSPLUG. The temporary transposition of two circuits, normally on a Jackfield. See also OVERPLUGGING.

CROSSTALK. Audible interference of one circuit upon another.

CUE. A small electric light, often green, used as a cueing signal.

CUE LINE. A circuit used to send cue programme to a distant contributor.

CUE PROGRAMME. The programme which contains a contributor's cue, generally to begin.

CUE SHEET. Documentation giving technical information and introductory script for programmes or insert.

CUME. Cumulative audience measurement. See REACH.

D   DB or dB. Decibel, Logarithmic measurement of sound intensity or electrical signal. The smallest change in level perceptible by the human ear.

DEAD SIDE OF MICROPHONE. Least sensitive area.

DEFERRED RELAY. The broadcasting of a recorded programme previously heard 'live' by an audience.

DIN. Plug or socket manufactured to standard of Deutsche Industrie Norm.

DIRECTIONAL. Property of microphone causing it to be more sensitive in one direction than in others. Also applied to transmitters, receiving aerials, loudspeakers etc. See also POLAR DIAGRAM.

DISC JOCKEY. Personality presenter of record programme, generally pop music show.

DOLBY SYSTEM. Trade name for electronic circuitry designed to improve the signal to noise ratio of a programme chain.

DOUBLE-ENDER. Length of covered wire with a Jack plug on each end used to connect pieces of equipment or Jacks on a Jackfield.

DOUBLE HEADED. Style of presentation using two presenters.

DRIVE TIME. Periods of morning and later afternoon which coincide with commuter travel and the greatest in-car listening.

DRY RUN. Programme rehearsal, especially drama, not necessarily in the studio, and without music, effects or movements to mic. See RUN THROUGH.

DROP OUT. Momentary drop in level or loss of quality in tape reproduction due to lack of contact between tape and repro. head.

DUB. To copy material already recorded. To make a dubbing.

DUCKING UNIT. Automatic device providing 'Voice-Over' facility. See V/O.

DYNAMIC RANGE. Measured in dBs, the difference between the loudest and the quietest sounds.

E   ECHO. Strictly a single or multiple repeat of an original sound. Generally refers to reverberation.

ECHO PLATE OR SPRING. Device for artificially adding reverberation.

EDIT. The rearrangement of material to form a preferred order. Particularly in the cutting of recorded tape.

EDITING BLOCK. Specially shaped metal guide which holds the tape in position during the cutting and splicing process.

EDITORIAL JUDGEMENT. The professional philosophy which leads to decisions on programme content and treatment.

EQUALISATION. The process which compensates for frequency distortion, e.g. at the receiving end of a landline.

EQUITY. The British Actors Equity Association. Actors' union.

ERASE HEAD. The first head of a tape recorder which cleans the tape of any existing recording by exciting it with a high frequency signal.

EXCLUDED CATEGORIES. Types of use of commercial records e.g. as signature tunes, specifically excluded from NEEDLETIME agreement. May also apply to review and illustrative use.

F FADE. A decrease in sound volume. (Fade down or out).

FADER. Volume control of a sound source used for setting its level, fading it up or down, or mixing it with other sources. Also 'POT'.

FADE IN. An increase in sound volume. (Fade up.)

FEED. A supply of programme, generally by circuit.

FEEDBACK. See HOWL-ROUND.

FEEDSPOOL. Tape recorder spool which supplies the tape to the recording head. (As opposed to 'take-up' spool.)

FIGURE OF EIGHT. See BI-DIRECTIONAL.

FILTER. Electrical device for removing unwanted frequencies from a sound source, e.g. mains hum, or surface noise from an old or worn recording.

FIRST GENERATION COPY. A copy taken from the original recording. A copy of this copy would be a second generation copy.

FLETCHER-MUNSON EFFECT. The apparent decrease in the proportion of higher and lower frequencies, with respect to the middle range, as the loudspeaker listening level is decreased. Significant in correct setting of monitoring level, particularly in music balance.

FLUFF. 1. Accumulation of dust on the stylus of gramophone pick-up.
2. Mistake in reading or other broadcast speech.

FLUTTER. Rapid variations of speed discernible in tape or disc reproduction.

FM. Frequency modulation. System of applying the sound signal to the transmitter frequency, associated with VHF broadcasting.

FOLDBACK. Means of allowing artists in the studio to hear programme elements originating elsewhere even while studio microphones are live.

FREELANCE. Self-employed broadcaster of any category – producer, contributor, operator, reporter etc. Not a permanent full-time contract. Paid by the single contribution or over a period for a series of programmes. Non-exclusive, available to work for any employer. See also STRINGER.

FREQUENCY. Expressed in cycles per second or Hertz, the rate at which a sound or radio wave is repeated. The note 'middle C' has a frequency of 256 Hz. The long wave transmitter in a wavelength of 1500 metres has a frequency of 200 kHz (200,000 cycles per second). Frequency and wavelengths are always associated in the formula

$$F \times W = Speed$$

Speed is the speed of the wave, i.e. sound or radio, and remains constant.

FREQUENCY DISTORTION. Distortion caused by inadequate frequency response.

FREQUENCY RESPONSE. The ability of a piece of equipment to treat all frequencies within a given range in the same way, e.g. an amplifier with a poor frequency response would treat frequencies passing through it unequally and its output would not faithfully reproduce its input.

FULL TRACK. Tape recording using the whole width of the tape.

FX. Sound effects created in the studio or available from grams or tape.

G GAIN. Expressed in decibels (dBs), the amount of amplification at which an amplifier is set. Can also refer to a receiving aerial – the extent to which it can discriminate in a particular direction thereby increasing its sensitivity.

GAIN CONTROL. The control which affects the gain of an amplifier, also loosely applied to any fader or volume control affecting the output level.

GRAMOPHONE, GRAMDECK or GRAMS. Turntable and associated equipment for the reproduction of records.

GUN-MIC. Microphone resembling a long barrelled shotgun. Highly directional, used for nature recordings or where intelligibility is required at some distance from the sound source e.g. OBs.

H HALF TRACK. Tape recording erase and recording applied only to the 'top'

286

half of the tape, as opposed to 'full track' which uses the whole width.

HANDOUT. Page of press information or publicity sheet issued to draw attention to an event.

HAND SIGNALS. System of visual communication used through the glass window between a studio and its control area, or in a studio with a 'live' mic. See WIND-UP.

HARMONIC DISTORTION. The generation of spurious upper frequencies.

HEAD AMPLIFIER. Small amplifier within a microphone especially capacitor type.

HEAD GAP. Narrow vertical slot at the front of tape recorder erase, record and replay heads.

HEADLINE. Initial short summary of news event.

HERTZ. Hz. Unit of frequency, one complete cycle per second.

HISS. Unwanted background noise in the frequency range 5-10 kHz. e.g. tape hiss.

HOWL-ROUND. Acoustic or electrical positive feedback generally apparent as a continuous sound of a single frequency. Often associated with public address systems. Avoided by decreasing the gain in the amplifying circuit, cutting the loudspeaker or in contribution working through the use of a clean feed circuit.

HUM. Low frequency electrical interference derived from mains power supply.

HYPER-CARDIOID. A cardioid microphone having a particularly narrow angle of acceptance at its front which decreases rapidly towards the sides.

I ID. Station identification or ident.

IFPI. International Federation of Phonographic Industries. International organisation of record manufacturers to control performance and usage rights.

IGRANIC JACK. Jack plug providing two connections.

IN CUE. The first words of a programme insert, known in advance. Can also be music.

INSERT. A short item used in a programme, e.g. a 'live' insert, a tape insert.

INTERCOM. Local voice communication system.

IPS. Inches per second. Tape recording term, refers to speed of travel past the recording and replay heads.

J JACK. Socket connected to an audio circuit. Can incorporate a switch activated by insertion of Jack Plugs – a 'break' Jack.

JACKFIELD or PATCH PANEL. Rows of Jacks connected to audio sources or destinations. Provides availability of all circuits for inter connection or testing.

JACK PLUG, or POST OFFICE JACK. Plug type used for insertion in Jack socket comprising three connections, a circuit pair plus earth, known as 'ring tip and sleeve'. See also DOUBLE ENDER.

JINGLE. Short musical station identification or commercial.

JOCK. See DISC JOCKEY.

JOINING TAPE. Adhesive tape used in tape editing.

K KEY. Switch.

KILO. Thousand. Kilo hertz – frequency in thousands of cycles per second. Kilowatt – electrical power, a thousand watts.

L LANDLINE. See LINE.

LAVALIER MICROPHONE. Small microphone hung round the neck. LANYARD MIC.

LAZY ARM. Small boom type microphone stand suitable for suspending a microphone over a 'talks' table.

LEAD SHEET. Basic musical score indicating instrumentation of melody. Used for microphone control during music balance.

LEAD STORY. The first, most important story in a news bulletin.

LEVEL. 1. A test prior to recording or broadcasting to check the volume of the speaker's voice, – 'take some level'.

2. Expressed in dBs, plus or minus, the measurement of electrical intensity against an absolute standard, – zero level (1MW in 600 ohms).

LIMITER. Device to prevent the signal level exceeding a pre-set value.

LINE. Post Office circuit between two points for programme or communication purposes.

LINE-UP. Technical setting up of circuits and systems to conform to engineering standards. Line-up tone of standard frequency and level used to check the gain of all component parts.

LIP MIC. Noise excluding ribbon microphone designed for close working e.g. OB commentary.

LOG. Written record of station output. Can also be recorded audio.

M   MARCHING BOX. Sound effects device comprising small box partially filled with gravel used to simulate marching feet.

MCPS. Mechanical Copyright Protection Society. Organisation which controls the copying or dubbing of copyright material.

MEGA. Million. Megahertz – frequency in millions of cycles per second. Megawatt – electrical power, a million watts.

MICROPHONIC. Faulty piece of electronic equipment sensitive to mechanical vibration – acting like a microphone.

MIDDLE OF THE ROAD. Popular, mainstream music with general appeal. Non-extreme.

MODULATION. Variations in a transmission or recording medium caused by the presence of programme. Often abbreviated to Mod.

MODULE. Interchangeable equipment component.

MONTAGE. Superimposition of sounds and/or voices to create a composite impression.

MOR. Middle of the road music.

MU. Musicians union.

MUSIC LINE. High quality landline suitable for all types of programme, not only music. Compare with CONTROL LINE.

N   NAB. National Association of Broadcasters. American trade organisation which secures agreement on standards of procedure and equipment, e.g. NAB spool, a professional tape reel type.

NAGRA. Trade name. High quality portable tape recorder.

NEEDLETIME. Expressed in hours or minutes per week, a station's permitted usage of commercial gramophone records. Its amount and cost is arrived at by negotiation between the broadcasting organisation and the record companies. See also EXCLUDED CATEGORIES, PPL.

NOISE. Extraneous sound, electrical interference, or background to a signal.

NOISE GATE. Amplifier which allows a signal to pass through it only when the input level exceeds a pre-set value.

O   OB. Outside broadcast.

OFF-MIC. A speaker or other sound source working outside a microphone's most sensitive area of pick-up. Distant effect due to drop in level and greater proportion of reflected to direct sound.

OMNI-DIRECTIONAL. A microphone sensitive in all directions. Also applied to transmitters and aerials.

288

ONE-LEGGED. 'Thin' low level quality resulting from a connection through only one wire of a circuit pair.

OPEN-ENDED. A programme without a pre-determined finishing time.

OUT CUE. Final words of a contribution, known in advance, taken as a signal to initiate the following item in a sequence.

OUT OF PHASE. The decrease in level and effect on quality when two similar signals are combined in such a way as to cancel each other.

OUTSIDE SOURCE. Programme originating point remote from the studio, or the circuit connection from it.

OVERLOAD DISTORTION. The distortion suffered by a programme signal when its electrical level is higher than the equipment can handle. When this happens non-continuously it is referred to as 'peak distortion'. Also referred to as 'squaring off'.

OVERPLUGGING. The substitution of one circuit for another by the insertion of Jack plug in a break Jack.

P PA. 1. Press Association. News agency.
   2. Public address system.

PAR. Paragraph. Journalists' term often applied to news copy.

P as B. Programme as broadcast. Documentation giving complete details of a programme in its final form – duration, inserts, copyright details, contributors etc.

PACKAGE. Programme or insert offered complete, ready for transmission.

PANEL. Studio mixing desk, control board or console.

PAN POT. Panoramic potentiometer. Control on studio mixing desk which places a source to the left or right in a stereo image.

PARABOLIC REFLECTOR. Microphone attachment which focuses sound waves thereby increasing directional sensitivity. Used for OBs, nature recordings etc.

PATCH PANEL. See JACKFIELD.

PATRONAGE. Term used in audience measurement to describe the total number of listeners to a station within a specified period. Market penetration. Reach.

PEAK DISTORTION. See OVERLOAD DISTORTION.

PEAK PROGRAMME METER. Voltmeter with a slugged delay time, designed to indicate levels and peaks of electrical intensity for the purposes of programme control.

PHASE DISTORTION. The effect on the sound quality caused by the imprecise combination of two similar signals.

PICK-UP. Gramophone record reproducing components which convert the mechanical variations into electrical energy, pu-arm, pu-head, pu-shell, pu-stylus.

PILOT. Programme to test the feasibility, or gain acceptance for a new series or idea.

PINCH ROLLER. Rubber wheel which holds tape against tape recorder drive capstan.

PLUG. Free advertisement.

POLAR DIAGRAM. Graph showing the area of a microphone's greatest sensitivity. Also applies to aerials, transmitters and loudspeakers. Directivity pattern.

POPPING. Descriptive term applied to 'mic-blasting', the effect of vocal breathiness close to microphone.

POST-ECHO. The immediate repeating at low level of sounds replayed from a tape recording. See PRINT-THROUGH.

POT. Potentiometer. Volume control or channel fader.

POT CUT. The cutting off of a tape during replay before it has finished by closing its fader – generally to save time. 'Instant editing'.

PPL. Phonographic Performance Ltd. Organisation of British record manufacturers to control performance and usage rights.

PPM. See PEAK PROGRAMME METER.

PREFADE. The facility for hearing and measuring a source before opening its fader, generally on a tape or disc reproducer or studio mixing desk.

PREFADE TO TIME. The technique of beginning an item of known duration before it is required so that it finishes at a precise time, e.g. closing signature tune.

PRESENCE. A sense of 'realistic closeness' often on a singer's voice. Can be aided by boosting the frequencies in the range 2.8 kHz to 5.6 kHz.

PRIME TIME. The best, most commercial hours of station output, e.g. 6.30 a.m. to 10.30 a.m.

PRINT THROUGH. The reproduction at low level of recorded programme through the magnetic inter-action of layers of tape due to their close proximity while wound on a spool. The cause of post and pre-echo. Often the result of tight winding through spooling at high speed, and storage at too high a temperature.

PRODUCER. The person in charge of a programme and responsible for it.

PROMO. See TRAIL.

PRS. Performing Rights Society. Organisation of authors, composers and publishers for copyright protection.

PUFF. Free advertisement.

Q QUAD. Quadraphony or Quadrasonic. Four channel sound reproduction providing front and rear, left and right coverage.

R RADIO MIC. Microphone containing or closely associated with its own portable transmitter. Requires no cable connection, useful for stage work, OBs etc.

RATINGS. Audience measurement relating to the number of listeners to a specific programme.

REACH. Term used in audience measurement to describe the total number of listeners to a station within a specified period. Also market penetration, patronage.

RECORD HEAD. The part of a tape machine which converts the electrical signal into magnetic variations and transfers them to the tape.

REDUCTION. Playback of a multi-track music recording to arrive at a final mix. Also mix-down.

RELAY. 1. Simultaneous transmission of a programme originating from another station.

2. Transmission of a programme performed 'live' in front of an audience. See also DEFERRED RELAY.

3. Electrically operated switch.

REPRO HEAD. The part of a tape machine which converts the magnetic pattern on the tape into electrical signal. Reproduction or playback device.

RESIDUAL. Artist's repeat fee.

REVERBERATION. The continuation of a sound after its source has stopped due to reflection of the sound waves.

REVERBERATION TIME. Expressed in seconds, the time taken for a sound to die away to one millionth of its original intensity.

REVERSE TALKBACK. Communications system from studio to control cubicle.

RIBBON MICROPHONE. High quality microphone on electromagnetic principle. Bi-directional polar diagram.

RIP 'N' READ. News bulletin copy sent by teleprinter, designed to be read on the air without rewriting.

ROT. Recording off transmission. Recording made at the time of transmission, not necessarily off-air.

RUNNING ORDER. List of programme items in their chronological sequence.

RUN THROUGH. Programme rehearsal.

S   SB. Simultaneous broadcast. Relay of programme originating elsewhere. Conveyed from point to point by system of permanent SB lines, or taken 'off-air'.

SCRIPT. Complete text of a programme or insert from which the broadcast is made.

SEGUE. The following of one item immediately on another without an intervening pause or link. Especially two pieces of music.

SIG TUNE. Signature tune. Identifying music at the beginning and end of a programme or regular insert.

SOLID STATE. Transistorised or integrated circuitry as opposed to that containing valves.

SQUELCH. Means of suppressing unwanted noise in the reception of a radio signal. See NOISE GATE.

STING. Single music chord, used for dramatic effect.

STOCK MUSIC. In-house library of recorded music.

STRINGER. Freelance contributor paid by the item. Generally newsman at outlying place not covered by staff.

STYLUS. Small diamond tipped arm protruding from gramophone pick-up. In contact with the record surface it conveys the mechanical vibrations to the cartridge for conversion into electrical energy.

SUSTAINING PROGRAMME. Programme supplied by a syndicating source or elsewhere to maintain an output for a station making its own programmes for only part of the day.

SYNC OUTPUT. Programme replayed from the record heads of a multi-track tape machine heard by performers while they record further tracks.

T   TALKBACK. Voice communication system from control cubicle to studio or other contributing point.

TALKS TABLE. Specially designed table for studio use, often circular with an acoustically transparent surface and a hole in the middle to take a microphone.

TAPE. Magnetic recording material.

TAPES. Journalist's term for copy received by teleprinter or paper strips on which such material is printed.

TBU. Telephone balance unit. Interface device used in conjunction with calls on a phone-in programme. Minimises risk of howl-round while providing pre-set level of caller to studio presenter and vice-versa. Isolates public telephone equipment from broadcaster's equipment.

TELEX. Telephone office teleprinter system.

TONE. A test or reference signal of standard frequency and level. For example, 1kHz at 0 dB.

TRACKING WEIGHT. The downward pressure of a gramophone pick-up transmitted through its stylus.

TRAIL. Broadcast item advertising forthcoming programme. On-air promotion or 'promo'.

TRANSCRIPT. The text of a broadcast as transmitted, often produced from an off-air recording.

TRANSCRIPTION. A high quality tape or disc recording of a programme intended for reproduction by another broadcasting service.

TRANSDUCER. Any device which converts one form of energy into another. e.g. mechanical to electrical, acoustic to electrical, electrical to magnetic etc.

TRANSIENT RESPONSE. The ability of a microphone or other equipment to respond rapidly to change of input or brief energy states.

TWO-WAY. Discussion or interview between two studios remote from each other.

U   UHER. Trade name of portable tape recorder.

UHF. Ultra high frequency. Radio or television transmission in the range of frequencies from 300 MHz to 300 MHz.

V   VHF. Very high frequency. Radio or television transmission in the range of frequencies from 30 MHz to 300 MHz.

VOICE-OVER. Voiced announcement superimposed on lower level material, generally music.

VOICE REPORT. Broadcast newspiece in the reporters own voice.

VOX-POP. 'The voice of the people'. Composite recording of 'street' interviews.

VU METER. Volume unit meter calibrated in decibels measuring signal level especially as a recording level indicator.

W   WARM-UP. Initial introduction and chat designed to make an audience feel at home and create the appropriate atmosphere prior to a live broadcast or recording.

WAVELENGTH. Expressed in metres, the distance between two precisely similar points in adjacent cycles in a sound or radio wave. The length of one cycle. Used as the tuning characteristic or 'radio address' of a station. See also FREQUENCY.

WILD or WILD TRACK. Term borrowed from film to describe the recording of atmosphere, actuality or effects at random without a precise decision on how they are to be used in a programme.

WINDSHIELD. Protective cover of foam rubber, plastic, or metal gauze, designed to eliminate wind noise from microphone. Essential on outdoor use or close vocal work.

WIND-UP. Signal given to broadcaster to come to the end of his programme contribution. Often by means of index finger describing slow vertical circles, or by flashing cue light.

WIPE. To erase tape.

WOW. Slow speed variations discernable in tape or disc reproduction.

FURTHER READING – A SELECTION

Historical Survey and Reference

Barnouw, Erik	*A History of Broadcasting in The United States.* Vol. 1. *A Tower in Babel 1966* Vol. 2. *The Golden Web 1969* Vol. 3. *The Image Empire 1971*	OUP, NY
Baron, Michael	*Independent Radio:* The story of independent radio in the United Kingdom.	Dalton, 1975
Black, Peter	*The Biggest Aspidistra in the World:* a personal celebration of fifty years of the BBC.	BBC, 1972
Boyle, Andrew	*Only the Wind Will Listen:* Reith of the BBC.	Hutchinson, 1972
Briggs, Asa	*The History of Broadcasting in the United Kingdom.* Vol. 1. *The Birth of Broadcasting 1961* Vol. 2. *The Golden Age of Wireless 1965* Vol. 3. *The War of Words 1970* Vol. 4. (in preparation)	OUP
Head, Sydney	*Broadcasting in America:* A survey of television and radio.	Houghton Miflin, Boston (3rd Edn), 1976
Lichty, Lawrence & Topping, Malachi	*American Broadcasting:* A source book on the history of radio and television.	Hastings House NY, 1975
Mansell, Gerard	*Broadcasting to the World:* Forty years of the external services.	BBC, 1973
Paulu, Burton	*Radio and Television on the European Continent.*	University of Minnesota, 1967
Reith, John	*Into the Wind.*	Hodder & Stoughton, 1949
Robertson, Edwin	*The Local Radio Handbook*	Mowbrays, 1974
Smith, Anthony	*British Broadcasting*	David & Charles, 1974
Snagge, John & Barnsley, Michael	*Those Vintage Years*	Pitman, 1972

Wheldon, Hugh	*British Traditions in a World Wide Medium.*	BBC, 1973

Broadcasting and Society

Curran, Charles	*Our Proper Concern.*	BBC, 1971
	Code or Conscience? A view of broadcasting standards.	BBC, 1970
	Broadcasting and Society.	BBC, 1971
Dinwiddie, M.	*Religion by Radio:* Its place in British broadcasting.	Allen & Unwin, 1968
Efron, Edith	*The News Twisters.*	Nash Publishing, Los Angeles, 1971
Fawdry, K.	*Everything but Alf Garnett:* A personal view of BBC school broadcasting.	BBC, 1974
Greene, Hugh	*The Broadcaster's Responsibility.*	BBC, 1962
	The Conscience of the Programme Director.	BBC, 1965
Hale, Julian	*Radio Power:* Propaganda and international broadcasting.	Paul Elek, 1975
Hood, Stuart	*Radio and Television.*	David & Charles, 1975
Katz, Elihu	*Social Research on Broadcasting:* Proposals for further development.	BBC, 1977
Lusty, Robert	*Bound to be Read.*	Cape, 1975
McLuhan, Marshall	*Understanding Media.*	Routledge, 1964 Sphere, 1973
Schlesigner, Philip	*Putting Reality Together – BBC News*	Constable, 1978
Scupham, John	*Broadcasting and the Community.*	C.A. Watts, 1967
Silvey, Robert	*Who's Listening?* The story of BBC audience research.	Allen & Unwin, 1974
Smith, Anthony	*The Shadow in the Cave:* Study of the relationship between the broadcaster, his audience and the State.	Allen & Unwin, 1973
Swann, Michael	*Freedom and Restraint in Broadcasting.*	BBC, 1976

Programmes and Personalities

Day, Robin	*Day by Day*	William Kimber, 1975
Dimbleby, Jonathan	*Richard Dimbleby.*	Hodder & Stoughton, 1975
Dougall, Robert	*In and Out of the Box.*	Collins & Harvill, 1973 Fontana, 1975
Draper, Alfred, Austin, John & Edgington, Harry	*The Story of the Goons*	Severn House, 1977
Friendly Fred	*Due to Circumstances Beyond Our Control.*	MacGibbon & Kee, 1967
Gallagher, Jock	*Twenty Five Years of 'The Archers'.*	BBC, 1975

Harris, Paul	*Broadcasting from the High Seas.*	Paul Harris, 1977
Jackson, John	*Monday's Prayer on the Air.*	Lakeland, 1976
Johnston, Brian	*It's been a Lot of Fun.*	W.H. Allen, 1974
Lawrence, Anthony	*Foreign Correspondent.*	Allen & Unwin, 1972
Manio, Jack de	*To Auntie With Love.*	Hutchinson, 1967
May, Derwent	*Good Talk:* An anthology from BBC radio.	Victor Gollancz, 1968
Miall, Leonard	*Richard Dimbleby, Broadcaster.*	BBC, 1966
Painting, Norman	*Forever Ambridge.*	Michael Joseph, 1975
Sanger, Elliot	*Rebel in Radio:* The story of the New York Times commercial radio station.	Focal Press, 1973
Savile, Jimmy	*As It Happens.*	Barrie & Jenkins, 1974
Talbot, Godfrey	*Ten Seconds from Now:* A broadcaster's story.	Hutchinson, 1973
Timpson, John	*Today and Yesterday.*	Allen & Unwin, 1976
Took, Barry	*Laughter in the Air:* An informal history of radio comedy.	BBC, Robson Books, 1976
Young, Jimmy	J.Y.	W.H. Allen, 1973

Radio Production

Aspinall, Richard	*Radio Programme Production:* A manual for training.	UNESCO, Paris, 1973
Bliss, Edward & Patterson, John	*Writing News for Broadcast.*	Columbia University Press, 1971
Burke, Richard	*The Use of Radio in Adult Literacy:* A training monograph.	Hulton Educational, 1976
Dawson, Stanley	*On a Point of Order:* A journalist's guide to local government.	Macmillan Press for the National Council for the Training of Journalists, 1973
	Who Governs? A journalist's guide to the British parliamentary system.	ditto, 1977
Evans, Elwyn	*Radio:* A guide to broadcasting techniques.	Barrie & Jenkins, 1977
Hall, Mark	*Broadcast Journalism:* An introduction to news writing.	Hastings House NY, 1971
Herbert, John	*The Techniques of Radio Journalism.*	A. & C. Black, 1976
Hilliard, Robert	*Radio Broadcasting:* An introduction to the sound medium.	Focal Press, 1975
Hills, George	*Broadcasting Beyond One's Frontiers.*	BBC, 1977
McNae, L.C.J. & Taylor, R.M.	*Essential Law for Journalists.*	Staples Press (5th Edn) 1972

McWhinnie, Donald	*The Art of Radio.*	Faber, 1959
Miller, G.M.	*BBC Pronouncing Dictionary of British Names.*	OUP, 1971
Milton, Ralph	*Radio Programming:* A basic training manual.	Geoffrey Bles, Collins, 1968
Quaal, Ward & Brown, James	*Broadcast Management.*	Hastings House NY (2nd Edn), 1976
Stahr, John	*Write to the Point:* A practical guide to the effective preparation of news releases and articles.	Collier-Macmillan, 1970
Taylor, Shervil	*Radio Programming in Action.*	Hastings House NY, 1967

BBC Booklets

Taste and Standards in BBC Programmes.	BBC Study Paper, 1973
The Task of Broadcasting News.	BBC Study Paper, 1976
Principles and Practice in Documentary Programmes.	BBC, 1972
Writing for the BBC: A guide for writers on possible markets within the BBC.	BBC (5th Edn), 1977
BBC Pronunciation: Policy and practice	BBC, 1974

Technical Matters

Aldred, J.	*Manual of Sound Recording.*	Fountain Press (2nd Edn), 1971
Borwick, John	*Sound Recording Practice.*	OUP, 1976
Briggs, Gordon	*Sound Reproduction.*	Wharfedale (3rd Edn), 1953
Diamant, Lincoln	*The Broadcast Communications Dictionary.*	Hastings House NY, 1974
Hadden, Burrell	*High Quality Sound Production and Reproduction.*	Iliffe, 1962
Hellyer & Sinclair	*Questions and Answers on Radio and Television.*	Butterworth, 1976
King, Gordon	*Beginner's Guide to Radio.*	Butterworth (7th Edn), 1970
Lyle, Garry	*Broadcasting.*	Batsford, 1973
Nisbett, Alec	*The Technique of the Sound Studio.*	Focal Press, (3rd Edn), 1972
	The Use of Microphones.	Focal Press, 1976
Oringel, Robert	*Audio Control Handbook.*	Hastings House NY

296

Other Bibliography Sources

British Broadcasting : 1922-1972 – a select bibliography.   BBC, 1972
Catalogue of Radio and Television Training Materials from   The British Council,
   the United Kingdom.   1977
Waller, Judith   *Radio:* The fifth estate.   Houghton Miflin
                                                                     Boston (2nd Edn)
                                                                     1950

Annual Handbooks published by the BBC and IBA.

INDEX